D0881050

Immigration and the
Political Economy of Home

AMERICAN CROSSROADS
Edited by Earl Lewis, George Lipsitz, Peggy Pascoe,
George Sánchez, and Dana Takagi

Immigration and the Political Economy of Home

West Indian Brooklyn and American
Indian Minneapolis, 1945–1992

Rachel Buff

UNIVERSITY OF CALIFORNIA PRESS
Berkeley · *Los Angeles* · *London*

University of California Press
Berkeley and Los Angeles, California

University of California Press, Ltd.
London, England

All photographs by author.

Library of Congress Cataloging-in-Publication Data

Buff, Rachel
    Immigration and the political economy of home :
West Indian Brooklyn and American Indian Min-
neapolis, 1945–1992 / Rachel Buff.
        p. cm. — (American crossroads ; 5)
    Includes bibliographical references and index.
    ISBN 0-520-21163-4 (cloth : alk. paper)—
ISBN 0-520-22121-4 (pbk. : alk. paper)
        1. Powwows—Minnesota—Minneapolis.
2. Indians of North America—Urban resi-
dence—Minnesota—Minneapolis. 3. Indians of
North America—Minnesota—Minneapolis—
Ethnic identity. 4. Carnival—New York
(State)—New York. 5. West Indians—New
York (State)—New York—Ethnic identity.
6. Immigrants—New York (State)—New York
(N.Y.)—Social conditions. I. Title. II. Series.

E98.P86 B84 2001
305.897'307765793—dc21
                                            00-064930

Manufactured in Canada

10   09   08   07   06   05   04   03   02   01

10   9   8   7   6   5   4   3   2   1

For Joe

Contents

Illustrations

PHOTOGRAPHS

Acknowledgments

This book started out as a dissertation project in 1988. Just as there has been a lot of living in the years since then, I have been lucky to receive many kinds of support from various institutions, colleagues, and friends. The names that follow are, of necessity, a partial list; I can't imagine I will manage to avoid leaving someone out. My apologies in advance. I have tried to acknowledge specific contributors to the work of researching and writing in a long note at the start of each chapter.

From the outset, both the Graduate College and the Program in American Studies at the University of Minnesota generously supported this work. I had support there in the form of a Thomas Stout Fellowship, a Harold Leonard Memorial Film Fellowship, a Doctoral Dissertation Fellowship, a Doctoral Dissertation Travel Grant, and travel grants from the Program in American Studies. Betty Agee, Executive Secretary of the Program in American Studies, provided consistent and much appreciated administrative support.

The Program in American Studies was the site of extraordinary collegiality and intellectual ferment. I learned as much from talking, from informal reading and writing groups, and from student activism as I did in the classroom. My thanks, in particular, to Carrie Krasnow, Vickie Munroe-Bjorkland, Mark Hulsether, Carla Bates, Mike Willard, Suzanne Dietzel Van Enstad, Amitava Kumar, Julia Mickenberg, Rebecca Hill, Michael Corbin, Dan Barclay, Frieda Knobloch, Jason Loviglio, and Joe

Austin. While at Minnesota, I was lucky to participate in a doomed but inspiring struggle to unionize graduate assistants

At Minnesota, I was also lucky to work with established scholars, such as Brenda Gayle Plummer, Roger Buffalohead, Dave Roediger, Maria Damon, David S. Noble, Prabhaka Jha, Jean O'Brien, Riv Ellen Prell, and George Lipsitz. Riv Ellen Prell read chapter drafts indefatigably, and has provided support and insight at crucial times throughout the duration of this project. George Lipsitz remained committed to this project even after his im/migration to California; he has been a consistent and stellar example to me of what a scholar-activist can be.

In doing oral history and participant-observation research, I have relied on the kindness and goodwill of many people. In Minneapolis, Dorene Day went from being my student at NAES (Native American Educational Systems) College to being a generous and patient teacher; I am grateful for her friendship. Bill Means shared his time and extensive knowledge of history and politics. Ellie Favel and Johnny Smith, both teachers at Heart of the Earth Survival School, shared their ample knowledge and deep commitment to Indian culture and education. In Brooklyn, Les Slater patiently explained the history of the steel drum. Randy Brewster and Tony Josephs taught me about mas' camps and pan yards. The Board of Directors at Sonatas Steelband tolerated my presence there during rehearsals and spent time trying to educate me on what I was seeing. Judy Henry showed me around Caribbean Brooklyn and was both an informative source and a good comrade in adventure. This book is indebted to the insights of many activists, students, teachers, musicians, dancers, and powwow and Carnival goers. I have tried to thank them by name wherever possible.

Helpful librarians and archivists aided the archival research presented here. Dave Klassen at the Social Welfare History Archive in Minneapolis first dug out a couple of boxes he thought might interest me; they did. In addition, I had excellent help from librarians at the Brooklyn Public Library, Local History Room; the Government Documents and Interlibrary Loan Departments at the University of Minnesota; the Schomburg Center for Research in Black Culture, and the Municipal Archives of New York City. It is also important to have somewhere to sleep while doing academic research. Sarah Johnson, Robert Danberg, Mary Biggs, Karl and Jean Kroeber, Ann Bailey, Pat Kaluza, Robert and Pam Goldman, Lisa Levine, Steve Root, and Art and Sandy Robbins have allowed me space in their homes during research trips; my thanks.

I have had good research support at Bowling Green State University. Under the fine stewardship of Department Chair Donald Nieman, abundant financial and collegial support has been available from the Policy History Program. In addition, I received a Faculty Research Council Grant to support revision work during the summer of 1998. A Younger Faculty Writing Group organized by Vickie Patraka of the Institute for Culture and Society has provided interdisciplinary intellectual engagement. My thanks to the members of this group, as well as other colleagues at Bowling Green, for reading various drafts of this work: Val Rohy, Laura Podalsky, Mark Hernandez, Steve Ziliak, Rebecca Green, Jeannie Ludlow, Eithne Luibheid, Joe Austin, Simon Morgan-Russell, and Vince O'Keefe. I am indebted to Rob Buffington for help on a key last-minute editorial decision.

In addition to being a collegial place to work, the History Department has provided me with excellent research assistance. Stuart Tart, Dave Haus, Sarah Hootman, Roy Smith, and Rob Smith graciously combed databases and compiled citations. I have also had the opportunity to work with talented graduate students who have helped me think about many of the issues discussed in this book; in particular, Leigh Corrette, Mary Farmer, Rob Smith, Julio Rodriguez, Yvonne Sims, Matt Young, and especially Andrea Kabwasa, whose work on "the border subject" sets a high standard.

Portions of this work have been presented at the American Studies Association (1990 and 1998); the Social Science History Association (1997); Black Popular Culture: Into the Twenty-first Century (University of Pittsburgh, 1995); the Caribbean Studies Association (1996); the Conference of Midwest Jewish Educators (1996); the Cultural Theory/Historical Practices Lecture Series at Carlow College (1997); the Conference on Holidays, Rituals, Festivals, and Public Display (Bowling Green, 1998); the Harvard University Young Americanists Conference (1998); a conference on West Indian migration at the Institute for the Study of Man (1999); and the Berkshire Conference for Women's History (1999). My thanks to the organizers and co-panelists of these various events, particularly: Dorothee Schneider, Donna Gabaccia, Matt Jacobson, Csaba Toth, Joseph Adjaye, Adrienne Andrews, Nancy Foner, and Werner Sollors.

A particularly grueling and unpleasant evening, by invitation of the Pittsburgh Center for Social History Seminar on Working Class History, nonetheless provided an invaluable education about the limits of collegiality.

Portions of this work have appeared in other publications. I am grateful to Eric Zinner of New York University Press for permission to use portions of "Gender and Generation Down the Red Road," which appeared in *Generations of Youth: Youth Cultures and History in Twentieth-Century America,* edited by Joe Austin and Michael Nevin Willard (New York: New York University Press, 1998). Portions of Chapter 3 appear in *Postcolonial America,* edited by C. Richard King (Urbana-Champaign: University of Illinois Press, 2000), and are used by arrangement with the publisher. A piece of Chapter 4 is from *Language, Rhythm, and Sound: Black Popular Culture into the Twenty-first Century,* Joseph Adjaye and Adrienne R. Andrews, Eds., ©1997 by University of Pittsburgh Press. Reprinted by permission of the University of Pittsburgh Press.

At the University of California Press, Monica McCormick has been an enthusiastic and patient editor. The book has been vastly improved by the efforts of the project editor, Sue Heinemann, and the copyeditor, Barbara Salazar. The efforts of the American Crossroads Series editors, George Lipsitz in particular, as well as the comments of Peter Iverson and an anonymous reader have challenged me to make this a book that speaks more powerfully and accessibly.

The places I call home have shifted during these years, along with the course of finding work in academia. Wherever I have been, the things I was fortunate to learn from my high school art teacher, Phil Russell, and my college mentor, Michael S. Harper, have accompanied me. I can only hope that my students learn some of the openness to the world that these early mentors instilled in me. During my time in Minneapolis, I was lucky to be involved with the short-lived Jewish Activist Minyan. The example of JAM continues to inspire me in thinking about a way of practicing and living radical politics. My thanks to all involved. My family has been supportive no matter where I lived: Jerry and Barbara Buff and my sister, Sarah; Joe Austin Sr. and my wonderful mother-outlaw, Tommi Nowlin.

The rigors of professional im/migration make good colleagues and friends all the more crucial. In Ohio, Laura Podalsky, John Crider, Jeannie Ludlow, Ruth Wallis Herndon, Michelle Clossick, Kristi Hannan, Mark Finnegan, and Denise Heberle have made it easier to land on that fine line between the Rust Belt and the Bible Belt. Across geographic remove, consistent and rewarding friendships with Lisa Levine, Rich Kees, Csaba Toth, Robert Goldman, Frieda Knobloch, Michelle Adams, and Laura Nelsen have inspired me to keep writing about the idea of home. Pat Kaluza's understanding and practice of radical subjectivity, her wisdom, and her generosity have been an anchor for me. Jason Loviglio read many drafts, co-authored an article on something completely different, and helped keep me sane during this long process. Lauren Fox's endless wit and insight via email gets me through many an uninspired workday.

This book is dedicated to Joe Austin, my life partner in love and work. Joe's grace and passion, his commitment to radical thinking in scholarship and daily life, are a continual source of joy and inspiration to me. He has always supported my work in the best ways possible: through intellectual collegiality and by including me under the rubric of his own high standards. Making a home with him has been the most important work of these years: a wild ride I wouldn't have missed for anything.

Im/migration, Race, and Popular Memory in Caribbean Brooklyn and American Indian Minneapolis, 1945–1992

TOWARD A POLITICAL ECONOMY OF HOME: DUAL CITIZENS, DENIZENS, THE DEAD

The government says that this land is of the nation, but then, we ask, "what is the nation, if not its people?" We are the nation, we are the ones that live here.

Zapatista Comandante Zebedeo, quoted in
Mariana Mora, "Changing Chiapas"

In August 1991 I listened to three West Indian women in Brooklyn discussing the recent deaths of Gavin Cato and Yankel Rosenbaum as we hurriedly prepared costumes for the upcoming Labor Day Carnival.[1] The storefront costume shop was just a few blocks from the corner that had come to symbolize Crown Heights to New Yorkers in the wake of these tragedies. The women were talking about recent events in their neighborhood, touching on long-standing municipal tensions over everything from parking spaces and police protection to a less visible but nonetheless palpable sense of belonging: denizenship.

The weekly police escort of Hasidic Rebbe Menahem Schneerson's procession to the grave of his wife figured centrally in their conversation, as it did in many other discussions of events in Crown Heights that month. A driver in this procession had fatally injured a young Guyanese-American boy, Gavin Cato. Many people in Crown Heights perceived the police escort as a symbol of Hasidic and Jewish privilege, something gained

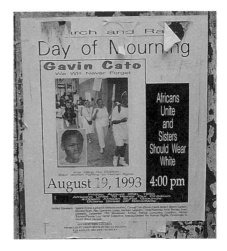

Photo 1. A poster on a Brooklyn wall demonstrates community resolve to remember Gavin Cato's death. In this interpretation, the Guyanese-American child is part of "African" historical memory.

at the expense of their African-American and Caribbean-American neighbors. Adding to this sense of injustice was the fact that one of the lawyers employed to defend the Hasidic driver of the vehicle that killed Cato had recently asserted that many of the Black people in Crown Heights were not really American, clearly suggesting that their grievances were less credible or important than those of "real" Americans (see photo 1).

"*We're* not really American!" scoffed one of the group of women, most of whom were legal residents or citizens of the country.[2] "*They* don't even bury their dead here!"

This was a brief and unequal exchange between individuals who were unlikely to meet: a lawyer, whose words were reprinted in the city's newspapers, mouthed by commentators, and received in court, and a Caribbean-American woman, speaking in an im/migrant community rarely even referred to in mainstream representations of the controversy over Crown Heights, as she labored to adorn a costume for that community's fantastic Carnival procession. Their words were infused by centuries of injustices in Brooklyn as well as in the larger arena of circum-Atlantic history.

As much as this exchange reveals differences in municipal empowerment, it also points to assumptions the two speakers had in common: about origins and return, citizenship and rights, belonging. It asserts that the practice of "burying their dead here" and the rights of citizenship are deeply connected.[3] In other words, these women were talking about a political economy of home. They understood that where people imag-

ine themselves to be most deeply and profoundly at home, with their ancestors, in the place of origin and return, relates to their socioeconomic
power and the kinds of rights they can claim there.

Garrett Hongo writes that his im/migrant Asian ancestors in Hawaii
buried their dead in the only land made available to them, on the sandy
boundary between island and sea. Plantation owners used more stable
inland acreage to grow sugar or to build their own houses and cemeter-
ies. So the im/migrants, those not possessing the rights to land owner-
ship and citizenship, buried their dead in the unstable place between land
and water.[4] There the dead, periodically, would become fugitive: "What
we didn't know, what the growers didn't know, was that the sea would
come and take our dead from us then, in the periodic raids of rips and
tidal waves from a swelling ocean."[5] For the living im/migrants in
Hawaii, then, the dead represented geographic and social marginality,
longing for home; the ability to straddle two worlds, and even to flee one
for another.[6]

Other commentators understand such connections as well. Like the
lawyer for the Hasidim, they express the need for limits, for a careful
policing of borders to defend the national character: exactly who is and
who is not American. Debates over immigration and citizenship have always been linked to the demand of U.S. employers for cheap labor, on
the one hand, and a simultaneous insistence on maintaining cultural uni-
formity, on the other. If a nation is an imagined community, the state
counts the rolls of this community in ways that reinforce the idea of cultural coherence, leaving many people betwixt and between.[7] To keep
producing a sense of national coherence, state bureaucracies such as the
Immigration and Naturalization Service have to bend the truth, producing statistics about illegal immigration that ring with an impossible
certainty.[8] At the same time, those at the borders of the nation-state in-
carnate their dead through cultural performance and political resistance,
amidst the columns of falsified statistics that are also the tallies of the
long war over the Americas.

Proper burials for the dead are also of concern to participants at
urban powwows held in Minneapolis. The American Indian Hearse Service often occupies a prominent place at these powwows, offering raffle
tickets and information. Created by urban Indian activists, the service
offers transportation for the dead, at no charge and "with dignity," back
to the reservation of their origin or enrollment. Like the West Indian
women in Brooklyn, clients of this service express the importance of
origins. There is a contradiction between where a body resides because

of economic and political exigencies and where it seeks its final resting place. Urban Indians retain ties to the reservation land base that was supposed to become obsolete; like New York West Indians, they dramatize the ongoing importance of these ties in the performative rituals of pan-Indian powwows.

Because of the conflict between Native Americans' allegiance to their homelands and the colonial administration of that land by the U.S. Department of the Interior, burial and the repatriation of ancestral remains is a complex issue. In recent years, struggles have developed over the final resting places of Indian remains: between upholders of official national culture, such as the Smithsonian Institution and state historical societies, and native people, who want to see their dead returned to their homelands. These struggles pit the forces of official history against those who have long been subjected to repression in the name of the nation. Activists struggling for the *repatriation* of their ancestors' remains assert their rights to inhabit a specific place. This means that native remains housed in national archives are, like Hongo's buried ancestors, fugitive denizens of an ill-defined state. And as such, they migrate across borders, becoming dual citizens of official and alternative nationalities. Pemina Yellow Bird and Kathryn Milun write: "In this light, Indian self-determination meant relocating the dead ancestors to a place where they would no longer serve as, literally, the repressed foundation of official state history. Reburied, the dead ancestors might stimulate stories of empowerment for the living."[9]

Struggles over interment and empowerment are concurrent with struggles over citizenship rights, as well as about something more elusive, which I call *denizenship:* the ways in which inhabiting a place, as much as the officially defined boundaries of that place, lead people to make claims on that place. The dead are dual citizens. They live in memory as well as inhabiting actual physical terrain. Joseph Roach writes of "the profoundly ambivalent emotions human beings harbor for the dead, who once belonged among the living but who now inhabit some alien country whose citizens putrefy but endure."[10]

Hearse services and funeral processions, then, are not only about making sure that the body has its final resting place somewhere that is home, but that the dead somehow inhabit both the place of interment and the expansive world of memory. And, in so doing, that they offer the living something as well: alternative practices of affiliation and membership.

While I was doing the research for this book, I spent four years commuting between New York, where I was born and raised, and Minneapolis, where I was working toward my doctorate. At the end of each summer, I would accompany my mother to the cemetery in southern Connecticut where her mother and grandparents, the im/migrant generation, are buried. There we would observe the custom of visiting the dead before Rosh Hashanah, picking up small stones on the overgrown path that leads into the Jewish cemetery. On the last visit, my mother took me past the graves we usually visited up a small hill now separated from the rest of the cemetery by a dump used by local contractors. On the hill we pushed back weeds and tall grass to reveal stones ornamented by the hammer and sickle: the Communists who had argued with my Workmen's Circle great-grandfather had chosen to be buried together, close to but just outside of the boundaries of the Jewish community. Time and the social processes of assimilation and forgetting had almost made them disappear. But this small geography of the dead speaks powerfully about the ways im/migrants stake claims to homelands real and imagined.

Processes of naturalization and border crossing, of course, become somewhat more complex when those who remember the dead are constrained within specific living physical and national bodies. The people I have mentioned are among those who honor the dead by crossing geopolitical boundaries as well as by their mourning. Such stories, as well as the practices governing citizenship—from green cards to border guards to the complex rules of "blood quantum" that govern tribal enrollment—often contradict lived experience. As Lisa Lowe writes, citizenship has always engendered loss for those passing into the hallowed ground of the nation: "In being represented as citizen within the public sphere . . . the subject is 'split off' from the unrepresentable histories of situated embodiment that contradict the abstract form of citizenship."[11]

Im/migrant performances like Carnival and powwow cross the borders between legitimated, forbidden, and imagined citizenship and denizenship. At Carnival, West Indian–Americans stake their claims to a transnational "Culture of Black Creation." They celebrate their concurrent pride in decolonized homelands in the Caribbean and in a hyphenated identity as West Indian–Americans. Similarly, at powwows, urban Indian people claim their right to return to reservations governed by the colonialist constructs of tribe as well as ongoing affinities to language, ancestors, and land (see photo 2). These performances interrogate and reinvent rhetorics of citizenship and race, ethnicity and municipal empowerment.

This book takes up and investigates an ongoing circum-Atlantic conversation about citizenship and denizenship, memory and boundaries.

Photo 2. The Grand Entry begins with flags, followed closely by special guests, veterans, and then dancers, beginning with the "traditional" styles favored by elders. This procession honors the multiple affinities of contemporary Indian people for Indian lands and historic identities as well as U.S. citizenship.

I listen for the different ways in which people in this hemisphere have inhabited and longed for "homelands" that are real and imagined; bordered and allotted; vanished, reinvented, and red-lined. Focusing on West Indian and Native American im/migrants in the post–World War II period, I attend to the diverse frequencies that signify and govern the experiences of migration and denizenship in the late twentieth century. The "utopian politics of transgression" present in performative moments is always in dialogue with the urban and national politics that so often regulate both local performance and im/migrant populations.[12]

Such questioning of rhetorics of displacement and placement is both crucial and timely. At a time when thousands of people every year die trying to cross an imaginary line between nations; when the health, welfare, and livelihoods of thousands more are put into jeopardy by draconian policies designed to police such borders, is it not crucial that we scrutinize the ways in which such borders are maintained? The rhetorics, imaginings, ideologies that make such lines have divisive and fatal consequences.

PERFORMING HISTORY

As an Indian woman in this country, I often find that
I have much in common with many of the immigrants

from other colonized lands who come here to make a
living, often as taxi drivers.

Joy Harjo, "Letter from the End of the
Twentieth Century," in
The Woman Who Fell from the Sky

This book is about social identity among racialized immigrants and migrants (im/migrants) to urban centers in the post–World War II period. In
it I compare urban Indian powwows in Minneapolis with the Caribbean
Carnival in New York. Unorthodox in terms of social science methodol-
ogy and the disciplinary lines that have separated immigration history
from Native American studies and the history of migration within the nation, this comparison emerges from my reading of (post)colonial history,
writ large, in the Western Hemisphere. As Joy Harjo explains in the quote
above, histories of colonization and resistance often connect individuals
from disparate parts of the globe. The long-term project of global capitalist hegemony overwhelms local political and economic structures and
destroys social connections, scattering friends and family through migration and loss. At the same time, survivors recognize each other and
create new forms of social connection. They remember their generations
of dead, broadcasting their stories beyond the boundaries of nation-
states.

Throughout their long histories in this hemisphere, the festivals that
are at the center of this book have responded to the violence of imperialism with social struggle and cultural creativity. These performances
translate local memories into long-standing symbols whose meanings
may be reinvented and added to over time. Created as "sites of memory" during the long contest over the Americas, carnival and powwow
perform historic origins at the same time that they dramatize ongoing
battles for municipal and hemispheric survival.[13] These are sites where,
as Stuart Hall writes, "the unspeakable stories of subjectivities meet the
narratives of history, of a culture."[14]

In the contested Brooklyn Carnival procession of 1992, municipal authorities worried about ongoing friction between Black and Jewish
denizens of Crown Heights. At the same time, many Carnival bands wore
extravagant costumes that celebrated the glories of Mayan and Aztec nations,
commemorating another conflict, the quincentennial of Columbus's arrival
in the Americas. The Association of Belizean Americans commemorated
the Mayan Indians whom they cited as the earliest inhabitants of Belize. Carnival King of this band was a "Mohawk Spirit Dancer" clearly
not indigenous to Belize at any time, but symbolizing native resistance

and survival, most recently, perhaps, in the conflicts at Oka in 1990. This was a year in Brooklyn when costume makers and steel bands had to battle increased surveillance and harassment from city police in the weeks leading up to the Carnival.[15] The Labor Day performance, then, became a site of memory for the long-term losses and survivals of history as well as the recent dead in Crown Heights.

In this book I follow three central themes in Caribbean and American Indian social experience: im/migration; historic and contemporary struggles over municipal empowerment at the local and national levels; and, in the twentieth century, the astounding quickness and reach of mass culture. These three things are, of course, linked: the forced migration of Africans in the Middle Passage resulted in their practice and remembering of cultures subject to vicious repression, first by slaveholders and later by the postemancipation hierarchies of Caribbean colonies. Forced west by pressure from Euroamerican expansion, Native Americans dealt with the losses and radical transformations of relocation.[16] Removal of eastern nations to Oklahoma, for example, resulted in alliances between Indian peoples who had previously been separated by considerable geographic distance.[17] Memory and performance are deeply connected in the Americas: circum-Atlantic culture encodes both the losses of colonization and migration and people's creative responses to them.[18]

POPULAR MEMORY AND MASS CULTURE

At the same time that they are sites of memory, these festivals are places where memory is disguised, reinvented, and sometimes lost altogether. The labor and land of African and Indian peoples was the basis for the rapid expansion of Euroamerican political and economic power in the eighteenth and nineteenth centuries. Simultaneously, their expressive forms played a crucial role in the development of the U.S. mass culture industry, which has always drawn heavily on both Afro-Atlantic music and native images from a mythical West. Roach writes: "Memories torture themselves into forgetting by disguising their collaborative interdependence across imaginary borders of race, nation, and origin. . . . To perform in this sense means to bring forth, to make manifest, and to transmit. To perform in this sense also means, though often more secretly, to reinvent."[19]

Circum-Atlantic performances such as Carnival and powwow, then, can serve as memories of silenced histories, or they can be used to silence history. In creating a story of proud national destiny, the early mass culture industry drew heavily on both Afro-Atlantic performative forms and the Indian imagery found in Westerns. Through mass culture, Euroamericans imagined that Black people were both the riotous children demeaning the Constitution in *Birth of a Nation* and the natural geniuses of music and sport recreated in blackface minstrelsy and its performative descendants; they saw Indians as the noble but doomed ancestors of the American democratic project fated to be removed by the exigencies of Manifest Destiny.[20] At the same time that the Ghost Dancers were performing their hopes for the land, Buffalo Bill's Wild West Show was traveling the country, making the native struggle for survival a spectacle before it was even finished. The Hunkpapa Lakota leader Sitting Bull, who traveled with the Wild West Show before being assassinated by Sioux tribal police, was so appalled by the poverty he saw on the East Coast of the United States that he gave away his wages in pennies to the children who would cluster around him. These were, in large part, the children of the "great wave" of immigration to the United States from Eastern Europe. The same children would grow up watching the silent movies that dramatized the last stand of Indians in the West; only in these films, no Indian would possess the humanity and insight of Sitting Bull, distributing his wages from the back of the circus wagon.[21]

At the same time that they presented racist imagery of African and Indian peoples, the road shows, silent films, and popular press of this nascent mass culture industry facilitated the diffusion and transformation of pan-Indian powwows and Caribbean Carnival. Mass circulation whited out popular forms, erasing their Indian, African, and im/migrant roots. But popular narratives retained traces of their vanished origins. As Mark Winokur argues, "This mainstream is at all times constituted, rather than contributed to, by immigrant [im/migrant] and ethnic cultures."[22] Winokur and other cultural critics have used critical theories derived variously from Marxist social thought, psychoanalytic theory, and poststructuralist theory to argue that such traces of repressed voices exist beneath the whiteout, and that we can glimpse them through close reading. This is an exceedingly important move, as it refocuses the ways in which we understand mass cultural texts to be produced, read, and disseminated. But it is also clear, in the cases of Carnival and powwow, that im/migrants themselves used mass culture to revise their relationship to the colonial enterprise. William Powers convincingly demonstrates that the Buffalo Bill show, with its racist representation of the struggle over the trans-Appalachian West, also influenced the form of

Oklahoma powwows.[23] Native performers adapted the vaudevillian spectacle of the Grand Entry, reorganizing the parade so that it demonstrated not the hierarchies of social Darwinism but the priorities of Native American life. Similarly, Paul Gilroy argues that the production of slave songs by the Fisk Jubilee Singers as mass cultural entertainment disseminated a new and important mode of Black expression throughout Britain and the United States.[24]

Mass cultural imagery, then, can be used as part of a temporary shelter against the colonial effort as a whole. Colonized peoples may appropriate the images of a racist mass culture to create their own meanings, using the impressive reach of the mass cultural apparatus to speak to one another and to broadcast alternative stories. The symbolic figures present in the postcolonial performances of Carnival and powwow do not stop the ongoing economic depredations of imperial capital. But they imaginatively reconfigure a mass-mediated universe. Hybrid figures such as the Yankee Sailor at Carnival, a parody of the nautical arm of colonial domination, and an ongoing commentary on the postcolonial relationship between the Caribbean and the United States indicate the ongoing slippage between categories of "mass" and "folk," "low" and "high" cultures.

At Carnival and powwow, Indian and Caribbean people assert identities created from the collection of roles and names available to them. For example, native veterans of U.S. wars join traditionalist elders in leading the Grand Entry powwow procession, which originates not in precolonial ritual but in the antic display of the Wild West Show. Both the soldier and the elder are figures that symbolize sovereignty, dignity, and self-respect, but they draw quite differently on indigenous traditions and Euroamerican images. A native veteran may be celebrated for defending a homeland whose boundaries are defined by treaty rather than by the geopolitical exigencies that separate the United States from Mexico and Canada. This collage of innovation, colonial forms, and "traditional" practices constitutes the often erased heart of modernity. Often taking place on terrain that modernity marks as cultural rather than political, such collages have long illustrated the diasporic history of the Americas.[25]

RACE, IM/MIGRATION, AND PUBLIC POLICY

While Carnival and powwow date back to the origins of conquest, slavery, and intercultural contact in the Americas, this book focuses on the post-1945 period. I compare the experiences of Caribbean im/migrants in Brooklyn after 1965 with those of Indian people who relocated to

Minneapolis after 1954. Brooklyn and Minneapolis are important sites for post-1945 immigration and migration (im/migration) history, for different reasons. New York City, long an im/migrant destination, has the largest concentration of Caribbean im/migrants in the United States.[26] The availability of service sector employment and strong African-American and Afro-Caribbean communities in Harlem and Brooklyn have attracted im/migrants throughout the twentieth century. Carnival on Eastern Parkway in Brooklyn in August is the largest Caribbean gathering in North America. While Carnival on Eastern Parkway has had increasing participation in recent years by im/migrants from the Hispanic and Francophone Caribbean, as well as by African-Americans, it is and has always been dominated by those from the Anglophone Caribbean, in particular by im/migrants from Trinidad and Tobago, Grenada, and St. Vincents.

While not among the officially designated relocation centers during the 1950s, the Twin Cities of Minneapolis and St. Paul developed a large urban Indian community in the post–World War II period. Located close to several reservation communities in Wisconsin, Minnesota, and South Dakota, the Twin Cities have long been a site of contact between native and Euroamerican peoples. In the postwar period, the urban Indian community in the Twin Cities developed Indian-run institutions out of pre-existing Indian communities as well as Great Society initiatives such as the Model Cities Program. The American Indian Movement began in Minneapolis in 1968 as a community initiative to watch the police, and, along with other urban Indian groups, worked to develop social and political institutions.

The parallel between Caribbean and Indian communities offers a window into the ways in which im/migrants connected their experiences of urban racial hierarchies with a developing postcolonial consciousness. Through urban social movements, im/migrants made rhetorical connections to histories of anticolonial struggle and hemispheric survival at the same time that they drew on vocabularies of race and rights to organize im/migrant communities within the nation-state.[27] The American Indian Movement, for example, drew on older forms such as the powwow to contextualize a continuous history of resistance. Powwows served to organize Indian communities around the comparatively new issues of municipal empowerment and antiracist struggle.

Im/migrant identity has always responded to the transnational circulation of workers and capital. In the post–World War II period, as the "empire" has increasingly come "home," im/migrants from the Third and Fourth Worlds have arrived in First World cities that have risen from their labor, their lands, and, simultaneously, their erasure. And in these cities, as Harjo tells it, Native American im/migrants encounter not only the Euroamerican society responsible for their displacement but other im/migrants from colonized places, who have their own stories of homes laden with familiar and new valences.

At the same time, im/migrants to the United States have always confronted the contradiction between democratic ideals and racialized practice. The very notion of liberal citizenship, as David Theo Goldberg and others argue, hinges on an idea of universality that has always, at the same time, delimited the emancipatory rights it promises.[28] Arriving in metropolitan centers, then, native and Caribbean im/migrants confront these discrepancies: the unequal distribution of goods, work, rights, access to the means of representation.

Both Indians and Caribbean immigrants, because of their racial positions and because of their diverse conceptions of citizenship and affinity, have not assimilated in the much-vaunted tradition of "white ethnics." Arriving in New York City in unprecedented numbers after 1965, Afro-Caribbean people confront a two-tiered racial hierarchy often concealed by ideologies of ethnic mobility and "model minorities." Caribbean immigrants enter the United States as foreign nationals subject to the vagaries of immigration and naturalization policy; as the proverbial "new ethnics" who compete for success and mobility in the urban order, often pitted against native-born minorities; and as Black people whose access to economic mobility is delimited by race.

Indians also moved to U.S. cities in unprecedented numbers during the 1950s and 1960s, responding to both official relocation and termination programs and unofficial but equally forceful regimes of systematic reservation underdevelopment and unemployment of the termination period. Federal rhetoric cast termination as an emancipatory project of giving the Indians full civil rights by removing them from presumably backward reservation communities. In the cities, Indian people came into contact with individuals from different Indian nations, forging an urban identity that relied multiply on previous contact between native people in cities, on reservations, and in boarding schools; on the Indian experience fighting in World War II; and on the exigencies of relocation, which often left Indian people in inner-city neighborhoods without the social services promised by the Bureau of Indian Affairs.

As Indian and Caribbean im/migrant communities grew in Minneapolis and New York during the late 1960s and early 1970s, local institutions increasingly sponsored cultural activities. However temporarily and conditionally Indian and Caribbean people accepted these cities as their new homes, they imported festivals that commemorated the traditions of their island and reservation homelands. And as urban Indian and metropolitan Caribbean communities grew and developed, the festivals they had brought changed along with them, creating places where cultural identity could be performed and revised.

Of necessity, Caribbean and Indian im/migrants respond to stories that hail them, variously, as workers, citizens, illegal immigrants, denizens, inner-city dwellers, minorities. Narratives of national community enact Roach's tortured acts of forgetting. In response, these intercultural performances remember and reinvent both past and present. Just as Carnival and powwow emerge from a colonial history of repression, these forms in the post-1945 period have changed to respond to the federal, transnational, and local politics that shape im/migrant communities.

For the Indian and Caribbean communities that are the center of this project, the historical experiences of geographic migration and cultural continuity, of creative identity formation and imaginative alliance challenge official paradigms of citizenship and identity. These experiences do not create singular citizens or unitary subjects; rather, they create individuals with multiple ideas about citizenship and complicated feelings of loyalty. There exists a social contradiction between nationalist ideas of citizenship and an increasingly transnational economy. An exploration of this contradiction is both crucial and timely, as both immigration policy and native sovereignty are increasingly the focus of national scrutiny.

In cultural spaces such as Carnival and powwow, urban ideologies of assimilation and mobility contrast with the long memories of resistance and survival carried in these performances. Im/migrants of color confront the powerful nationalism that so depends on their exclusion as well as their labor.[29] These festivals are ethnic social forms in a racialized urban landscape. As Stuart Hall writes: "The term ethnicity acknowledges the place of history, language and culture in the construction of subjectivity and identity, as well as the fact that all discourse is placed, positioned, situated, and all knowledge is contextual."[30] Carnival and powwow respond to ideologies of national harmony by asserting a social difference uniquely grounded in both recent local memory and long-term hemispheric histories.

Producing a stable sense of national identity for some engenders fragmentation, removal, and loss for others. Carnival performances allow West Indians in New York to straddle the contradiction between the neocolonial economic exigencies that bring them to the city and allegiances to Caribbean "homelands" that many second- and third-generation im/migrants have never seen. As revelers march down Eastern Parkway at the West Indian American Day Carnival, they dramatize the issues of citizenship and empowerment so salient to their lives in this hemisphere.

American Indians, whose claims on this place based on long-standing cultural affiliation and ancestral ties are unimpeachable, nonetheless have a long and vexed relationship to citizenship rights. Today's urban pow-wows take place in a pan-tribal context that is both a direct response to the neocolonialist programs of termination and relocation instituted after World War II and a strategy employed by native activists to stake a claim to urban political power and social services.

This comparison between Caribbean immigrants and Native American migrants to U.S. cities points to hemispheric parallels in the construction of racial identities and postcolonial narratives. These parallels, in turn, demand that scholars reconceptualize our notions of immigration and ethnic formation to reflect hemispheric processes of transmigration as well as the struggles of Third and Fourth World peoples for geopolitical and cultural sovereignty.

"STORIES THAT COULD BE TRUE": SOME NOTES ON SNACKING AND METHOD

One of the most terrible implications of the ethnographic approach is the insistence on fixing the object of scrutiny in static time, thereby removing the tangible nature of lived experience and promoting the idea of uncontaminated survival. This is how those generalized projections of a series of events that obscure the network of real links become established. The history of a transplanted population, but one which elsewhere becomes another people, allows us to resist generalization and the limitations it imposes. Relationship (at the same time link and linked, act and speech) is emphasized over what in appearance could be conceived as a governing principle, the so-called universal "controlling force."

Edouard Glissant, *Caribbean Discourse*

The summer of 1991 was my first summer of dissertation research in Brooklyn.[31] That summer, in August, the deaths of Gavin Cato and Yosef

Lifsh caused city-wide anxiety about the relationship between Blacks and Jews in Crown Heights, a neighborhood neatly bisected by Eastern Parkway, the route of Carnival since 1969. The two deaths took place in August, just a couple of weeks before Carnival was set to take place. The costume shops (mas' camps) and the pan yards, where steel bands practice, were at their customary August full tilt. Against the somewhat aggressive advice of various friends and family members, I continued my research in Crown Heights.

I had become accustomed to being one of a very few white people on the street in a predominantly Black, and less commonly Asian, part of the city. Both on blocks dominated by the Hasidim, where I appeared neither as a "Jew" by neighborhood definition nor as a member of the Black majority, and in the rest of Crown Heights and Flatbush, I was generally a racial "other." A certain Euroamerican common sense perceives this to be a dangerous situation. In my experience, what was endangered, both before and after the conflict in Crown Heights, was much less my physical safety, which is always an issue for a woman in any context, than the map, the cultural geography that is part of my heritage as a suburban "white" New Yorker. This map draws lines around areas that are considered safe and unsafe, virtually guaranteeing, as the Black alien in John Sayles's film *Brother from Another Planet* discovers on the subway, the segregation of daily life.

Apart from the subtext of tension and anxiety that followed the conflicts in Crown Heights, preparations for Carnival continued at their customarily rapid August pace. In late August, many Caribbean im/migrants and their Caribbean-American offspring take their vacation time, leave temporary jobs, or come to Brooklyn from other boroughs, states, or the islands; they stay with friends or relatives. People stay up late to make costumes and learn the music for Panorama, often practicing until the early morning hours. Mas' camps and pan yards, often small storefronts, alleys, or basements, are crowded, industrious, and festive.

Into all of this activity one afternoon stepped a Euroamerican reporter and photographer from the *New York Times*. Working on deadline, they came to the storefront that holds the registration office of the West Indian–American Day Carnival Association as well as the Culture of Black Creation mas' camp. They were looking for information about how recent events in Crown Heights might affect the upcoming Carnival. Would there be violence? Were Caribbean people angry?

In a room full of Afro-Caribbean and African-American people, the reporter, Andrew Yarrow, directed his questions at me. I, in turn, directed him and the photographer, Sara Krulwich, to Randy Brewster, a famous costume maker who runs the Culture of Black Creation. Brewster's costumes are exhibited in the city's American Museum of Natural History; he has been involved in the Brooklyn Carnival for some twenty years. After a brief conversation with Brewster, the reporter came back to talk to me. Randy laughed and waved to me. "You go ahead," he said.[32]

I spoke to Yarrow briefly, emphasizing again that I was a student, and that I was just beginning to learn about Caribbean life in Crown Heights. He asked what my dissertation was about, and then asked me to speculate on what was happening in the neighborhood. I gave him the names and phone numbers of some of the Brooklyn activists I had interviewed in my research, and told him that they might be better equipped to answer his questions than I was. I'm not sure whether he ever called these people; reading the *New York Times* carefully that month, I never saw an article referring to any of them.[33]

If this introductory chapter emphasizes the ways the nation has always been defined at its transnational margins, this anecdote makes it clear that a racialized citizenship frames the stories that explain public life in the nation. Because of an identity based on skin color, the *Times* reporters could easily imagine that I was a citizen of their public sphere; they thought I was someone who could inform them about the communities of Crown Heights and Flatbush. The Caribbean people in the room that day became, then, silent, to be heard only through the ventriloquism of my expertise or that of the *New York Times*.[34] Silent people do not speak in newspapers, except possibly as statistics; they are not asked their opinion; they are not thought of as newspaper readers or as political constituents. This incident constitutes a moment in the ongoing construction of whiteness as bearing the authority of citizenship and voice— ironically, in this instance, being deployed to describe the experience of multiethnic blackness in Crown Heights.

The truth, of course, is that no one standing in the storefront that day knew whether there would be "more violence" on the Parkway at Carnival. Incidents like the ones that took place in Crown Heights that August are not planned. They reflect complex tensions over municipal empowerment and cultural space. These tensions exist in a constantly moving field of everyday life, public policy, and cultural practices where identities are created, deployed, and erased. What the *Times* reporter and photographer were seeking that day, I think, was some way to understand these more elusive issues. It is significant, then, that they came to the mas' camp, which is a site where Caribbean identity is invented, transformed, and performed, looking for information about urban conflicts over territory and identity.

At the mas' camp, Krulwich, the photographer, engaged in the most extended interaction either of the two had with any Caribbean-American person there by talking to a group of women about where to get the best roti and dried mangos, not an unusual response from Americans confronted with the complexities of cultural difference. After summers of research in Flatbush and Crown Heights, I had developed my own theories about where to get good roti and other delicacies in the area. Many of my walks around Crown Heights and Flatbush, as well as some of my interviews and friendships, began by sharing these foods.

It is not the practice of roti eating that is at issue here, but rather the system of power in which this consumption is embedded. Dan Simon, a Vincentian sociologist and calypsonian, emphasized the social boundaries drawn around practices of eating and ethnography:

> One thing I would like to mention, which is very important, is how you were able to come into the Caribbean community. Observe, or write, or whatever you did. And, although you had maybe reservations in terms of how you were going to be accepted, you were accepted and you felt comfortable, you ate a roti and you were there. Now, if the roles were reversed, and let's say there was something happening in the Village, or somewhere else and somebody of color was to want to do that, I think it would not be as easy an assimilation.

Simon insists that ethnographic practice and the expertise it generates are always conditioned by social power; that even the seemingly simple practice of eating lunch is multiply conditioned by hierarchies of race, nationality, and class. My experience doing the research that forms the center of this book, as well as my discomfort at being asked to profess expertise about a roomful of people, indicates to me that the idea of a monolithic ethnographic authority is a component of the modernist paradigms that have long obscured the complexities of Western history. The representatives of the *New York Times* wanted to construct me as an authority in a room crowded with people far more knowledgeable than I am, because the racialized logic of expertise told them that I would be able to speak in a language they would understand. In turn, then, my comments and their rendering of the afternoon in Crown Heights were to become the transcript of the official record, the time after the incidents between "Blacks" and "Jews"; the time before Carnival, 1991. The roomful of Black people, the neighborhood of heterogeneous reactions to this most recent display of racism and anti-Semitism in the city, the cross-cultural tensions and pleasures of roti eating all drop out of the account, or at best form a backdrop to the stage of history.[35]

I did the oral history and participant-observation research for this book between 1991 and 1994. I spent the summers in Brooklyn and the academic year in Minneapolis where, in addition to being in graduate school, I came into contact with the American Indian community by teaching at NAES (Native American Educational Systems) Community College and living in an apartment close to the Minneapolis Indian Center.

In both cities my research was conducted through informal networks. In Brooklyn I first met people by hanging around at the Culture of Black Creation mas' camp, where Randy Brewster tolerated my less than perfect sewing skills and introduced me to many of the people who became friends and contacts later on. In Minneapolis, my friend and former student Dorene Day became an important source of stories and contacts among Indian powwow goers. Besides relying on the knowledge and kindness of friends, I attended powwows, meetings, steel band practices, and concerts, talking to the people I met there who were willing and interested. When a name or an institution came up repeatedly in these conversations, I tried to make contact with the people mentioned.

As much as possible, I have tried to reflect the sense of what people told me. I have quoted them directly and supplemented people's remembered stories and interpretations with archival and secondary source research. As a writer and researcher, I have been most interested in the ways history gets written in both local and institutional practices, and what this writing of history means to the lives of the im/migrants, citizens, and denizens of this hemisphere.

Juxtaposing popular performance, state policy, and im/migration historiography, this book focuses on denizenship and citizenship as they are practiced. Trying to listen to the diverse stories about these issues, I draw on interviews and observations, along with archival research and textual criticism. The questions that arise in this project, then, center on the politics of representation; on narrative practices and their comparative audibility.

Part One, "Im/migration History," begins by exploring the ways im/migrants have retained and revised cultural practices that contest the imposition of national boundaries. Chapter 2, "Playing for Keeps: A Brief Colonial History of Carnival and Powwow," compares the ways Caribbean and Indian people have interpreted their histories through these performances from colonial to postcolonial times. Deliberately set up to echo the rhetorical inversion suggested by "A Political Economy of Home," Chapter 3, "Im/migration Policy, the National Romance, and the Poetics of World Domination, 1945–1965," reads federal policy as a story written by the state about home. This story, of course, deploys much more physical force and political power than those told in Carnival and powwow.

Part Two, "Performing Memory, Inventing Tradition: Colonial Optics and Im/migrant Locations," includes a closer reading of the colonial and contemporary histories of these festivals. Chapter 4, "Performative Spaces, Urban Politics, and the Changing Meanings of Home in Brooklyn and Minneapolis," traces the history of Carnival and powwow by looking at cycles of migration and urban development as well as at the changes in these festivals that came about with their move to the cities. As transmigrant Indian and Caribbean people brought these festivals into Minneapolis and Brooklyn, the festivals became sites for the writing of alternative notions of citizenship and subjectivity. Chapter 5, "Sounds of Brooklyn: Pan Yards as Im/migrant Social Spaces," and Chapter 6, "Generation and Gender Down the Red Road," are case studies in the practice of alternative sovereignties. In both I am looking for the ways im/migrants claim home in these cities, and how they are affected by dominant narratives of nationality and citizenship. These chapters illuminate the complex negotiations between generations of im/migrants, and between men and women, over cultural forms that are both resistant to and entwined with domination. Such historical contradictions are at the heart of any story about home.

PART I

Im/migration History

CHAPTER 2

Playing for Keeps

*A Brief Colonial History of
Carnival and Powwow*

COMPARATIVE COLONIALISMS

This chapter compares Carnival and powwow, framing them as responses to colonialism. I trace the history of Carnival in Trinidad from
slavery days through emancipation in 1838 and the subsequent colonial
administration of a profoundly mixed-race society. I follow pan-Indian
culture through the 1880s, when the Dawes Act allocated Indian lands
during the final phase of military conflict over the western frontier, and
into the twentieth century, with its history of federal attempts to assimilate or eradicate native peoples and culture. The chapter continues a
short way into the twentieth century, concluding with a description of
Carnival and powwow in their contemporary im/migrant incarnations
in Brooklyn and Minneapolis.

Throughout their long histories in this hemisphere, Carnival and powwow have responded to three central themes in Caribbean and Indian
social experience: migration, colonial administration, and, in the twentieth century, the astounding reach and celerity of mass culture. These
three things are, of course, linked: the forced migration of Africans in the
Middle Passage resulted in their invention and re-membering of a culture
that was subject to vicious repression first by slaveholders, later by the
postemancipation hierarchies of Caribbean colonies. American Indians
were forced west by pressure from Euroamerican expansion. Removal
of eastern nations to Oklahoma, for example, resulted in the formation

of alliances between Indian nations that had previously been separated by considerable geographic distance. As much as the labor and land of African and native peoples were the basis for the rapid expansion of U.S. political and economic power in the eighteenth and nineteenth centuries, their expressive forms also played a crucial role in the development of the U.S. mass culture industry, which has always drawn heavily on both Afro-Atlantic music and mythologies of the frontier West.[1]

Both Helen Safa and Errol Hill suggest that the inability of Africans to return to their actual geographic homelands has a lot to do with the richness of Afro-Creole culture in the New World. Rooted in the concept of culture, rather than any specific place, slaves and their descendants forged a uniquely "indigenous culture," as Hill phrases it.[2] While the respect given by these Caribbeanists to the power of diasporic memory is appropriate in light of the tremendous syncretic capacity of Afro-Atlantic cultures to remember and reinvent history, the example of Native American experience in the United States provides an illuminating parallel, connecting feats of cultural memory with geographic removal.

Rather than being barred from returning home, American Indians have had the experience of being interned and administered on their own land. They have been removed from or legally deprived of specific places that their nations held sacred; relocated to "Indian territories" on reservations or in Oklahoma; and then administered through the culturally genocidal practices of Indian boarding schools and the prohibition of Indian religions. As both Gloria Anzaldúa and John Martínez Weston point out, native and mestizo peoples often inhabit lands that are historically theirs but have been reshaped by colonial power.[3] Ties to the land are important as practice, much as ties to Africa or to a syncretic Afro-Creole culture are the products of historical struggle. "It is the land," asserts Gail Guthrie Valaskakis, "real and imagined, lived in heritage and current political process, and expressed in discourse, which constitutes the connection between nature and culture for Indians."[4] As evidenced by contemporary struggles at Black Mountain, the Paha Sapa (Black Hills), and Mole Lake, to name only a few, simple geographic proximity does not necessarily facilitate access to cultural practices of the land.[5] Patterns of im/migration and administration partially determine the relationship of diasporic peoples to their homes. I will discuss these two strands of Indian and Caribbean history together, and then move on to consider the role of mass culture in what Robert Orsi calls "the inner history" of im/migration.[6]

HEMISPHERIC MOVES

For both Indian and Caribbean people, moves to New York City and Minneapolis after World War II were only the most recent phase of ongoing migrations. People have moved throughout the history of this hemisphere, responding initially to the pressures of colonization and slavery that moved Indians west and brought Africans to the New World, and, in the twentieth century, to the hemispheric politics of labor and resources. Im/migration involves cycles of regional and hemispheric economic development; political restrictions such as immigration policy and official relocation programs; and local negotiations about municipal empowerment. The international economy has always pulled local versions of identity into a broader dialogue: race and class, ethnicity and nation are powerful narratives told both within and beyond the borders of the nation at different historical junctures.

From colonial conflicts over land up to the present-day pattern of leaving the reservations to find employment, migration has been a central feature of the experience of Indian people. The historical exigencies of such geographic mobility have brought about, in turn, cultural invention and change. The relocation of many nations to "Indian territory" in Oklahoma after 1830 brought different Indian cultures into close proximity. Such proximity, as James Howard and others have argued, led to the development of a pan-Indian culture in Oklahoma.[7] This pan-Indian culture centrally featured the powwow, which had long been a site where Indian nations have met to socialize.[8] As both William Powers and Carol Rachlin point out, the development of a pan-Indian culture in Oklahoma did not extinguish specific tribal cultures; nor does it signal the inevitability of assimilation. "There is no renascence of Indian culture in central and western Oklahoma," Rachlin argues, "because Indian culture there never died in order to be reborn."[9]

Relocation to Oklahoma brought diverse Indian peoples together. Before the Dawes Act (1887), the federal government used Oklahoma as a place to exile defeated Indian nations from the Midwest, South, and Southwest. Many of the newly arrived exiles, then, carried along with them the recent memory of pan-Indian political alliances, such as the one in the Ohio River Valley between Shawnee, Potowatomie, Miami, and Delaware nations in the early part of the nineteenth century, or other struggles, such as the Apache-Comanche resistance in Arizona and New Mexico.[10] At a powwow in Hinckley, Minnesota, during the summer of

1994, eleven-year-old Little Miss Shawnee Oklahoma proudly explained to me that her nation, the Shawnee, were among the last Indians to be relocated to Oklahoma, because of their historic resistance to Euroamerican expansion. The development of pan-Indianism in Oklahoma, then, was not consonant with assimilation or necessarily with the loss of specific tribal cultures. The powwow, a gathering that traditionally provided a space for contact among Indians of diverse nations, became a significant social form in this intertribal context.

It is important here to distinguish between assimilation, which denotes the gradual melting of different cultural groups into Americans, and acculturation, which signals the ongoing process of cultural adaptation and change. Many scholars have written about the ways Indians used Christian and federal institutions (churches, schools) to further their survival in an increasingly Euroamerican context and simultaneously to preserve native cultures.[11] Indians often drew on Euroamericans' efforts to assimilate them for their own ends; federal boarding schools in the twentieth century, as both K. Tsianina Lomawaima and Brenda Childs have documented, served Indian parents in hard times when they could not provide for their children's well-being, as well as becoming sites of resistance, where children from diverse tribes educated one another in their religious beliefs and languages, intermarried, and forged new political alliances.[12] Pan-Indian practices, such as the Ghost Dance of the 1880s and 1890s, allowed for the circulation of traditional Indian forms of dance, song, and culture around the fragmented geography of this time period. The Ghost Dance Movement used the trains and mail service to circulate people and ideas; many of its leaders, educated in missions or in off-reservation schools, used English as a movement lingua franca.[13] Both boarding schools and other pan-Indian forms, such as the Ghost Dance and the Native American Church, the Society of American Indians, and even the notorious Wild West shows aided in the circulation of cultural forms between Oklahoma and the Plains, and from these two centers of colonial pan-Indianism throughout Indian nations in the United States and Canada.[14] Michael Rynkiewich traces the spread of the Grass Dance from Oklahoma tribes such as the Pawnee to the Dakota by the end of the nineteenth century, and east to Minnesota and Wisconsin Ojibwa in the early twentieth century.[15] Pan-Indian diffusion combines with local tradition and invention in complex forms such as the Grass Dance, which is danced to local forms of drumming by dancers who wear costumes bearing both local and intertribal markings.

With the end of the period of removal and the implementation of the reservation system, Indian people were relegated to small pieces of land. Because the Dawes Act allotted land to individuals rather than along traditional lines, the reservation system after 1887 resulted in loss of land to entrepreneurs who offered quick cash for ancestral holdings; to swindlers who swapped paper titles for farm and forest land; and to outright theft by federal agents and Euroamerican settlers. In addition, the reservation system often broke up existing family and band alliances. Lakota individuals from a band near Pine Ridge, for example, might find themselves enrolled on the Rosebud or Standing Rock reservation. This tendency of the reservation system to break up existing social ties was exacerbated by the blood quantum standard, which mandated that individuals had to prove one-quarter lineage from a specific reservation to be officially recognized as Indian. The reservation system disrupted indigenous political organizations: the systems Indian people had devised to deal with cultural contact and trade. Aware of the potentially devastating effects of allotment on Indian life, both traditional leaders and a newer generation of reservation "progressives" struggled to maintain native lands and identities.[16] And, as Harold Hickerson argues, this colonial displacement brought about an emphasis on cultural organizations, such as drum societies and local councils, in Indian social life.[17]

Federal Indian policy attempted to break up native relationships: to the land; to social organizations of band and nation; and to religious and cultural practices. Because of their association with Indian military resistance, many religious and cultural forms were driven underground. Noel Dyck contrasts the efforts of Indian people to maintain their lands and culture to the impetus of U.S. and Canadian policy in implementing reservation systems in the late nineteenth century, explaining that federal policy assaulted all forms of Indian community in the interests of promoting the individualism necessary for capitalist development.[18]

At the same time that federal policy assaulted existing practices, it stressed the assimilation of Indian people during the postallotment period.[19] Colonel Richard H. Pratt had founded a boarding school at Carlisle, Pennsylvania, in 1879 with the motto "Kill the Indian and civilize the man."[20] Indian boarding schools attempted to silence and shame Indian students, and to prevent them from speaking their languages or practicing their cultures and religions, going so far as to force Indian boys to dress as girls until they spoke English.[21] The standard curriculum at federal boarding schools, half days in the classroom and the rest at manual labor, had, in fact, originated at the Fort Marion prison as part of a program to civilize Arapaho, Cheyenne, Comanche, and Kiowa prisoners there.[22] Bill Means, director of the American Indian Industrial Opportunities Center (IOC) in Minneapolis and a longtime activist and member of the American Indian Movement, explained the effects of federal policy on Indian people in this way: "Through missionary schools, the assimilation process, you know, boarding schools, having that pretty much disallowed. Not only religiously, but culturally and linguistically as well. Weren't allowed to speak our language. So that generation, two or three, four generations, it all, almost, left us."[23]

By forcing geographical and cultural relocation, the boarding schools attempted cultural genocide in the name of assimilation and progress. At the same time, the boarding schools created a group of English-speaking intellectuals. Many of these bicultural individuals were involved in political pan-Indian reform efforts, such as the Indian Reform Association, founded in 1882.[24] Like the relocation to Oklahoma, the boarding schools forced Indians from diverse regions and cultures together. In addition to the class of reformers who emerged from the boarding school experience, the many Indian students went back home with common experiences and with a cultural pan-Indianism forged out of the immediate exigencies of institutional life. Lomawaima writes: "Tribal and pan-Indian identity were reinforced, not diluted, in Indian schools."[25] Along with Buffalo Bill's Wild West Show, the boarding schools, most of them located in the Midwest, helped to disseminate and popularize Plains Indian traditions as pan-Indian style.[26]

Indian people responded to forced relocation and cultural prohibitions with syncretic invention and historical alacrity. Similarly, the history of Carnival illuminates the ongoing struggle of Caribbean people as they created a home in exile from their diverse nations of origin. The history of Carnival begins in Trinidad and then travels, along with various migrations, throughout the Caribbean and later to Britain, Canada, and the United States.

Characterized by an eighteenth-century observer as "the sinkhole of the Eastern Caribbean," colonial Trinidad was a refuge for diverse populations of escaped slaves, renegade revolutionaries, and Catholics who did not fit into the British colonial order of other West Indian colonies. The island was settled by French, Spanish, and British colonists; by French republicans fleeing Napoleon's ascendancy; by generations of Creole and African slaves as well as free Blacks, some of whom had served in the British forces in Virginia; by Africans escaped from slave ships or freed from service in the

British West Indian Regiment; by Arawak and Carib Indians who had fled east from colonization and sugar cultivation, as well as native traders from the Latin American mainland; by East Indian laborers, who came as indentured servants after the slaves were freed in 1838; and by Chinese, Portuguese, Syrian, and Lebanese trading minorities.[27]

Carnival has traditionally been a site where the complex class and ethnic relationships among this diverse population have been articulated through inversion, parody, and imagination.[28] Where American Indians were "removed" out of the way of the developing United States, Afro-Creole slaves and their European owners were forced into an uneasy cohabitation on plantations as well as in cities. Because of its liberal colonization policies and the comparatively late introduction of sugar, Trinidad did not have the same rate of absentee plantation landlords as other colonies, such as Cuba and Santo Domingo. In addition, the presence of a sizable population of free people of color complicated the race question, both before and after emancipation. The colonial administration of culture provided symbolic resolution to questions of race and power, much as it did in the case of the federal Indian policy. Because the Afro-Creole and African populations were a much larger proportion of their populations in the Caribbean than Indians were in North America, the African influence permeated Caribbean culture; its effects on Carnival after emancipation were difficult to ignore. Supposedly disappearing but noble Indians came to symbolize a virtuous republican past in North America, but it was harder ideologically to sweep colonial cultures free of the African. Throughout Trinidadian history, Carnival and other public processions, such as the Madrasi Hindu festival of "fire pass" and the Muslim festival of Muhurram, have been focal points for this struggle between cultural invention, appropriation, and suppression.[29]

Initially imported to the island by the French, the Carnival preceding Lent during slavery days featured the cross-dressing and class inversion of European Catholic festival days. Slaves were not permitted to masquerade, though it is likely that they performed for their masters. Certainly Caribbean masquerading traditions—"playing mas'," as it is called today—retain as many African influences as they do European ones, although, because of the ongoing repression of the African in Trinidadian history, it is harder to document them.[30] British authorities, in command in Trinidad after 1797, banned drumming altogether in their colonies, starting in Jamaica in 1792. Drums sounded threatening and unfamiliar to European ears, and were associated by Africans and their descendants with Shango, the Yoruba god of war and fire.[31]

Free Blacks and the Creole working and middle classes celebrated Carnival in the period between 1797, the beginning of British rule, and 1838,
when the four years of indenture after emancipation in 1834 expired.
Fearing the disorder caused by drinking and dancing in the street, the
British passed a law in 1808 requiring police permission for Blacks to
hold parties after 8 P.M.[32] The Creole middle class in Port of Spain obtained police permission to hold balls, although they still faced a curfew
at 9:30 P.M. and were expected to carry lanterns.[33] The French Catholic
upper classes preferred house parties and costume balls. In the ongoing
cross-racial exchange of the Americas, which Eric Lott has so aptly
dubbed "love and theft," the upper classes favored costumes portraying
field and house slaves, while Black celebrants, according to contemporary descriptions, often dressed in mock-European finery as kings and
queens and English mummers.[34]

Although they had been prohibited from participating in Carnival before emancipation, slaves had maintained and invented their Afro-Creole
culture in the small gaps in colonial administration. In *canboulay* (from
cannes brûlées, French for burning sugar cane), for example, slaves
would march to the fields to extinguish sugar cane fires, carrying torches
and singing songs. Along with command performances for the slave owners, canboulay was a rare opportunity for slaves to perform without sanction. After emancipation, canboulay transcended its function as a slave
fire squad, becoming an important site for Afro-Creole invention. Groups
of revelers would march with their lit torches through the street in the
early hours of Carnival morning; this pre-Carnival festival, called *j'ouvert,* or break of day, has been a site of suppressed Afro-Creole practices
throughout Trinidadian and, as we shall see, Brooklyn history. As freed
slaves moved away from the countryside and into urban centers, Carnival became more African during the 1860s and 1870s, driving respectable European and Creole classes away from a street festival that
had become a festival for the "urban black underworld."[35]

In 1881, as Ghost Dancers prepared themselves to fight for a land
newly replenished with buffalo and rid of whites, Black working-class
canboulay revelers clashed with police in Port of Spain in what have come
to be know as the Canboulay Riots. Predominantly Afro-Creole revelers
clashed with police in Princess Town in 1884 and in Cedras in 1885, and
a struggle between Islamic Asian Indians celebrating Muhurram (Hosay)
with the colonial authorities in 1884 resulted in twelve deaths and approximately one hundred injuries.[36] British colonial authorities responded
to these incidents by abolishing canboulay and fixing the time for the start

of Carnival at 6 A.M. in the so-called Peace Preservation Act of 1884. Commissioner Hamilton went so far as to recommend that the British fleet be anchored off Trinidad during Carnival season.[37]

Throughout Trinidadian history, Carnival has been the focal point for encounters between the colonial administration and the impetus of grassroots imagination. In the 1870s, as colonial authorities began clamping down on the new Afro-Creole practice of masquerading at Carnival, they banned the Madrasi Hindu "fire pass" festival; in the 1880s, such restrictions resulted in both the Canboulay Riots and the Muharram Massacre.[38] At the same time that these festivals were sites for working-class Black and East Indian performances of social unrest, sometimes resulting in physical clashes with the police, these conflicts marked and reinforced fears of working-class culture among both white Creoles and the colored middle class.[39] The latter groups responded by participating in Carnival in limited ways, holding private parties and sometimes taking advantage of the masquerading tradition to attend Carnival unnoticed, avoiding the social sanction that could come from such participation.[40] Civic efforts to police Carnival, to make it safer and more respectable, resulted in an ongoing struggle between working-class Blacks with their Afro-Creole cultural forms and the colored middle class, which favored a more European, regulated Carnival, with contained performances of more Africanized forms.

Carnival forms such as calypso and steel drums originated in the increasingly urbanized Black working class,[41] while the European origins of costuming mingled with African retention and New World invention in both the themes and designs of the costumes. In 1846 an observer of Carnival masquerades reported seeing pirates, Turks, Scottish Highlanders, Wild Indians, the Angel Gabriel, and Death portrayed at Carnival. He observed a group of Black Trinidadians "as nearly naked as might be, bedaubed with a black varnish. One of this gang had a long chain and padlock attached to his leg, which chain the others pulled. What this typified, I was unable to learn; but, as the chained one was occasionally thrown down on the ground and treated with a mock bastinadoing, it probably represented slavery."[42] By the 1860s, the Black urban working class had taken over Carnival in the streets.[43]

The social organization of Carnival reflects the historical development of urban Black working-class spaces in tenement yards: mas' bands (groups of people wearing thematic costumes); pan yards (places where the steel drums are made and played); and even "tribes" of "Wild Indians" who wore costumes that separated them into groups of black, red,

blue, and white Indians and spoke a language unintelligible to out-
siders.[44] Donald Hill discusses the importance of the "yard and the road"
in Carnival history: the rural yard had been the center of plantation life
for the slaves, while the yards in Black working-class neighborhoods
were the focal points of urban social life. The road became a place where
the Carnival forms developed in urban yards would compete, both symbolically and sometimes with actual physical conflicts in stick fighting
and steel band rivalries. Calypso tents, on the other hand, developed as
a middle-class response to these working-class spaces of yard and road:
like the mas' bands, they provided the middle class with a more shel-
tered, controlled place to enjoy Carnival.[45]

Many members of early steel bands during the 1930s and 1940s were
also supporters of labor struggles in the predominantly Black oilfields.[46]
The emergence of road and yard forms such as the steel band into mainstream Trinidadian Carnival and its appropriation from the "grass roots"
by the "national" marks a cultural negotiation over class, race, and national identity.

At the same time that Carnival has been marked by conflict over racial
meanings between Europeans, the Creole middle classes, and the Black
working class, it has also helped to consolidate a national identity based
in an African heritage. The development of calypso and the steel band
in the 1930s and 1940s in Trinidad as grass-roots forms critical of class
and colonial domination pushed the African aspects of Caribbean culture into the political foreground of Trinidadian life. Donald Hill writes:

> If fancy mas' was a harbinger of colored Creole power for the middle class,
> the steel band was a forerunner of a re-afrocreolization of the entire Creole
> complex, a development that eventually led to political independence. Car-
> nival was once again being pushed by the grass roots, as in the 1880s. These
> groups tended to retain Afro-Creole culture to a greater degree than the mid-
> dle and upper classes. The fusion of the new steel-band Carnival to the struc-
> ture of the middle-class fancy mas' Carnival that had been evolving for fifty
> years resulted in a modern, truly Creole-Trinidadian popular culture, a
> re-afrocreolized culture.[47]

The steel band movement has been significant for the development of
Trinidadian nationalism, at home as well as in New York. Often appropriated from the grass roots to speak of an entire nation, Carnival forms
have been intricately linked with the development of a national identity.
Black working-class neighborhoods such as Laventille, then, become simultaneously places of national origin and invention and "bad neighborhoods" of denizens that need more discipline.[48] Since decolonization,

Carnival has become a national symbol, a site where, as the saying goes, "all o' we is one." In such a small and diverse country, such a motto takes on a charged and contradictory meaning. East Indian and other strands in the rich multiethnic society of Trinidad tend to be obscured by the promotion of an Afro-diasporic national identity. Such strands are only slowly evident in the acknowledgment of the contributions of East Indian music to calypso, the participation of East Indian people in Carnival bands, and the evolution of "chutney soca" and the coronation of non-Black carnival queens and kings.[49]

Because Trinidad has always been a profoundly multicultural society, with a high rate of in- and out-migrations, Carnival did not remain a strictly Trinidadian cultural form. Both Dawn Marshall and Elsa Chaney delineate four stages of Caribbean im/migration: interterritorial movement after emancipation as former slaves left the plantations, primarily for English-speaking islands; movement toward the Hispanic Caribbean and, in smaller numbers, to the United States in search of work during the late nineteenth and early twentieth centuries; a slower rate of migration during World War I and the Great Depression; and the massive emigration to the United Kingdom, Canada, and the United States after World War II. Four million Caribbean people left the region, primarily for the United States and Canada, between 1950 and 1980.[50] Cultural forms, such as the calypsos and costumes of Carnival, must have circulated through the Caribbean and reached the United States well before the arrival of the largest wave of Caribbean immigration, after 1965. And as Carnival cultures spread, they change to suit their locales, becoming variously a means of ethnic expression, a link to home, and a source of racial or pan-African solidarity and pride.[51] If "All o' we is one" was a popular slogan in Brooklyn as well as Port of Spain in the 1990s, the questions "Who is we?"; "Who is all?"; and "Under what circumstances does 'we' come together as 'one'?" are profoundly political im/migrant questions.

THE LONG PAST AND THE CHANGING SAME

Indian and Caribbean people came to the U.S. urban landscape with cultural traditions that had long been articulated in the contexts of migration and repression. The revivals that have taken place in Minneapolis and New York during the post–World War II period are part of these traditions, which are always in dialogue with places known and affectively experienced as "home," even for those who have never visited the specific island nation that they claim, or who do not have the blood quantum for enrollment on a rural reservation. The carnivals and powwows that urban Indians and Caribbean migrants celebrate in New York and Minneapolis, like the festivals of the past, negotiate oppressive political and socioeconomic hierarchies.

"Tradition," in this context, is always contradictory, invented at the same moment that it lays its claims on the past. Tradition can be politically mobilized by the hierarchical authority of national, racial, or patriarchal formations, as it has been at various times. Mined with the multiple contradictions of a multicultural and migratory history, traditions also contain space for negotiation and reinvention.

New powwow forms invented in the post–Dawes Act period brought together Euroamerican style with native concerns. The Jingle Dress Dance, for example, was based on the dream of an Ojibwa elder about how to heal his sick daughter in Mille Lacs, Minnesota, in 1919.[52] The dress, an elegant cotton dress with a tiered skirt, was adorned with jingling metal cones made from Copenhagen chewing tobacco cans. When the women dancers move with a dignified step around the powwow circle, the cones make a jingling noise; the wearer creates a movement that both looks and sounds beautiful. The Jingle Dress Dance spread throughout Ojibwa country on reservation powwows during the 1920s; it also made a comeback during the 1950s.[53] Perhaps the dance's metaphorical message, about using the implements of mass culture to heal a sickness of Indian people, held great appeal in these periods of cultural deprivation and enforced assimilation.[54]

Ellie Favel, a guidance counselor and teacher at Heart of the Earth Survival School in Minneapolis, explained contemporary jingle dress stories among Indian people in the northern United States and Canada: "Well, the jingle dress story, the one that the elders gave me the right to tell, is from the Lake of the Woods area. And there's three that I heard: one from that lake, Red Lake, that area. And there's even one I heard from Sisseton, South Dakota. And they're all a little bit different, but they're all, you know, special, because they're visions and dreams, and the vision was a gift from the Creator."[55]

Individual tellers are given permission to relate specific stories about the jingle dress, as well as about other powwow forms, such as the Grass Dance. Those who tell these stories publicly always announce the origins and partiality of the story, leaving room for the multiple layers of historicity these forms carry.[56]

As much as tradition is entwined with the historical exigencies of invention, the preservation of Carnival folk arts has been increasingly involved with the development of the mass culture industry in the twentieth century. Just as Caribbean and Indian people negotiated the repressive effects of colonial administration and migration, they also deal with the increasing power of mass culture as it not only commodifies and exoticizes their cultural practices but also allows for the huge increase in the reach and speed of specific forms.

Recent scholarship has documented the dependence of emergent mass culture at the turn of the twentieth century on working-class popular forms. Early films drew on the popularity of immigrant theater and vaudeville, much as the minstrel shows, with their love, hate, and theft of Black culture, provided the grounds for a white audience for Afro-diasporic cultural forms. As early as 1910, Victor Recording Companies was recording Trinidadian calypsos for a New York audience that was made up of both West Indian immigrants and white socialites.[57] In Los Angeles during the same time period, Chicanos, Jews, and Italians found work in the emergent film industry; movies depicting frontier conflicts needed extras to play Indians, but avoided hiring Indian people, because of their supposed volatility.[58]

The early mass culture industry drew on narratives of migration and transformation as they were encoded in Afro-Atlantic performative forms. Tin Pan Alley songwriters, for example, drew on the "coon songs" of Black and white performers, including the most famous African-American musical comedy star, a Bahamian immigrant named Bert Williams, to write the tunes that came to embody American urban glamour and power.

Music, in particular, would continue to cross over between Afro-Caribbean performers and Euroamerican mass audiences. The song that became popular as "Rum and Coca-Cola," for example, originated as a Martiniquan folk song, and became popular in Trinidad during the 1890s. In the 1940s, Lord Invader put new lyrics to the tune and popularized it throughout the Caribbean. Decca Records, a U.S. company that had been recording West Indian calypsos and folk songs during the 1930s, released an Andrews Sisters cover of "Rum and Coca-Cola" during World War II. This popular song helped sustain Decca through the war and a protracted musicians' strike, and revived the popularity of calypso music in North America.[59]

The title proclaims the mixing of Yankee ingenuity—Coca Cola, possibly the most widely marketable product of U.S. capital—with a well-known

Caribbean intoxicant. That the two are both sugar-based products is interesting, as Eric Williams, the first prime minister of Trinidad, has noted: "Strange that an article like sugar, so sweet and necessary to human existence, should have occasioned such crimes and bloodshed!"[60] But the song also tells the story of a more contemporary colonial mixture: Yankee capital and Caribbean labor. Here Caribbean women earn their "Yankee dollars" by working to please U.S. soldiers stationed on their islands. The song, as well as the pattern of postcolonial economic development, feminizes labor.[61] In addition, it narrates the close connection between economic and cultural circulation in the Western Hemisphere.

The rise of a mass culture industry facilitated the spread of both pan-Indian powwows and Caribbean Carnival at the same time that it influenced changes in these forms. Buffalo Bill's Wild West Show, which toured the country with Indian dancers, drummers, and such famous warriors as Sitting Bull, spread Plains Indian cultural forms throughout the Indian United States, resulting in the diffusion of such practices as the Grass Dance and of the Lakota war bonnet to other cultural regions. Sitting Bull, as well as Chief Joseph of the Nez Percé, Jack Red Cloud, the son of the famous Lakota chief, and Métis veterans of the Riel Rebellion of 1886 all toured in the show.[62] Because the popularity of the Wild West Show coincided with the final military conflicts over the intermountain West, Plains Indian forms came to symbolize resistance to other Indian people.[63] In addition, the Wild West Show introduced elements of non-Indian origin into powwow practices: the Master of Ceremonies figure, the Grand Entry Procession, the contest powwow, and the Indian Princess competition, all central elements in contemporary powwow culture.[64] Some of the major powwows in the country date back to the turn of the twentieth century. William Powers writes of the influence of the Wild West Show on Indian performances:

> The famous Wild West shows of the latter part of the nineteenth century, which partly gave rise to the notion of War Dance, also created for the next century the idea of the Indian musical performer as showman. Along with this newfound role came attributes of the theatrical performer—a calendar of events, performance outside the usual setting—the rodeo arena, coliseum, auditorium, theatrical stage.[65]

Another "tribe" of Indians influenced by the Wild West Show, the Mardi Gras Indians of New Orleans, combined Afro-Atlantic Carnival performances with their interpretation of both their own mixed bloodlines and of the touring anticolonial Plains heroes.[66] "Playing Indian" is an old Caribbean Carnival tradition, dating back to the appearance of

Indian laborers at Carnival during the 1840s. Latin American Indians, probably from the Orinoco Delta of Venezuela, traded in Trinidad up until they were barred during the 1920s. Rural communities in Trinidad and throughout the Caribbean claim Indian ancestry, as did a few of the people I interviewed during the course of my research.[67] By the end of the nineteenth century, as local Indian identities were obscured and half-forgotten in Afro-Creole culture, the images of North American Indians replaced those of Caribbean Indians.[68] While much has been written about the prevalence of native imagery at Carnival, I think two factors are salient: first, the persistence of native communities, such as Arima, in Trinidad through the early nineteenth century and the intermarriage of Trinidadian as well as mainland Latin American Indians with Venezuelan migrant workers; second, the organization of secret West African societies during slavery into "regiments," featuring kings, queens, and mock-European military uniforms.[69] These two strands of historical memory inform the prevalence of "Indians" at Carnival, from the nineteenth century to the present.

Wild Indians were among the most popular Carnival bands throughout Trinidadian history. Their descendants, the often spectacular "Fancy Indians," remain popular today among master costume designers as well as among those who want to slap something together quickly to wear on Carnival morning. People who "play Indian" at Carnival explain their costumes variously. They talk about the tradition of Carnival Indians, about the Carib Indians in the Caribbean, about the multicultural history of Trinidad, and, in the United States, sometimes about the struggles of Native Americans against colonization. One costume designer I met in Brooklyn during the summer of 1993 showed me his Carnival king, a ten-foot-tall Indian figure. Two years after the Mohawk resistance at Oka made headlines throughout the country, the Carnival king of the Association of Belizean Americans was called "Mohawk Spirit Dancer."

Narratives of frontier conflict have long been a staple of American popular culture. In addition to Fancy and Wild Indians, two other popular Carnival figures emerge from frontier conflicts. The Trinidadian tradition of the Midnight Robber, derived from the icon of the masked cowboy, "holds up" onlookers and must be paid off in contributions of change. Although this costume has diverse incarnations, Daniel Crowley's folkloric research led him to speculate that the probable source of imagery for the Midnight Robber figure was the pulp or "Texas" magazines, an early form of the Western genre, with its romanticized cowboys and noble Indians, popular in the 1890s.[70] Another extremely popular figure at Carnival, the

Fancy Sailor, originates from working-class parody of the endless procession of colonial occupiers: French, British, and, after the visit of the American fleet in 1907 presaged the ongoing presence of U.S. troops in Port of Spain, Yankee Sailors. "Sailor mas'" bands, which in the 1940s often sported long noses in the shape of U.S. fighter planes, were closely associated with the evolution of the steel band in working-class Black neighborhoods of Port of Spain.[71]

Mass culture must be seen as a part of the colonial enterprise. Tourism has been almost as ongoing a source of interest in Caribbean and Indian cultures as hunger for land, resources, and labor. Rarely situating Indian and Caribbean people in their actual historical circumstances, films exoticize and objectify them. Frontier narratives rewrote the history of the West at the same time that the nascent music industry bleached the Afro-Atlantic origins of much popular song. Mass media images of contemporary immigrants and urban Indians are almost inevitably negative: one more piece of a seemingly formidable colonial arsenal that breaks apart colonized nations and national minorities, and with them cultures and memories. It becomes difficult to separate mass media images of waves of poor brown and Black people mobbing the shores and cities of the United States from the equally surreal policy initiatives designed to "deal with them."

At the same time, mass culture imagery can be appropriated as part of a temporary shelter against the colonial effort as a whole. Midnight Robbers symbolically mug people at Carnival, demanding a share of the loot, while drunk and dirty Yankee Sailors cavort, offering entertainment and a reminder that imperial force is made up of men who depend on Port of Spain for their pleasure. The Master of Ceremonies at powwows is likely derived from the imperialist spectacle provided by Buffalo Bill Cody, but today he is also likely to talk about red power and rallies for treaty rights. These symbolic figures, by themselves, do nothing to oppose the ongoing depredations of imperial capital; but they imaginatively reconfigure a mass-mediated universe.

Carnival in New York and powwow in Minneapolis encode a history of resistance to colonial administration. But I want to conclude this chapter on the colonial past of these festivals by skipping forward in time to look at the ways these festivals carry on the traditions of invention and resistance in these urban contexts. Grass Dancers and Midnight Robbers, jingle dresses and steel bands: all arrive in an urban landscape that offers Indian and Caribbean people only partial access to power and citizenship. These festival denizens, bearing their complex and potent historical legacy, signify richly about alternative notions of citizenship, nationality, and home.

Just as the Midnight Robber and the Yankee Sailor costumes reflect the circulation of popular imagery throughout the United States, Canada, Britain, and the Caribbean, the meanings of Carnival in metropolitan contexts shift. Alma Guillermoprieto notes the rediscovery of Zumbi, the leader of the maroon community Palmares, in the late 1970s by Brazilian Carnival designers. Emphasis on Zumbi in Carnival floats paralleled contemporary Afro-Brazilian interest in Black history and cultural pride.[72] Similarly, Abner Cohen, in his detailed study of Notting Hill Carnival in London, talks about how Rastafarian themes emerged as the festival became both more dominantly West Indian and more explicitly political during the 1970s. Cohen explains these changes by emphasizing the role of Carnival in immigrant identity formation. "London carnival was continuously transformed, within certain cultural and social conventions, into an expression of, and an instrument for, the development of a new homogeneous West Indian culture that transcended affiliations to islands of origin, to confront the economic and political realities of contemporary Britain."[73]

In Brooklyn, contemporary Carnival practices deploy different structures of meaning than the same practices would elsewhere. As Philip Kasinitz points out, eating a roti on Eastern Parkway on Labor Day in Brooklyn takes on an ethnic significance it lacks in Trinidad.[74] At the same time, the meanings of costumes and music are always in dialogue with the Caribbean as well as with other metropolitan festivals, inventing local practices both traditional and specific to New York. The name of the mas' camp and front office for the West Indian–American Day Carnival Association in 1992, "The Culture of Black Creation," has a different meaning in Brooklyn than it would have had in Port of Spain or London. Brooklyn Carnival emphasizes West Indian Black ethnic identity against the background of a predominantly African-American city. The name "The Culture of Black Creation" carries both ethnic and Afrocentric pride. Gesturing to second-generation Caribbean-Americans and to African-Americans with a broadly inclusive pan-Africanism, the name simultaneously points out to Caribbean immigrants that their culture is as Black, and can be as proud, as the African-American culture that surrounds them. It also points to the geographical segregation in New York of Afro- and Indo-Caribbean im/migrants. One year and several blocks from the 1991 Crown Heights conflict, the name of the mas' camp also announced its origins and alliances to those passing by the building.

The tendency of Trinidadian Carnival bands to memorialize actual and imagined pasts was amplified in the 1950s, when the designer Harold Saldenha began to draw on contemporary Hollywood imagery to create themes rooted in past empires—Romans, Greeks, and Asians.[75] Carnival designers have always done extensive research into the themes and sartorial specifications of their bands; through Hollywood productions, images of cultures elided in British canonical histories became available.[76] More recently, Carnival themes have turned to imagining great non-European empires of the past, particularly in Brooklyn.

In Brooklyn as in Trinidad, Indian, Asian, and African empires are especially popular. The celebration of empire on Eastern Parkway carries resonance of im/migrant national pride. Carnival in Brooklyn, after all, falls on or directly after Trinidad's Independence Day; many of the sound systems move down the parkway on floats that proclaim Panamanian, Belizean, or Grenadian pride and solidarity. At the same time, in the context of contemporary Afrocentricity in Brooklyn, the celebration of non-Western empires also relates directly to a politicized geography of Blackness that draws heavily on the ideas of Egyptian and ancient African splendor. "I wouldn't even break it down in terms of Caribbean," one pan player argued. "I think what you see happening, especially in our community, is African."[77]

As Kasinitz argues, the strength of Carnival has always been in its multivocality, its refusal to speak in what sounds like a unified, political voice. While it frustrates politicians who attempt to support Carnival as representing a monolithic community, such multivocality allows for the existence of multiple layers of history. Such layers of history, in turn, constitute the grounds for the formation of a new urban identity; both Kasinitz and Frank Manning argue that Carnival is the space where West Indian immigrants mark an identity that is at once Black and distinct from the African-American community; ethnic but generically West Indian, rather than identified with any specific Caribbean nation.[78] In the cultural space of Carnival, then, immigrants and their children negotiate various claims of assimilation, racial identification, and dual loyalty.

At Brooklyn Carnival in 1992, the popular Hawks mas' band celebrated the Columbian Quincentennial by playing Empires of the Americas, with vast sections devoted to the Aztec, Inca, and Mixtex empires. The Culture of Black Creation mas' camp was dressed in the theme of Sophisticated Africa. A Trinidadian immigrant and an artist who makes the copper masks used by the large Carnival bands explained the importance of designing such costumes, connecting the Sophisticated Africa theme with the quincentennial work of reimagining history in general. This reimagining takes place in the contexts of local, regional, and international hierarchies of race and imperial power. "I am trying to imagine Africa in the years when Africa was a powerful nation," he said. "In order to do certain things, you have to use certain words, and people tend to get the wrong impression. But as soon as you say 'tribal,' people say that you are savage."[79]

Like Brooklyn Carnival, Trinidad Carnival in 1992 also featured bands that portrayed pre-Columbian splendor, illustrating Shadow's calypso hit of that year, "Columbus Lied." Such parallels indicate the constant circulation of contemporary Caribbean culture, from sending nation to metropole and back again. The popular historiography of Carnival involves the transatlantic transmission of intellectual currents, of dreams and imaginings of exile and homecoming. At the same time, the great popularity of such bands as Sophisticated Africa in contemporary Brooklyn and the rows of stalls along Eastern Parkway that sell Caribbean food along with contemporary Afrocentric commodities such as kente clothe and cowrie shells indicate the growth of a Caribbean-American Carnival culture that negotiates boundaries of race, ethnicity, and nationality to stake out a Caribbean identity in Brooklyn.

Like West Indians in Brooklyn, Indians in Minneapolis navigate the multiple hierarchies of contemporary urban life. As I have argued, pan-Indian culture in the United States developed in response to the exigencies of serial relocations, as well as the boarding school experience, the cultural imperialism perpetrated by Wild West shows and the Western genre of popular novels and films they influenced. In some cases, as Gail Guthrie Valaskakis writes in her political memoir about growing up in Lac du Flambeau, Wisconsin, the preservation of tradition mingled with pan-Indian performance in the context of tourism. The powwow at the Lac du Flambeau reservation, according to Valaskakis, became more tourist-oriented during the 1950s, as automobiles proliferated with postwar affluence, and with them the development of the white middle-class family vacation.[80] At the same time, according to Jim Clermont of the Lakota Porcupine Singers, the diffusion of automobile travel also helped proliferate powwow singing styles, as more Indians visited reservations during their annual powwows.

The knitting of traditional practices into the fabric of Indian life in Minneapolis required adaptation into an urban, intertribal context. Along with the memories woven into the fabric of daily life, Indian people in the 1950s and 1960s inherited a history of direct repression of

Indian religion and cultures.[81] Many practices had been partially lost as a result of the boarding school experience and the "civilizing" imperatives of reservation missions.[82] While many aspects of Indian culture flourished in spite of official repression, Indians in the cities were often hesitant to display what they knew. In 1955 the newsletter of American Indians Inc., an intertribal social group that held powwows in dance halls and community centers, noted of a recent event: "Even though there were but few costumes in evidence, everyone joined in for a good time."[83] Five years later the *American Indian Center News* exhorted those attending the center's monthly powwows: "You should have your Indian regalia on when you dance on the floor. At least men should have some kind of Indian dress. Ladies who are dancing should at least have an Indian feather in their hair. Many of our Indian dances have a meaning—and should be danced with a spirit of reverie."[84]

In attempting to reinvent this spirit of reverie, Twin Cities Indian organizations confronted a long history of repression. Bill Means described the early days of the American Indian Movement during the 1960s, when AIM organizers decided to include drumming and singing in their demonstrations. He recalled: "See, when AIM first started, we used to have to go get the singers out of bars and—because a lot of our Indian people didn't even want to sing, because in some ways they were kind of ashamed, unless if they had a few beers. And then they said, 'Oh, wow, let me be an Indian.'" In creating a politicized cultural revival in Minneapolis, Indians drew on their diverse cultures, bringing them together into an urban pan-Indian form.

According to both Clermont and Powers, the move from the reservation to the cities changed the ways people sang and danced. Migrants brought their songs to the cities and shared them; by 1962 the Upper Midwest Indian Center boasted a singing group with members from the Crow, Chippewa, Sioux, Arapaho, Gros Ventre, and Canadian tribes. Powers argues that relocation changed singing styles because people who were not known for their singing in reservation communities often got involved in it in the cities, changing and reinterpreting traditional songs.[85]

With the mobility brought partially by relocation, singing groups traveled to various reservations. Groups such as the Porcupine Singers, traditionally based in Standing Rock and Pine Ridge, traveled around, teaching and performing. When the Porcupine Singers began to travel around the northern United States and Canada in the 1960s, Clermont recalled, they spread the Lakota singing style to diverse urban and reservation communities, "mainly in Canada. A lot of their powwows sat idle for many, many years. And, by us going and visiting powwows that started up on different reserves in Canada, a lot of the young boys learned our songs when we went up there to sing. . . . So a lot of the young boys, after we left, they said, 'Well, let's start a drum group.' "[86]

Today a popular drum group at both urban and reservation powwows is the Boyz. Jim Clermont's son, Hokie, started the group, along with Opie Day, who is a Nett Lake Ojibwa. Like the Porcupine Singers, the Boyz travel to reservations and urban powwows. Also like the Porcupine Singers, they influence other drum groups through the recordings that people make at powwows by standing around the drum group with small, portable tape recorders held high in the air. Unlike the Porcupine Singers, though, the Boyz are urban Indians: they sport the fade haircuts popular with their African-American contemporaries and listen to rap music at the same rate that they play tapes of drum groups at powwows. Their name, with its echoes of popular films like *Boyz in the Hood,* indicates the multiple influences of contemporary urban Indian culture.

The Boyz's participation in powwows marks their commitment to Indian culture, but as Valaskakis points out, this is not a simple maintenance of an uninterrupted tradition. Rather, urban Indians continue to transform a tradition that has survived largely because of the creativity and ongoing commitments of Indian people. Because Indians residing in urban areas often return to reservation communities for extended visits, to live, or for short periods during the summer "powwow trail," when Indians from all over the nation travel to weekend powwows held in rural communities, the urban Indian revival is in constant dialogue with reservation life as well.[87] Some years ago the Red Lake Nation changed its guidelines for the Red Lake Nation Princess competition. Previously, young women who wanted to represent the nation had to reside on the Red Lake Reservation; because many young women enrolled in the reservation live in the Twin Cities or in Bemidji, the competition was opened to women living in urban areas. Such changes indicate the ongoing "intertwining," as Valaskakis calls it, of contemporary Indian reality with local interpretations of tradition.

Means explained, "The powwow has become that link to our homeland and to the past for the urban area. On the reservation, where you live in that setting . . . of course they have a lot of powwows, and I think that for the urban Indian the powwow is really a chance to come together and to recreate that. In the past and to their home."[88]

As Carnival and powwow change to reflect and create new narratives of identity, these forms are also in dialogue with the urban environment.

Carnival and powwow move from being celebrations of a specific home culture to being expressions of emergent urban identity. As such, these festivals are in dialogue with the narratives about class, race, and ethnicity generated by state policy.

Chapter 3 discusses the foundational fictions of immigration and termination that brought Caribbean and Indian people to the cities during the 1950s and 1960s. This national romance operates at a local level through discourses of ethnic empowerment and machine politics: new immigrants to the cities work their way into municipal power by constituting themselves as the latest ethnic group to be absorbed into local opportunity structures. Of course, the conversion of foreign immigrants to white ethnics is race-based; these accommodations are less available to nonwhite immigrants.[89] The transnational cultures of such groups as urban Indians and Caribbean immigrants respond to racialized hierarchies. By maintaining and reinventing ties to home, these im/migrants use the ethnic model against itself, participating in nation-building "back home" and using their identities as a basis for local empowerment. Linda Basch, Nina Glick Schiller, and Cristina Szanton Blanc write: "Transmigrants simultaneously participate in nation-building in their home country and in processes of nation-building in the U.S. that are ordinarily subsumed under the rubric 'ethnicity.' "[90] The question, then, is the role that emergent pan–West Indian and pan-Indian identities play in the struggle for municipal power, for citizenship, or a role in the national romance. Racial and ethnic identity in Minneapolis and Brooklyn bear heavily on the positions of these communities in the urban order.

Im/migration Policy, the National Romance, and the Poetics of World Domination, 1945–1965

DECOLONIZATION AND IMPERIAL SLEIGHTS OF HAND: THE NATIONAL ROMANCE

This chapter analyzes the ways in which im/migration policy attempted to write Indians and immigrants into dominant imaginings of U.S. life during the postwar period. In those years a reexamination of national borders became ideologically significant, in light of emergent movements for self-determination and sovereignty among former colonies as well as minority groups within the country. The emergence of the United States as an international power after World War II makes possible the tremendous mobility of capital today. Historians and cultural critics must respond to this mobility by considering the powerful narrative of the nation, and what is done in its name.[1]

At the close of World War II, the United States consolidated its position as a world power. Like his European counterparts during the nineteenth century, the American publisher Henry Luce could now proclaim an "American century," in which the sun would never set on the busy whir and hum of an internationalized economy. Geopolitically, the nation had ascended to the leadership of the "free world," while domestically, the military-industrial complex had expanded and consolidated, using war production as the machine to pull the national economy out of the Depression. The spatial fix so crucial to capitalist development was available abroad as far as the imperial gaze could contemplate.[2] Unlimited Third World markets clamored for glitzy American products; and workers throughout the world could labor in microelectronics and undergarments plants, coffee and banana plantations. From the newly consolidated anti-communist alliance of NATO to the U.S. backed SEATO in Asia; from hemispheric domination perpetrated by single companies and backed by the CIA in Latin America to a developing mission to stop the spread of communism in Africa, the United States would dominate resources, diplomacy, and internal politics throughout much of the so-called free world. This geopolitical consolidation presented an ideological challenge: how could the same narratives that supported U.S. domestic and international imperialism also appear to foster egalitarian democracy?

American hegemony in the postwar period was a matter of controlling the flow of international labor, as well as extending the development of national resources to include lands guaranteed to Indian peoples. This hegemony, generally associated with the Cold War against communism both internally and externally, was crucially reliant on immigration and Indian policy: im/migration policy. By creating a national romance of assimilation and unity through citizenship, im/migration policy both authored and responded to formative discourses of race and ethnicity in this period. As Nikhil Pal Singh writes: "Anti-communism was the modus operandi for a political project in which a racial animus and an imperial ambition remained paramount, if sublated."[3] The assimilation of disparate cultures and politics into a harmonious national family was a key part of the rhetoric of corporate liberalism; social conflict would no longer be necessary in the technological progress guaranteed by capitalist democracy.[4] Cold War im/migration policies took the idea of bringing im/migrants into this family as a keystone of social order.

This notion of assimilation was part of a more general "foundational fiction" of national identity in the postwar period. "Foundational fictions," according to Doris Sommer, attempt to reconcile social inequalities by creating romantic fantasies of collective national destiny. Inevitably, these fictions betray their origins: they are specifically gendered, highly racialized imaginings of national unity that rely on a familiar cast of characters for their heroes, villains, and walk-ons. The importance of Sommer's work is that it teaches us about what she calls "the inextricability of politics from fiction in the history of nation building."[5]

The enduring rhetorical accomplishment of the foundational fiction of federal im/migration policy in the postwar period was to translate claims to civil rights and sovereignty into a language of ethnicity and assimilation. Because assimilation and racial hierarchy are both rooted in liberal political theory, policies designed to "assimilate" "aliens" into the national body will generate inequality, even as they seek to absolve it.[6] Just as different denizens of the state were required to take different routes to citizenship, the liberal idea of citizenship for all is always undercut by the racialization of public policy.[7] And im/migration policies generated resistance from the communities that were subject to them. As Richard H. Thompson writes: "the dialectic between ethnicity and the state . . . must be seen, at root, as a struggle over the institutional forms the new society will embrace."[8]

In the post–World War II period, the extractive power of First World capital increasingly involved the transformation of Third World workers into domestic laborers; in other words, workers around the world were recruited for the parts they would play in the national romance: as suitors (appropriate or inappropriate), servants (faithful or treacherous), or, simply, insignificant extras. This recruitment happened in plants built by multinational corporations in newly decolonized home countries; through austerity and "import substitution" programs implemented by the World Bank and other international development agencies, and through the emigration of large sections of the labor force away from the Third World and into the United States. At the same time, the national romance increasingly wrote Indians—the "domestic dependent nations" of nineteenth-century jurisprudence—into the national family, not as domestic dependent nations but as potential family members in need of domestication.

It is important to note that the policies aimed at the transformation of Indians and immigrants in this period had only partial success. Both groups attempted to use federal policy initiatives to advance alternative agendas of tribal land claims, expanded civil rights, and social and economic mobility. Attempts to modify denizens' lives from the top down often met with consequences that surprised politicians and policy makers. As K. Tsianina Lomawaima puts it, "no institution is total, no power is all-seeing, no federal Indian policy has ever been efficiently and rationally translated into practice, and much of the time produced unpredicted results anyway."[9]

At the same time that the U.S. consolidated domestic and international hegemony, nations all over the world were engaged in decolonization struggles. National liberation movements begun before World War II won political victories after 1945 in Asia, the Caribbean, and Africa. Weakened by centuries of colonial rule, nations such as Egypt, Senegal,

India, and Vietnam would nonetheless define themselves as politically independent. At the 1955 Bandung Conference in Indonesia, these African, Middle Eastern, and Asian nations asserted their commitment to economic and political sovereignty, and to resisting neocolonialism.[10] While they met with little success in combating a world system based on maintaining the economic benefits of colonialism, these decolonized nations did limit the ability of First World nations such as the United States to intervene, at least overtly, in their affairs of state.[11]

The rhetoric of decolonization abroad had substantial echoes within the borders of the United States. For Native Americans, the immediate postwar period was a time of changing consciousness. Like other minority veterans, native veterans such as Ira Hayes and the 382nd Platoon of Navajo code talkers returned from distinguishing themselves in defense of democracy to diminished opportunities, and to a national community that recognized them as citizens only in theory. The Dakota linguist Ella Deloria wrote in 1944: "The war has indeed wrought an overnight change in the outlook, horizon, and even the habits of the Indian people—a change that might not have come for many years yet."[12]

In the immediate postwar period, such organizations as the National Congress of the American Indian (NCAI), founded in 1944, contested the status of Indian people under federal law. The NCAI brought together, according to its first president, Napoleon Bonaparte Johnson, "a cross-section of Indian population: old and young, full-bloods, mixed-bloods, educated and uneducated Indians from allotted areas and others from reservations," all of whom "were dissatisfied with many phases of the government's administration of Indian affairs."[13] Many Indians initially supported a shift in policy, thinking either that the Bureau of Indian Affairs (BIA) was at last making good on the promise of self-rule made under John Collier in the 1930s or that they could best manage their own affairs as individual citizens of states. Urban California Indians, for example, favored termination, as it allowed them per capital settlements on lands from which they were dispossessed.[14] Eventually, however, the problems with termination and relocation policies catalyzed the formation of new alliances between Indians on reservations and in cities, and the emergence of a new generation of Indian activists.

Similarly, a coalition of ethnic, religious, and civil rights groups fought the imposition of restrictive immigration legislation throughout the 1950s. A diverse coalition opposed the McCarran-Walter Act (the Immigration and Nationality Act of 1954). African-American organizations such as the NAACP contested the racialized basis of the law. Civil rights groups were well aware that U.S. citizenship constituted a terrain of struggle, as the Reverend William J. Harvey noted at the NAACP's forty-third Convention in 1952: "We want you, our guests, to know that nearly every privilege of citizenship which we now enjoy has been fought for." The NAACP's yearly resolutions between 1952 and 1964 called for immigration reform and "the fair and equal treatment for all immigrants and prospective immigrants."[15]

African-American groups, because of the presence of Caribbean-Americans in civil rights organizations as well as the influence of pan-African and anticolonial discourses in the Black community, recognized the interdependence of Northern and Southern hemispheres. While Congress debated immigration reform, Representative Adam Clayton Powell Jr. (D-N.Y.) presented a bill in the House in 1961 calling for unlimited immigration from the British West Indies and the nascent West Indian federation.[16] Powell, whose participation at Bandung had been controversial in both Black and diplomatic communities, grounded his civil rights leadership in a background informed by internationalist movements such as the 1955 conference and his work in the Council on African Affairs during the 1940s.[17] Ethnic organizations such as the Sons of Italy and the Anti-Defamation League of B'nai B'rith, as well as Christian organizations such as the Church World Service, sought a more liberalized policy of admission for Southern and Eastern Europeans, hardest hit by the aftermath of the war.[18]

As it has done throughout U.S. history, immigration policy balanced concerns about domestic security with the need for cheap labor. The Displaced Persons Act of 1947 allowed 100,000 European refugees into the country: a drop in the bucket, according to their relatives in the United States and refugee social service workers. The McCarran-Walter Act attempted to resist the globalization of the labor force by reverting to the highly restrictive national origins quotas of 1924. Until the Hart-Cellar Act (the Immigration and Nationality Act of 1965) repealed national origins quotas, allowing immigration by family and employment preference, many potential immigrants, particularly those from Africa, Asia, Latin America, and the Caribbean, would be virtually excluded from legal admission to the country.

But an ongoing need for cheap labor drove a whole other set of policies. The Bracero Program, operative from 1946 until just before the passage of Hart-Cellar in 1964, provided temporary work visas for Mexican men. These braceros, or hired hands, would be denizens of the workforce not eligible for marriage into the national family of citizens.

Many braceros, of course, were part of a cohort of cyclic migrants between the United States and Mexico; they understood their rights and
claims on each place quite differently than did policy makers' attempts
to regulate immigration. During the 1950s, largely because of the "pull"
of ongoing demand for agricultural, domestic, and nonunion factory
labor, illegal immigration from the Caribbean and Latin America increased. And while panic erupted intermittently over the "hordes"
"infiltrating" the U.S.-Mexico border, it was increasingly clear to legis-
lators as well as to immigrants themselves that there existed an ongoing
need for labor in the cities, factories, and farms of the postwar United
States.[19] The direction of both postwar labor and citizenship policies
meant that many new arrivals would be unlikely to be officially included
in the national family. At the same time, corporate liberal rhetoric of inclusion and progress proclaimed that a piece of postwar prosperity would
be available "for everyone."

As the paradigmatic new Americans, immigrants, particularly those
fleeing communism, were expected to assimilate into the "American
way" much less problematically than Native Americans. Immigration
policy was charged with screening out "undesirable immigrants" who
would not make good citizens. "Undesirable immigrants" were those
whose loyalties were questionable on grounds of their ties to other nations or political systems, or those who sought refuge in the United States
not for access to democracy but for economic opportunities. The drive
to immigrate or naturalize could be a matter of only "political" rather
than economic or social coercion.[20] Determining competency for citizenship, then, was not a matter of individual preparation, as it was with
Indians. Instead, the assimilability of new immigrants rested on their political loyalties. The pressure to receive immigrants democratically and
to be the traditional "golden door" to the poor and oppressed of the
world was mitigated by an overarching Cold War concern for national
security. Senator Patrick McCarran (R-Nev.) argued that immigration
policy should err on the side of security:

> Our entire immigration system has been so weakened as to make it often im-
> possible for our country to protect its security in this black era of fifth col-
> umn infiltration and cold warfare with the ruthless masters of the Kremlin.
> The time has long since passed when we can afford to open our borders in-
> discriminately to give unstinting hospitality to any person whose purpose,
> whose ideological aim is to overthrow our institutions and replace them with
> the evil oppression of totalitarianism.[21]

Cold War ideology translated the mythologized democracy of the western frontier into Third World skirmishes as actively as possible. But the reinvention of America as a land of opportunity was contradictory. Many of the actual opportunities for new immigrants were maintained by agribusiness and industry at the minimal wage made possible by cheap labor provided by the Bracero Program.[22] The logic of assimilation here was contradictory: For many new immigrants, particularly those of color, it would be difficult or impossible to participate in what Daniel Bell touted as a classless society.[23]

Calls for immigration restriction during this period were also couched in the rhetoric of civic responsibility and anticommunism. Demanding restriction of immigration and naturalization in 1951, McCarran "indicated that the bill would call for a careful 'screening' of persons seeking to come to the United States to see if they were 'adapted to our way of life' . . . [under the current system] proof of good moral character, adaptability to our way of life, and general conduct have been most laxly dealt with."[24] While the call to restrict immigration echoes similar arguments of an earlier period, the language here is decidedly that of the Cold War. Immigration policy during the 1950s became one more site of struggle against invisible threats to the national body.[25] Im/migrants, then, would have to be transformed before they could safely become citizens.

Cold War federal Indian policy attempted to resolve the long-standing, messy business of relations with Indian nations, "domestic, dependent" peoples defeated in the nineteenth century. The Bureau of Indian Affairs established the Indian Claims Commission (ICC) in 1946 to resolve unsettled land titles, clearing the way for unrestricted exploitation of western lands. This move was initially supported by many Indian leaders, who saw the ICC as a way to finally address native land claims that had long been pending.[26]

Debates about the "special status" of Indian peoples in the 1950s linked the rhetoric of Indian wars with contemporary anticommunist rhetoric: Michael Rogin's useful term "red scares" points to the continuous need in U.S. political thought to cohere around a perceived threat from an "other," whether internal or external.[27] In attempting to deal with the "red threat" posed by communalistic Indian nations claiming valuable western lands, Congress during the 1950s implemented a policy known as termination: the ending of the trust relationship between Indians and the federal government. Under termination, reservations would disappear into local counties, and the dual claims of Indian people to citizenship in the United States and in Indian nations concurrently were to be resolved by the assimilation of Indian people into the national family. Termination policy, or Public Law 280, was to complete the "breakup of the tribal land mass" begun by the Dawes Allotment Act in the late nineteenth century.[28] In addition, the termination project included a relocation program, which was to bring Indians off the reservations and relocate them in cities. In the context of the Cold War, New Deal Indian policies such as the Indian Reorganization Act seemed dangerously communistic, encouraging dual loyalties to "nations within" rather than the development of safely individualized citizens.[29] Congress devoted time and energy into debating with an absent Eleanor Roosevelt, who had written a letter to the *Washington Times* opposing termination. John Collier, the former BIA director and architect of the Indian Reorganization Act (IRA), whose vocal criticism of termination and relocation appeared in newspapers as well as government debates, was largely branded as too left-leaning to be taken seriously.

At the same time that the code talkers and the war hero Ira Hayes brought Indians into the public consciousness, allowing the discourse of national policy to scrutinize them as both "first Americans" and potential citizens, the war had also turned national economic attention to the West. Federal expenditures on economic development in the West increased, in California by as much as ten times. Resisting the sway of internationalist arguments, cold warriors such as McCarran and Arthur Watkins (D-Utah) eyed native land claims, arguing that the United States could become self-sufficient if only it were to fully develop the resources within its borders.[30] Kenneth Philp writes:

> McCarran emphasized that (these) energetic European homesteaders had turned "wild wastelands" into "productive, wealth-creating, revenue producing property." Furthermore, the entire edifice of the Indian Bureau was built on "the fiction of tribal political organization and the constitutional delegation to the federal government of power to deal with Indian tribes."[31]

McCarran's language is worth noting here; the "fiction of tribal political organization" clearly contradicted his attempts to write another foundational fiction of national cohesion.

While Indian people had become citizens by national law as of 1924, federal termination policy attempted to "integrate" them into the social, political, and economic life of the nation, "emancipating" them from the federal trust relationship that protected their treaty rights to the land.[32]

Emphasizing on *Meet the Press* in 1953 that Indians' current nonassimilated status made them inferior Americans, Douglas McKay, secretary of the interior, stated: "Any time anybody lives as a ward of the Government, they are of no value."[33] Fear of Indian dependence readily slid into the rhetoric of anticommunism: in 1946 Congressman George Schwabe (R-Okla.) stated that it would be a good idea "to get rid of the Indian Bureau as soon as possible, it is a drain upon the taxpayers and . . . a poor guardian for the Indians. I think it tends to encourage paternalism and socialistic and communistic thinking."[34] In this way of thinking, Indian groups such as the NCAI could clearly be nothing more than Communist front organizations.[35]

By no coincidence, many of the most strongly pro-termination congressmen belonged to a coalition of political and corporate interests that saw the postwar West as the site of a new America. Indians stood in the way of this progress, and the termination-era Bureau of Indian Affairs, under Dillon S. Myer, former head of the War Relocation Authority, consistently supported the claims of local white ranchers and farmers to land and water claimed by Indian people. In the case of the controversy over water rights at Pyramid Lake, the BIA did this in direct contradiction to a 1944 Supreme Court settlement in favor of Paiute Indian claims.[36] The development of the West promised American economic autonomy and the certain replication of a familiar foundational fiction. McCarran wrote: "The West today is the land of empire, of opportunity, of destiny. Today, more than ever, the West is plain every day American for 'opportunity.' "[37] The West had water and uranium to support growing urban populations and an emerging nuclear state; in addition, the West has long had tremendous ideological capital in the national imagining of freedom and destiny.[38] If this glorious and familiar future was to be realized, of course, the rich "opportunities" that existed on Indian land would have to be made available to the national project. "Emancipation" of Indians through termination of the federal trust relationship would allow for the exploitation of Indian lands.

Ann Stoler comments perceptively about the way racial discourse "invariably draws on a cultural density of prior representations that are recast in new forms."[39] In its concern to cast the United States as a free nation in a world threatened by communist totalitarianism, in its use of nineteenth-century racial categories to explain the necessity of termination, federal Indian policy in the 1950s and early 1960s very much paralleled contemporary immigration policy. Both im/migration policies attempted to select individuals who would enter the national family as

worthy potential citizens; both were ultimately concerned with the health
not of im/migrants themselves but of the larger body politic suffering the
threat of a red scare. As Singh points out, the Cold War can be seen as
the first of many postwar culture wars; with federal im/migration policy, we see the nation attempt to select qualified citizens to make a co-
herent nation.[40]

Citizenship, as the racialized grounds for inclusion in the national
family, became a contested terrain—a culture war, in Singh's terms—for
public policy during the immediate postwar period. At the same time
federal policy makers set out to create a safe way of filtering the addition of internal denizens and external émigrés into the national body,
im/migrant groups organized to press for inclusion on their own terms.
With this conflict, the narratives governing inclusion would shift
throughout the 1940s and 1950s, finally yielding in the 1960s to renewed
calls for reform and a transformation in the ideas of what citizenship
would mean.

The foundational fictions informing immigration and Indian policies
in the postwar period can be divided into different chapters, according to
how they created citizens. Sometimes citizenship was written as a narrative of *descent,* in which citizens are produced through the bodies of other
citizens, through biological reproduction and the socializing institution
of the family.[41] In the case of naturalization, however, citizenship becomes
a narrative of *ascent,* in which the legitimating body of the nation stands
in for the actual bodies and genealogies of subjects. In the case of naturalization, the state is the parent bringing already existing individuals into
the national fold. These various origins of citizenship point to different
constructions of race and ethnicity in the postwar period.

Immediately after the war, between 1945 and 1952, policy debates
focused on bloodlines and reproduction, and the ways new citizens were
related to the actual bodies and immediate families of those who were
already members of the national family. Policies concerning nonnational
"war brides" and the families of returning Indian veterans in this period
emphasized lineage and reproduction.[42]

After 1952, the attention of social scientists and policy makers shifted
away from the military heroics and physical depredations of war. Social
fictions in this period did not correspond so directly to bodily incarnations of citizenship. As they considered the domestic ramifications of "the
American century," the authors of im/migration policy turned to the legal
production and naturalization of new citizens, and cultural conceptions
of race and citizenship came to supplant biological distinctions.

Finally, as the coalitions that opposed both termination and immigration policies during the 1950s challenged these restrictive practices, a more liberalized approach to assimilation emerged. Reformed Indian and immigration policies after 1965 would emphasize ethnicity over race, liberalizing the terms of inclusion in the national body. Where termination and immigration policy adopted racialized definitions of culture, reform efforts responded to the influence of the civil rights movement by implementing an ethnicity-based model of access to economic and political rights. These different models of citizenship and assimilation overlap to a great degree: while reforms changed the immediate racial hierarchy of existing policies, they maintained continuity with racialized social thought and continued to limit democratic access to full citizenship. Lisa Lowe writes: "While the nation proposes immigrant 'naturalization' as a narrative of 'political emancipation' that is meant to resolve in American liberal democracy as a terrain to which all citizens have equal access and in which all are equally represented, it is a narrative that denies the establishment of citizenship out of unequal relationships between dominant white citizens and subordinated racialized noncitizens and women."[43] In other words, while racial paradigms change, influencing social policy, conflicts over citizenship and inequality remain because of a lack of real redistribution of power and resources.[44] These different chapters of the postwar romance do point to the limited romantic resolutions possible within the national fictions of capitalist democracy.

WE ARE FAMILY: CITIZENSHIP EMBODIED

In 1945, as Congress was beginning to debate issues of national origin, immigration, and ancestry, the War Brides Act passed both houses and was signed into law by President Truman. Under this law, the spouses and minor children of United States citizens serving in the military were allowed to enter the country as nonquota immigrants. Because of the long-term barriers to the naturalization and citizenship rights of Asian-Americans, servicemen of Asian descent were the exceptions to this policy, but the law was amended to include them in 1947. McCarran-Walter legislation, passed seven years later, maintained this special right for families of GIs.[45] Women married to American servicemen and the children of these marriages were beyond the racialized scrutiny applicable to other refugees and immigrants.[46]

The War Brides Act rested on two assumptions about the family and citizenship: first, American GIs, the defenders of democracy, would be

unlikely to select wives who would make bad citizens; second, these foreign women, because of their gender and their status as wives, were unlikely to be the same kind of immigrants that Congress worried would
"not leave behind them their loyalties to foreign governments and foreign ideologies."[47] Both of these assumptions suggest, as did later immigration reform strategies, that the family was to function as a crucible
for assimilation and for the screening of loyalties to the nation. At the
same time, im/migration policy would reshape gender relations among
the groups subject to it.[48] This reshaping was a key part of the transformation of im/migrant groups into the postcolonial labor force so necessary for U.S. hegemony in the postwar period.[49]

At the same time that war brides were admitted as potential U.S. citizens, Congress debated the status of American Indian veterans. Because
of the federal trust relationship, Indian veterans were not eligible for Veteran's Administration mortgages.[50] House Resolution 1113 in 1947 ad-
dressed this problem:

> The Secretary of the Interior is authorized and directed, upon application of any
> Indian who shall have served honorably in the armed forces of the United States
> in time of war, to remove all restrictions upon the lands, interest in lands, funds,
> or other properties of such Indian, and, if such lands or interests in lands are held
> in trust for such Indian, to issue an unrestricted patent in fee therefore.[51]

While veterans had shown themselves to be worthy of inclusion in a
country that they had fought and died for, Congress saw fit to amend
the initial bill providing for the removal of restrictions on the land of Indian veterans by requiring them to take a competency test. A veteran
over the age of twenty-one could "apply to any naturalization court for
the area in which he resides for a 'writ of competency.' "[52] A second
amendment, debated at length in Congress, restricted the rights of citizenship to the *individual* Indian veteran who successfully applied, grant-
ing the offspring of Indians who had achieved competency the right only
to apply for citizenship on becoming twenty-one. In other words, Indians were capable of becoming citizens, but not of engendering them;
being an Indian born in the United States did not necessarily grant an individual the right to claim citizenship in the national body. This policy
gave Indians the same status as immigrants before naturalization.

The "emancipation" of Indian veterans through competency tests set
a precedent that would be at the center of termination policy: Indians
had to be transformed in order to enter the national family. This re-

quirement affected Indian families as well as Indian nations. Representative Francis Case of South Dakota argued that when individual Indians became citizens, they should be allowed to become the legal guardians for their minor children.[53] Entrance into the national family here entitled prospective citizens to responsibility for their biological families. In a parallel gesture, Senator Barry Goldwater (R-Ariz.) used the debate over Indian citizenship and competency as a platform to argue for transforming the racial definition of Indian status. Just as Indians needed to prove their competency to become U.S. citizens, Goldwater argued, they should be required to be of full-blood status to claim any Indian identity at all.[54] This assertion contradicted the laws and practices of both Indian nations and the federal government. What it attests to, however, is the importance of bloodlines and reproduction in this debate over membership in the national body.

The national romance, as it was written into the War Brides Act and House resolutions for competency testing of Indian veterans, centered on a national family constructed on actual biological descent, shored up by federally adjudicated competency. In a minor but illuminating subplot of this postwar romance, House Resolution 2108 in 1949 allowed refugee doctors, ordinarily prevented from practicing medicine in this country by the complexities of passing national certification tests, to practice in Indian hospitals.[55] Citizen/subjects deemed incompetent to operate on the bodies of full citizens were allowed to practice on Indian bodies. In turn, Indian bodies needed legal operations to enter the national family.[56]

Indian people took note of the discussion of their status in Congress, and responded to its qualified promises of liberation. The NCAI dubbed House Resolution 1113 the "phony emancipation bill." José Carpio, governor of Isleta Pueblo, pointed out the injustice of such policies:

> In our recent struggle for freedom from European aggression, many Indian boys donned the uniforms of Uncle Sam to fight the threats of the aggressors. But it seems that it resulted in vain, because by the so-called "emancipation bill" many are going to be affected to the end of our natural lives. It seems like our white brother is shaking us with his left hand and stabbing us with his right.[57]

In 1949 the NCAI's Sixth Annual Convention's resolution on "emancipation" pointed out the bill's problematic construction of Indians as "foreigners" and its inherent unconstitutionality:

> This bill operates under a false premise: namely, that Indians are foreigners who must apply and prove their competency; no other native citizen is required to humiliate himself to prove his competency; this again, is in conflict with the rights of native-born citizens as prescribed within the framework of the United States Constitution; the whole tone of the bill stresses the approach that the Indian is inferior and not really a citizen; for example, he is put on the same level as aliens. . . . [58]

Here the NCAI points to the central contradiction in the policy of naturalizing Indians. The BIA attempted to resolve this contradiction through the civil rights rhetoric of "emancipation" and "desegregation" of American Indians. At the same time, immigration policy would implement a biologically based discourse of race, screening immigrants for their potential assimilability by the restrictive policies of national origins quotas and loyalty tests.

THE RECOMBINANCE OF RACE:
NATURAL SELECTION OF CITIZENS

The reliance of the national romance on the physical family and on explicitly biological constructions of race and citizenship gave way after 1952 to a model of the nation as a homogenizing social body. The actual bodies and families of American GIs could not be the only incubators of good American citizens. Increasingly, the national romance relied on discourses of assimilation and selection for the integration of new bodies into the national family. This discursive shift, in turn, made room for different strategies of resistance on the part of immigrants, Indians, and their political allies.

The McCarran-Walter Act was the culmination of debates on immigration that took place between 1947 and the passage of the act into law under Eisenhower in 1952. Like the termination policy pursued during the same time period, immigration policy under McCarran-Walter legislation gestured toward American egalitarianism while at the same time mandating a racialized selection process for the assimilation of new citizens. Harry N. Rosenfeld, commissioner of the Displaced Persons Bureau, pointed out that the law "would remove racial barriers from our current laws but would tighten the provisions for admissions and deportation on security grounds."[59] While the law did continue to eliminate restrictions against the naturalization of Asians as citizens begun during the war, it also implemented national origins quotas that applied the "Nordic race theory" of immigration restriction from the 1920s. In accordance with Nordic race theory, this law gave preference to immigrants of Northern European backgrounds. Quotas diminished in size moving down the scale to Southern European, Latin American, Asian, and African nations; newly decolonized nations such as Mali were granted a yearly quota of 100.

In concert with the Internal Security Act of 1950, McCarran-Walter legislation set up strict and subjective loyalty tests for potential immigrants.[60] Finally, and most important in terms of foundational fictions of citizenship, assimilation, and national inclusion, the law distinguished between political and economic immigrants and refugees.[61]

The enduring ideological success of the McCarran-Walter Act, even after its abrogation by the Hart-Cellar Immigration Reform Bill of 1965, lay in its ability to conflate racial distinction and political loyalties. From the 1950s through the present, immigration and refugee policy take as a given the distinction between economic and political refugees that McCarran-Walter legislation recognized. Under this policy, individuals fleeing "Communist-totalitarian" regimes are given preference and considered "political" refugees. This ironic Cold War vote of confidence in the economies of the Eastern Bloc left other refugees fleeing "friendly" governments such as Antonio Salazar's Portugal, Reza Shah Pahlavi's Iran, and Anastasio Somoza's Nicaragua designated "economic" refugees. This distinction between political and economic migrants is what David Theo Goldberg calls a "racialized exclusion": "If it is reasonably clear that some institutional practice gives rise to racially patterned exclusionary or discriminatory outcomes, no matter the institutional aims, and the institution does little or nothing to avoid, diminish, or alleviate these outcomes, the reasonable presumption must be that the institution is racist or effectively promotes racism of a sort."[62]

Conceiving of "political" immigrants as rational subjects, able to assess their situation and opt for the democratic freedom offered by the United States, immigration policy posits "economic" immigrants, almost without exception nonwhite people from developing countries, as part of push/pull cycles of hemispheric and international migrations, not as viable democratic citizen/subjects. In this Cold War fiction, "political" immigrants assess their situations in an analytical manner, whereas "economic" immigrants seem to wash up on our national shores, out of control of their lives, family economies, and destinies. Ironically, the political "freedom" touted in Cold War discourse is largely economic: the freedom of the free market, the abundance of economic opportunities for hardworking and deserving families.

Controversy over McCarran-Walter preceded its congressional approval and accompanied the law's thirteen-year dominance of national immigration policy. Support for the bill came from the same western senators who backed termination, from Dixiecrat cold warriors such as Senator James O. Eastland (D-Miss.),[63] as well as from such eastern conservatives as Francis Walter (R-Pa.). These policy makers saw the postwar epic arising from western lands and domestic ingenuity.

But this romance of national development through isolationism and selection contradicted the logic of postwar capitalist development. By 1956, even John Foster Dulles had concluded that national health and racial selection were incompatible. The national origins system, he argued, "which draws a distinction between the blood of one person and the blood of another, cannot be reconciled with the fundamental concepts of our Declaration of Independence."[64] National homeostasis needed to be maintained, but the discourse of blood and competency was to be transformed into a discourse of social assimilation.

As the national economy boomed during the 1950s, riding the "peace-time conversion" of military-industrial development into consumer goods, the family assumed ongoing importance as a social and economic unit. Cold War economics as well as political rhetoric depended on a fiction of "the American way of life," which in turn took family life as its moral and cultural justification.[65] Notions of assimilation and "emancipation" came to replace the ideas of race and national origins prevalent during the immediate postwar period. During the 1950s, Cold War concern for the loyalties of citizen/subjects coincided with racially laden ideas about the assimilation of minorities into "mainstream" American society. For example, Secretary of the Interior Douglas McKay argued that Indian nations should not have a right of "consent" to termination policies outside of their rights, as American citizens, to vote for candidates for elective offices. In a 1955 letter, McKay conflates his distaste for Indian self-determination with a Cold War aversion to nongovernmental political organizations:

> The issue of consent has most serious Constitutional implications . . . for Indians would thus be given over and above the normal rights of citizenship, a special veto power over legislation which might affect them. . . . No other element in our population (aside from the President himself) now has such a power, and none has ever had in the history of our country . . . it would be extremely dangerous to pick out any segment of the population and arm its members with the ability to frustrate the will of the Congress which the whole people have elected.[66]

Termination, then, was presented as the emancipation of Indians from their segregated status as owners of reservation land and self-determining politics. The national romance here offered Indians the chance to marry into the family, to emerge from their more primitive relationship with the federal government into full rights as citizen/spouses. Pro-termination statesmen such as Senator Hugh Alfred Butler (R-Nebr.) compared Indian emancipation to civil rights for African-Americans: "Let me say frankly that I do not believe Negroes should be segregated, and I do not believe Indians should be segregated. Any institution or any public policy which strengthens and enforces segregation for these two minority racial groups in my judgment is wrong."[67] Self-determination meant different things to Indian people and policy makers in this period. To Indians, it meant a chance to control their individual and collective destinies outside the administration of the BIA. Indian supporters of termination, including the NCAI until 1953, tended to see it as removing a level of bureaucracy and allowing Indians to administer their land and lives directly. Many Indian veterans, for example, wanted federal restrictions removed from their lands so that they could be eligible for Veteran's Administration loans. For non-Indian proponents of termination, however, self-determination meant, strictly, individualism; all communal claims to land and governance had to be renounced in order that Indians might finally "become Americans."[68]

Like many marriages, however, Indian emancipation required the restructuring of the economics and social life of one of the partners. Lomawaima calls the education of Indian girls in federal boarding schools "training in dispossession under the guise of dependency."[69] The paternalism of termination policy, as well as its disciplinary intentions, were well expressed by Assistant Secretary of the Interior Bill Warne, who said at a meeting with the Association of Indian Americans in 1949: "What we need most is the knowledge which will enable us to awake in our Indian fellow citizens a desire to move away from the past of their fathers into the future we have arranged for every youngster."[70] Gendered metaphors of transformation indicate the ways the state was to minister: to real Indian families, and as an agent of naturalization into the national family.

Many Indian people did desire economic and social progress, though their ideas for achieving these ends did not include giving up the land. At a statewide conference on Indian affairs in Minnesota in 1950, Joe Vizenor, White Earth Ojibwa, stressed the need for a jobs program on reservations, so that Indians could become economically self-reliant. Keying in to one of the central contradictions of termination policy, he noted: "Removal of the Indians from the reservation centers will not solve their employment problems. Most of them that have left the reservations are returning because of unemployment."[71] But a reservation jobs program would not have had the same allure to congressional policy makers; smacking of federal support for Indian sovereignty, it contradicted the assimilationist, states'-rights policy of termination.

To some people, Indian self-determination meant that they "no longer feel attached to tribal custom [and] are leaving the reservation to make their own independent way in the world."[72] But many Indian organizations and non-Indian policy makers wondered how Indian citizens would fare off the reservation. Concern centered on how members of the Klamath and Menominee nations, the first to be targeted for termination, would spend their allotment money and what kinds of households they would establish off the reservations. In 1961 each Klamath to accept termination was eligible to receive $43,000.[73] The Reverend Harvey Zeller, who worked in a Methodist mission on the Klamath reservation from 1945 to 1963, reassured *New York Times* reporters that "the Klamaths are behaving just like white men. Some blew their cash, others put it to work. Some bought new cars, lots are buying new houses."[74]

Marriage into the national family required the ministering of a coalition of university social scientists and state, county, and government agencies. This coalition saw the attachment of American Indians to their land and culture as typical "laboring class psychological problems [that] often come from the lack of requisite practical social skills, or from lack of opportunity to fulfill white middle class goals—not from a reluctance to adopt them or inability to fully assimilate them."[75] The psychologization of Menominee resistance to termination by this coalition is worth quoting at length here, because it exemplifies how the romance of assimilation dealt with different conceptions of citizenship and subjectivity.

> Most Menominees would prefer to maintain the present federal guardianship status rather than accept termination. The widespread belief that they were bribed or coerced into accepting termination is a poor psychological foundation for a program which demands the utmost cooperation and efforts of the tribal membership. . . . Underlying this feeling is the strong attachment that the Menominees have for their "homeland," a birthright that they feel is worthy of and entitled to protection. This feeling is reinforced by the exceptional beauty of the Reservation forest, streams and lakes, the passion of the Menominees for hunting and fishing, and its symbolic significance for them as Indians; and on the human side, the fact that the Reservation psy-

chologically represents an island in the white man's world, where one is relatively certain to be treated in a friendly and permissive way.[76]

Not surprisingly, the termination coalition attempted to override these sentimental objections, implementing assimilation by drawing on the related discourses of citizenship and family. The BIA offered Menominee adults classes in citizenship and government, and employed a home agent to help Menominee women prepare their households for termination and relocation. The *Menominee News,* a pro-termination paper, carried regular tips on sanitation, canning, and gardening, as well as advice on how to buy appropriate clothing for children attending integrated county or city schools.[77] In his monthly column, Relocation Officer George McKay offered fatherly advice on home economics: "We all desire to have something better for our home, to improve our living conditions, but we must work and save in order to obtain this type of living."[78]

Just as allotment and termination policies individualized Indian land holdings by taking them out of federal trusts, relocation policies emphasized the success of individual Indians in mainstream American society.[79] Pursuing the goal of Indian assimilation, federal policy during the 1950s and 1960s focused on individual Indians. Programs often rested on individualistic assumptions about success and motivation, discounting cultural context and values as important factors. Joan Ablon, a social scientist who researched relocation for the BIA extensively in the early 1960s, thought that even the family was too large a unit to take into account when the potential success of the individuals being relocated was considered: "The importance of the personal psychological characteristics of the individual relocatee cannot be overstated in their influence on the future of the relocation experience, and are so varying that they can rarely be figured in as a generalized 'given' when planning for the individual or family unit."[80]

Evaluations of relocatees' success often focused on individual factors, such as previous arrest record, marital status, and even blood quantum. One study even suggested an inverse relationship between degree of Indian ancestry and successful employment.[81] Another social scientist found that successful relocatees were most likely to "take their Indianness lightly."[82] The assumptions here about Indians come from both the assimilationist paradigm of the relocation programs and a traditional U.S. emphasis on the reform of the poor, rather than from any thought of economic redistribution.[83] Criteria for fitness for termination and relocation

flouted the careful attention of earlier reformers, such as Collier, to Indian culture and sovereignty; rather, they reflected Cold War assumptions
about appropriate homogeneity and assimilation.[84] While termination-
era rhetoric spoke of freeing Indians, the termination project inscribed Indian people into a racialized narrative of progress. Citizenship, in this
context, has much more to do with subjugation than with liberation.

In 1950 the Minnesota governor's Human Rights Committee reported
that the estimated 1,000 Indians in the Twin Cities area were following the
time-honored immigrant path of concurrent assimilation and nostalgia:[85]

> Those Indians who have become "acculturated" to city life have, by defini-
> tion, ceased in all ways but appearances to be Indian. Many of them, hating
> childhood memories and dreaming of a new life for their children, think this
> is just as it should be. However, there is a growing number of city Indians
> who have passed through and beyond the pains of cultural rebirth and are
> now emotionally and economically able to be nostalgic about better things
> from their past.
>
> Perhaps the future of city Indian life is to be seen in the ways of these
> people: Craftsmen and laborers whose children attend neighborhood schools,
> they make a point of learning and using the labors of their fathers, and they
> master the old arts and crafts and dances—but only for Saturday night.[86]

The writer of this report was not only concerned with Indians' economic success in the city and the viability of federal policy that it would
imply. Rather, Indians' success, and thus the success of the termination
project, had something to do with the memories, dreams, and entertainment of individuals. In becoming citizen/subjects, Indians had to
progress from collective cultural identification to the individualized life
of consumers in the American empire.[87]

Under pressure from the termination coalition, Wisconsin Public Law
399 changed the legality of Indian inheritance in 1956. In contrast to
Goldwater's earlier concern that only full-bloods be considered Indian,
this law made it possible for all legal heirs, not just those eligible for
tribal enrollment, to receive a "certificate of beneficial interest." A share
of tribal property, then, would be passed on to all legal heirs.[88] This law
concerning inheritance undermined the limited legal sovereignty of the
trust relationship, and allowed for the eventual dissolution of the
Menominees' land claims, along with their seemingly inevitable intermarriage into white society. The termination coalition here made war on
the internal frontiers of Indian self-determination, opening sovereign
nations to literal and figurative marriage and the social and economic
exploitation accompanying both.

Under termination, the national romance replaced its emphasis on bloodlines and kinship with the legally administered conversion of citizens. The state adopted a therapeutic attitude toward Indian people in the 1950s: they would be converted into citizens through social psychology and political education. The "internal frontiers" here are no less racialized than those based on biological conceptions of race. Instead of operating through the exclusions of biology and reproduction, however, they emphasize culture and social standing. As Donald Fixico points out, "the real circumstances of terminating trust relations set the stage for scrutinizing the Indian ability to exchange traditional life for that of dominant middle class values."[89] The coalition of state, federal, county, and university forces in this period authored a narrative of transformation. Under their scrutiny, Indians were to give up their national identity and through the ministrations of the therapeutic state become singular American citizens.

In their work on East Indian colonial history, Kumkum Sangari and Sudesh Vaid describe policies closely parallel to those of termination and relocation in the United States: "Such ostensibly gender-neutral land settlements . . . in fact, began a process of social restructuring which was simultaneously and necessarily a process of reconstituting patriarchies in every social strata."[90] Termination and relocation policy wrote Indians as the child brides of the state, emerging from the infancy of the trust relationship into citizenship and wifely maturity. These policies, ultimately designed to abolish the separate national and cultural status of Indian people, offered a citizenship that was specifically gendered and racialized. National Indian organizations such as the National Congress of American Indians (NCAI) and the Association on American Indian Affairs (AAIA), as well as activists in specific reservation communities from Oklahoma to Wisconsin to Montana, resisted the narrow choices that termination ultimately represented.

Federal im/migration policy during the Cold War always deployed race and gender, categories of personal identity, as technologies for securing the expansion of state power. Anticommunism, in other words, was necessarily rather than incidentally racist and sexist. The McCarran-Walter Act, by far the most important immigration legislation of the immediate postwar period, combined an anachronistic focus on "national origins" with a Cold War discourse of national loyalty and potential subversion. The biological aspects of Nordic race theory and their continuing influence through the Cold War discourse of political and economic motivations for migration provided the grounds for the coalition that challenged the basis of nationality quotas and immigration restriction throughout the 1950s. This coalition succeeded in overturning these policies with the Hart-Celler Immigration Reform Act in 1965. Just as termination policy moved away from a concern with bloodlines and physical reproduction toward a discourse of therapeutic social amelioration, immigration policy in this period also replaced the controversial idea of national origins with an emphasis on family reunification and the productive health of the nation.

In 1958, Governor Averell Harriman of New York used his Columbus Day address to support changing the racialized basis of the law, calling for a "new age of discovery" and progress in the United States based on "continuous infusion of new vigor and new ideas from other countries. . . . Italians and peoples from other countries of southern and eastern Europe have added enormously to our culture, our progress, our strength."[91] Columbus Day speeches like this one wrote a narrative of ethnic assimilation onto the story of heroic national origins.

For ethnic associations, the romance of assimilation was key to their claims to citizenship for themselves and their friends and relatives in Europe. In order to write themselves into this narrative of assimilation, ethnic groups such as Jews and Italians emphasized their good citizenship and downplayed any potential rivalries for their loyalty to the nation. In a heated exchange with Representative Emanuel Celler at the Democratic National Convention of 1956, Clarence L. Coleman, president of the American Council for Judaism, insisted that being Jewish was a religious rather than a national matter, and that Jews had no extranational loyalties. He argued: "We regret the Zionist thesis that all of the Jewish faith by virtue of being Jews hold a common Jewish nationality."[92]

Similarly, organizations such as the Sons of Italy argued for enlarging the quotas for their ethnic group, rather than against the idea of national origins itself.[93] Claiming citizenship for themselves and potential citizenship for other immigrants, they emphasized their assimilability. While they were temporarily allied with African-American groups in achieving reform, their identifications were, for the most part, as "white ethnics" who wanted to allow their friends and relatives into the country.[94]

Immigration reform was also supported by a coalition of eastern and midwestern congressmen. This coalition sought greater immigration, in the words of Senator Jacob Javits (R-N.Y.), "not only in the name of humanity but in our own enlightened self-interest."[95] In contrast to the coalition that supported termination and immigration restriction in Congress, supporters of immigration reform saw postwar prosperity founded on increasing internationalization of both capital and labor. Javits stressed the increased productivity that new laborers would bring to the country, as did John F. Kennedy's popular, posthumously released book, *A Nation of Immigrants.*

Pro-termination congressmen, who in general also favored immigration restriction, saw the sovereignty of the nation within its geographic borders as all-important. They sought to extend state hegemony over separately governed Indian land, creating a return to a heroic national economy. Immigration reformers such as John F. Kennedy and Herbert Lehman were more likely to see national progress wedded to the international expansion of markets and the ingenuity and hard work of immigrants. "Who can say how far ahead in science we would be today," asked former congressman Lehman in 1959, "if Congress had not created so many immigration barriers and kept out of our country so many individuals of ability and promise. The loss is not only in the scientific field but in the whole fabric of American life."[96]

In the vision of immigration restriction, national interest lay in strictly policing both internal and external frontiers. A *New York Times* editorial worried in 1956 that the days of the "golden door" for immigrants were over: "There are no new lands on which they might settle; no unpopulated prairies, no shores where orchards have never been planted."[97] In 1959 a proposal was made in Congress that control over immigration be moved to the House Committee on Un-American Activities (HUAC), so that potential threats to the national order might be nipped in the bud. Richard Arens, the chairman of HUAC, commented, "If the liberal groups succeed in the destruction of the immigration system, it will be the destruction of the first line of defense of this country."[98]

The contradictions between the ideological needs of state and nation to maintain sovereignty by screening new immigrants and the internationalization of labor and capital in the postwar period were resolved domestically through discourses of social assimilation. Just as actual competency tests and immediate family members proved to be too limited a method of screening individual Indians for their readiness for "civilized" life, national origins quotas were controversial as well as unrealistic in light of the increasingly hemispheric economy of the Americas and the Caribbean. Traditional immigration restriction had been part of the historic pact between capital and organized labor since 1924. After World War II and the reorganization of capital and labor, unauthorized immigrant labor became particularly important, particularly in the Southwest.[99]

Like similar conversations about Indian policy, debates on immigration policy during the late 1950s and early 1960s focused on discourses of family and productivity to ensure national stability and allow new immigrants to provide the inexpensive labor needed for economic expansion. Immigration reform efforts consolidated around family reunification and meeting the needs of the domestic labor market, as well as continuing the Cold War aim of providing refuge for persons fleeing persecution or disaster abroad. This new set of immigration restrictions was implemented in the Immigration and Nationality Amendments of 1965. The law specified that these restrictions were to apply to Eastern Hemisphere immigrants, while a general ceiling and a nation-by-nation quota remained in effect for Western Hemisphere immigrants until 1976, when they were included in general policy. The reforms of 1965 set limits of 120,000 immigrants from the Western Hemisphere and 170,000 from the Eastern Hemisphere. For Western nations, a national quota of 20,000 each was established. This provision amplified by 100 percent the numbers of Caribbean people eligible to immigrate, and, along with Great Britain's restriction of immigration from its former colonies in 1962, accounts for the increase of immigration from the Caribbean during the late 1960s and 1970s.

In 1959 Senator John F. Kennedy proposed amending immigration policy by allowing unrestricted immigration to relatives of citizens and resident aliens. Family reunification, as a central component of immigration policy, would "make it easier for future immigrants to assimilate into the United States and eliminate much of the bitterness engendered by the present system."[100] The discourse of family reunification attempted to counter fears that immigration would get out of control. As Guillemina Jasso and Mark Rosenzweig point out, the assumption of family reunification policy is consonant with Cold War policies that sought to screen out unsuitable immigrants. "If the characteristics of family members are similar, then given that priority in sponsorship is provided to naturalized immigrants, who presumably have had some success in the United States, the family preference system will select new immigrants who are also likely to succeed."[101]

Like the War Brides Act, family reunification, a central component of immigration reforms since 1965, presumes that the family is a competent crucible for selecting likely citizens. Unlike the War Brides Act, however, family reunification is administered by the Immigration and Naturalization Service, drawing on a complicated set of laws governing relationships and their relative priorities for admission. As in termination policy, the discourse of family value and home economics here stands in for a therapeutic state. Potential citizen/subjects are operated on under the auspices of this state.

In a parallel move that did not draw on this discourse of family and was ultimately politically unacceptable, Senator Claiborne Pell (D-R.I.) proposed a "new seed" program in 1961. Immigrants would have to pass physical tests similar to those for entrance into the Army. In addition, the state would settle immigrants in areas appropriate to their potential assimilation; immigrants would be "prevented temporarily from settling with their own ethnic groups or where jobs are scarce."[102] What this rather toothless subplot of the national romance suggests is that the welfare of actual families was not so important to state policy as the use of a discourse of family unification as an arena where the confluence of national and private good allow for the intervention of a therapeutic state apparatus in planning assimilation. Family reunification as a policy, of necessity, favors a culturally specific notion of family relationships. Immigrants attempting to use family reunification policy to gain entrance into the United States would have to draw on a culturally acceptable model of kin relations.[103] By 1988, for example, more than one-third of all adult immigrants who did not come under refugee/asylum status got visas through marriage.[104]

The second component of the immigration reform that supplanted national origins was a discourse of "special skills" and "domestic labor market needs." This component of the law gave preference to professionals and skilled workers who could find employers to vouch for their importance on the job. As Whitney Young observed in an *Amsterdam News* editorial, this idea of special skills "is likely again to discriminate in favor of the industrialized nations of Europe, while excluding those from Africa and Asia, which are not as highly developed."[105]

Even though the particular provisions of immigration reform maintained a national romance of assimilation through the discourses of family and work, the 1965 amendments largely satisfied the coalition backing reform. Kennedy's *Nation of Immigrants,* itself a foundational fiction of the diverse nationalities that had come together to form the United States, was widely acclaimed as endorsing a more tolerant immigration policy. Praising the talents and hard work of America's immigrant stock, Kennedy celebrated the marriage of new blood into the family of the nation: "Somehow the difficult adjustments are made and people get down to earning a living, raising a family, and building a nation."[106]

FICTIONS OF EMPIRE: TOWARD REVISION

In the 1950s and 1960s Congress and the Bureau of Indian Affairs, in concert with social scientists and western business interests, installed policies that undermined Indian sovereignty and cultural self-determination in the name of epic narratives of democracy and progress. Immigration policy implemented a racially based national origins quota system and used political loyalty tests to determine the eligibility of potential immigrants for the American way of life.

State policy draws on and imposes the foundational fictions of national life. The termination and relocation policies of the 1950s used the epic of the national struggle for freedom to claim to "emancipate" Indians from "primitive" reservation conditions. Correspondingly, immigration policy invoked narratives of upward mobility and American love of freedom, screening immigrants on the basis of whether they would "assimilate" into the national community. At the same time, of course, to emancipate Indians was to open their land to development; to assimilate new immigrants was to accept those who were presumed to become loyal citizens and a docile labor force.

Viewing state policy as a story allows for elaboration of the practices and politics of specific regimes. On the one hand, state policies construct disciplined populations. Both Indian and immigration policy in the post–World War II period extended an institutional gaze to marginalized populations, studying their preparedness for emancipation and assimilation. Indians and immigrants were carefully studied in this period, so that their social lives, their very existence as subjects of the state and citizens of the nation might be remade. In this context, social policy provides "a technique of power/knowledge that enabled administrators to manage their institutional populations by creating and exploiting a new kind of visibility."[107]

Immigration and federal Indian policy were and are part of a complex system of global and hemispheric domination. Of necessity, the struggle to reform repressive policies takes place in a national arena. The contradiction here is that the factors that make immigration such a crucial source of cheap labor, the reasons that Indian lands are perennially sought after by western land and mineral developers, are part of much larger, more global processes. The national results of these processes are still under way, as many states consider legislation like California's Proposition 187 and the Save Our State initiative in Florida. Congress passed highly restrictive immigration reform bills in 1990 and 1996.

In embodying a fiction of national unity based on social assimilation and family values, the immigration reforms of 1965 ignored the contemporary realities: increasing dependence on both cyclic and permanent migration of workers from Latin America, Asia, and the Caribbean; racial barriers against the access of many of these immigrants to the rights of full citizenship in this country; the feminization of the labor force. It would not be long before the rediscovery of those shadowy outlaws of the national romance, the undocumented, pregnant fugitive and her brothers, the dark hordes sweeping "out of control" across the border, would make defending the national family through immigration restriction seem a crucial next act.

Similarly, the national movement toward antifederalism and block grants to the states threatens to undermine the limited sovereignty that native peoples have achieved within the confines of the United States. An irony of federal Indian policy, from termination through the present day, is its attempt to provide civil rights for Indian people through an increasing political emphasis on states' rights, which has historically meant the delimiting of native sovereignty.

Understanding state policy as a discursive field allows for the use of this field for the articulation of oppositional claims. If the state writes foundational fictions of the nation, it also provides an arena where these fictions may be edited, revised, or altogether rewritten by social movements and by groups that do not have access to hegemonic power. While termination policies articulated a discourse of emancipation, Indian groups such as the National Congress of American Indians were able to use the contradictions in social policy to argue that *true* emancipation should not mean the end of the federal trust relationship and relocation of Indians from their land to cities, but rather broader access to their constitutional and treaty rights. Similarly, groups opposed to restrictive immigration policies drew on discourses generated by the Civil Rights Movement to demand equal status under the Constitution for people of all races.

At the same time that resistance to termination and restrictive immigration policies were crucial to their subsequent reform, the kinds of reform available, authored through the racialized discourses of national citizenship, maintained continuities with the discriminatory policies of the immediate postwar period. Where the nation claims a subject in the form of a citizen, alternative imaginings of citizenship status undermine the totalizing claims of nationalist ideology. Instead of identifying with the national narrative of assimilation, new immigrants often think of

themselves as citizens of more than one homeland; similarly, Indians in
the 1950s and 1960s systematically refused to be pushed into the mainstream of national life. Any time the nation creates a foundational fiction,
that fiction gives life to the discursive struggle to write alternative narratives. Until we have a new story, one that recognizes that multiple experiences of citizenship and denizenship are part of international capitalist hegemony, we will be repeatedly confronted by the dazzling solidity
of colonialist fictions.

In the postwar period, im/migrants from all over the world and from
Indian reservations within the national borders arrived in U.S. urban centers in record numbers. Pushed by federal policy as well as under-
developed reservation economies, American Indians came to cities in
search of the democratic opportunities that the war was fought to defend. Refugees from war-torn Europe waited in the relocation centers
and devastated cities of their homelands for permission to migrate to the
United States. As newly consolidated U.S. power reshaped the world political economy, Third World people were pulled to seek opportunities
away from the ravaged economies of their home nations. These im/mi-
grants joined communities that had existed in the United States as long
as the intrahemispheric, intercultural economies of colonialism had been
bringing North American and Caribbean Indians into contact with Euroamerican settlers and African slaves; as long as immigrants had come
back and forth across the oceans in search of economic opportunity and
political liberties; as long as im/migrant peoples had had to leave their
homes for temporary work, from which many of them never returned.
The historical experiences of Indian and Third World peoples in this
hemisphere brought these im/migrants to identify home with multiple
political geographies, some of which were not illustrated on the maps
available in the Cold War United States

Almost by definition, the narrative of the nation can't recognize the
dual identities maintained by groups of people whose historical experiences position them in places where the claims of dominant foundational
fictions are less convincing than those of alternative discourses of nation
and community. The existence of citizens with cultural and political loyalties tied to more than one homeland challenges liberal ideas of what
the state is, as well as its relation to the nation. Assimilation, as Howard
Winant points out, is part of a modernist framework for understanding
social relations. Equality and social harmony are presumed to come
about as various classes, races, and ethnicities grow to be alike under the
generalizing rubric of the nation.[108] Emancipation is part of the enlight-

enment project that sought to discipline various ethnic, class, and regional factors into national harmony through education and the gradual absorption of difference.

With all its historic discontents, citizenship became a crucial site of political struggle in the 1950s and 1960s. African-Americans drew on the discourse of national consolidation to claim the equality promised to them as citizens under the Thirteenth Amendment and reaffirmed by Truman's desegregation of the military in 1948. The achievement of the civil rights movement in asserting African-Americans' claims to citizenship and equality rearranged the field in which foundational fictions of the nation could be written. Similarly, the celebration of Indian veterans as American heroes changed the ability of Indian political organizations such as the NCAI to make claims in nationalist discourse. At the same time, decolonization created newly conscious citizens who had struggled for their identities; immigrants from these countries were unlikely to easily accept melting pot paradigms of assimilation and national unity. Both im/migrants and citizens working for civil rights accepted the ideological claims of Cold War egalitarianism at the same time that they used these claims to pressure the state for additional rights. This refusal to let the state manage the terms of national ideology set up a challenge to primary U.S. foundational fictions in this period.

The next chapters examine the ways in which Caribbean and Indian im/migrants have defined themselves against the narrow parameters of citizenship established for them by the state. Drawing on historically complex identities, these im/migrants have created social institutions and cultural narratives that resist the discourse of social assimilation offered to them by federal policy. For this reason, termination resulted not in the end of the trust relationship between Indian nations and the federal government but in a renewal of claims to the land and in demands for rights for Indian people who relocated to cities. In Brooklyn, Caribbean people contested discourses of assimilation that erased their identities as Black citizens of newly decolonized nations and of neighborhoods struggling for municipal empowerment.

PART 2

Performing Memory, Inventing Tradition

Colonial Optics and Im/migrant Locations

Performative Spaces, Urban Politics, and the Changing Meanings of Home in Brooklyn and Minneapolis

NEOCOLONIAL SLEIGHTS OF HAND AND THE MEANING OF HOME

The neocolonial sleights of hand of postwar federal policy translated, for Indian and Caribbean people, into great demographic and social transformations. Restrictive immigration legislation in 1924 and 1952 had slowed the influx of Caribbean workers into the country, although circulation through travel, study, and temporary migration under work permits continued throughout this period. By abolishing the national origins quotas of the McCarran-Walter Act, the Hart-Celler Immigration Reform Act opened the door in 1965 to a dramatic increase in immigration from the Caribbean. The foreign-born Black population of the United States doubled between 1960 and 1970, and increased more than two and a half times between 1970 and 1980. By 1980 almost 20 percent of New York's Black population was foreign-born.[1]

Increasingly during and after World War II, Indians moved between reservations and urban communities, living and working in both places.[2] The American Indian population of the Twin Cities area increased, from less than 1,000 in 1920 to 6,000 by the end of World War II.[3] Both Indian and Caribbean urban communities were transformed by the federal policies designed to recruit cheap labor, obtain the rights to Indian land, and assimilate im/migrants into the national family.

Federal immigration and Indian policies operated, as I have argued in Chapter 3, on assumptions about assimilation shaped by ethnicity theory.[4] According to this theory, im/migrants hold onto older, "ethnic" identities as they gradually become Americanized. Ethnicity theory had shaped the thinking behind the removal, internment, and gradual relocation of Japanese-Americans during World War II.[5] In the postwar period, Bureau of Indian Affairs policies moved away from efforts to promote native self-determination, as John Collier had attempted to do during the 1930s. The termination project, initially endorsed by many Indian people as a way to gain more control over their lives and lands, saw Indian peoples not as nations or tribes but as individuals to be relocated into cities and gradually educated into social and economic conformity. Immigration reform under the Hart-Celler Act of 1965 responded to the needs of the U.S. labor market by allowing for an increase in immigration from the Third World. Native and Caribbean im/migrants would be regulated by the dual pressures of the open market and the policy romance of the national family.

The gap between the stated aims of federal policy and its consequences for im/migrant experience turns on the contradiction between ethnicity theory and the reality of life in a racist society. Changes in federal Indian and immigration policy in the postwar period, although couched in the rhetoric of emancipation and assimilation, were based on the economic needs of the United States. Ethnicity theory does not address the historic roots of inequality, or of identity. Constructed on a model designed to explain the experience of European im/migrants in the early twentieth century, ethnicity theory assumes that group identities will gradually weaken as im/migrants find their way up the socioeconomic ladder and into full political participation. As im/migrants of color, Caribbean and Indian people had quite limited access to such socioeconomic mobility, as well as to full citizenship rights.

In many ways, federal policy in the postwar period operated under a rubric of ethnicity theory to reinforce racialized inequalities. As policy makers looked at Indian reservations, they saw not sovereign nations but isolated colonies of unassimilated Americans, some of whom occupied resource-rich or strategically useful lands. Indian people came to cities in this period because of reservation unemployment, and because of policies designed to assimilate them, in BIA Commissioner Dillon S. Myer's words, "even though Indian cooperation may be lacking in certain cases."[6] Caribbean people were allowed into the United States in great numbers after 1965, in part to serve as cheap labor for northeastern factory and service industries. And, as low-paid workers and as Black im/migrants, Caribbean people have always been subject to the vagaries of immigration restriction, clamp-downs on illegal immigration, and popular anti-immigrant sentiment.

Im/migrants responded to these policies by creating cultural, social, and political coalitions that allowed them to resist assimilation, respond to local racial hierarchies, and struggle for municipal empowerment. Paul Gilroy writes: "Where state institutions impose racial categories, the struggle against racism will be a struggle against the state."[7] In Minneapolis and Brooklyn, im/migrants of color created alternative categories of identity, and struggled to found institutions to reinforce these identities and help them in their quest for municipal empowerment.

Caribbean im/migrants in New York after 1965 initially socialized and thought of themselves by nation: as Trinidadian, Grenadian, Barbadian, or Jamaican; sometimes as British subjects. More slowly, they came to speak of themselves as Caribbean or West Indian, African, Black, or Third World people; as inner-city dwellers struggling for economic self-determination and cultural liberation. Similarly, as Indian people moved to Minneapolis in increasing numbers in the late 1950s, they initially made contact with other Indians through the existing bonds of reservation and Indian nation. Gradually these contacts combined with the exigencies of urban Indian life to create a pan-Indian or what Stephen Cornell calls a supra-Indian identity: a "pan-ethnic" identity based on shared histories of responding to racist federal Indian policies, and on a syncretic culture of tribally specific, intertribal, and newly invented Indian traditions.[8]

This transformation took place slowly. Caribbean immigrants came to New York at a time when decolonization was changing geopolitical maps to accommodate new entities such as independent Trinidad and Tobago, Jamaica, Belize, and the short-lived West Indian Federation. Indians left reservation communities that had come into being after allotment and the reservation system strained existing bonds of family, band, and nation, and after the limited sovereignty and attendant political fragmentation of the Indian Reorganization Act. As they moved to the cities, the ongoing struggle for self-determination took on a pan-Indian political identity on an unprecedented scale. The tribal and national identities that these im/migrants brought to the cities had been constructed out of historical necessity. As what was necessary changed in metropolitan contexts, so did the social and performative narratives that people related about themselves, their communities, their histories, and their futures.

During the time of increased migration from reservations and Caribbean nations to U.S. cities, the very idea of home was changing for both Indian and Caribbean people. The struggle for decolonization brought about a renewed awareness of the African roots of Caribbean cultures. The writings of West Indian, African, and African-American anticolonial thinkers circulated among Caribbean people at home and in Great Britain, the United States, and Canada. These anticolonial politicians and intellectuals drew on the force and invention of Afro-Atlantic cultures to argue for national traditions linked to a broader, pan-African history, overturning the cultural Eurocentrism and political dominance of colonial rule. Carnival culture, especially steel band music, became a central symbol in Trinidadian nation formation, signifying the invention and genius of Afro-Creole culture against colonial repression. At the time of decolonization back home, popular cultural forms also took on a new symbolic importance for Caribbean people in New York.

Caribbean im/migrants to New York after 1965 were aware of anticolonial developments, both because of their recent experiences at home and because the im/migrant community in New York had been actively involved in struggles for national liberation.[9] Unlike American Indian im/migrants in this period, they also drew on their pride and identification with newly legitimized political entities called home: specific Caribbean nations that had successfully struggled for sovereignty. While Indians also staked claims to sovereign homelands, pan-Indian political and cultural resurgence was not represented by the boundaries of newly decolonized, sovereign nations. Caribbean anticolonial struggle and cultural pride wrote nationalist narratives, but Indian nationalism inscribed no political boundaries of territory and law. At the same time that they defended claims to existing reservation geographies, Indians in the 1950s and 1960s imagined a common terrain that linked isolated reservations and urban Indians of diverse tribal and reservation homelands.

The struggle against termination on the Menominee and Klamath reservations, as well as among many other bands slated for the program, brought a new generation of reservation leaders to political consciousness in the 1950s.[10] This consciousness raising took place outside the contours that had been established by the Indian Reorganization Act in 1934. Cornell explains how contradictions in federal Indian policy simultaneously reinforced tribal consciousness and pride and created the preconditions for a broader, Indian consciousness: "The survival of the tribe required an *Indian* consciousness, the ability to act as Indians and thus confront federal policy on its own terms. Indian policy, through its own organizations and implications, had turned tribal politics into Indian politics, and in so doing had greatly increased the tribe's political capacities."[11]

Cornell explains the growth of supratribal organizations such as the National Congress of American Indians (NCAI), the National Indian Youth Congress, and the American Indian Movement (AIM) after 1950 as an Indian strategy to respond to and resist the racialized practices of federal Indian policy in the postwar period. He grants the importance of traditional powwows, dress, and dancing in the 1940s and 1950s as expressions of emergent Indian pride after the cultural desiccation of the boarding school system. But ultimately, he sees supratribalism as a political phenomenon, lacking the deep roots in Indian culture and history that could allow it to inspire a people often besieged by attempts to assimilate or eradicate them, or to exoticize and commodify their culture. This chapter argues that powwow culture was an essential part of the formation of a pan-Indian community in Minneapolis, and the refashioning of the idea of home among native peoples in cities and on reservations. As Joan Nagel argues, this refashioning of identity was a political response to federal policy.[12]

As Indian and Caribbean im/migrant communities grew in Minneapolis and New York during the late 1960s and early 1970s, local institutions increasingly sponsored cultural activities. Tentatively accepting these cities as their new homes, Indian and Caribbean people imported festivals that commemorated the traditions of their island and reservation homelands. And as urban Indian and metropolitan Caribbean communities grew and developed, the festivals they had brought changed along with them, creating places where transformed identities could be performed.

Blending a global anticolonialism with an awareness of local constructions of race, these im/migrants used Carnival and powwow to assert ideas about identity and home that provided alternative plot lines to the foundational fiction of national homogeneity and assimilation. Pan-Indianism in the postwar period wrote an Indian racial identity as a counternarrative; an indigenous national romance that rejected the arranged metaphorical marriage of Indian people to upstanding American citizens. Afro-Caribbean im/migrants held onto cultural and political connections to "home" at the same time that they negotiated a Black ethnic identity in Brooklyn.[13] The ethnicity theory that informed exploitive im/migration policies does not describe the postwar histories of Caribbean Brooklyn and Native American Minneapolis. Rather, both groups created identities responsive to local racial hierarchies as well as to the long sweep of popular memory

NATURALIZING IM/MIGRANTS: BROOKLYN AND MINNEAPOLIS AS RECEIVING COMMUNITIES

One irony of the assimilationist rhetoric of postwar im/migration policy is the way it sought to absorb im/migrants into an economy that had already started to vanish by 1952.14 Relocation of Native Americans was an urbanization policy in a nation rapidly suburbanizing in response to the postwar housing crisis, federally subsidized by Veterans' Administration funding and a somewhat skewed interpretation of the Housing Act of 1949. Immigration policy drew Caribbean people seeking upward mobility to urban economies that increasingly provided low-paid service-sector employment in contrast to the mobility offered by a booming industrial sector a century earlier.15 By the 1950s, industry had begun to relocate away from core cities, seeking cheaper tax rates on the suburban periphery, where workers drove to plants and office buildings on state-subsidized highways instead of riding now-neglected public transportation to work in the core city. Because of this contradiction in the stated intent of policy and the demographic, social, and economic reality of postwar America, im/migration policies virtually ensured that im/migrants would struggle with the problems of more established urban minority groups: high unemployment, neighborhood redlining; and the flight of white residents and municipal funds.

The first generation of West Indian im/migrants to the United States in the 1910s and 1920s had responded to the extreme racial segregation they encountered in the United States by nurturing dual identities. Like many of their southern migrant neighbors in Harlem, Caribbean people were new to the neighborhood. Many Caribbean im/migrants to New York maintained cultural and political links to their home islands, much as African-Americans kept ties to communities in the South.16 Entering a society that saw them primarily as Black regardless of their class or regional origins, Caribbean immigrants resided, worked, and often became politically active in the African-American community while cultivating economic, political, and imaginative ties to their home islands.17

Caribbean im/migrants used these dual loyalties to define themselves against a model of ethnicity and assimilation that would not easily accommodate im/migrants of color. Whether these im/migrants should become citizens was the subject of much debate in Harlem, by both native-born and Caribbean Blacks. For African-American organizations, the question of naturalization for Black im/migrants was about gathering strength in numbers of voters. As Irma Watkins-Owens details, many Caribbean im/migrants declined to be naturalized, arguing that "they had more rights as foreigners than native Blacks had as citizens." The Jamaican journalist Wendell Malliet wrote a series of articles for the *Pittsburgh Courier* in 1927 titled "Why I Cannot Become Americanized."[18] Caribbean immigrants were far less likely than European immigrants of the same period to become citizens.[19]

Conflict over naturalization, as well as stereotyped ideas of hard-working immigrants who managed to succeed while native-born Blacks could not, sometimes resulted in tensions between American Blacks and those of West Indian ancestry.[20] Such sociologists as Thomas Sowell have long perpetuated a myth of West Indian exceptionalism, arguing that limited West Indian success in the United States is proof that culture, rather than race, impedes African-American economic progress. But, as Philip Kasinitz points out, statistically, West Indians of this first generation were economically closer to African-Americans than to white workers, whether immigrants or native-born.[21] Similarly, Linda Basch, Nina Glick Schiller, and Cristina Szanton Blanc point out that this model, bounded by the political geography of the nation-state, fails to account for the global and hemispheric racial orders, which keep Black immigrants both mobile and poor.[22]

Speaking in Harlem in 1923, Chandler Owen, editor of the *Messenger,* delineated an African-American case against Black West Indians:

> There are three reasons that are the cause of the friction between the American and the West Indian. First, undermining. The West Indian will accept lower wages, and when he gets into a place will bring in all of his friends and crowd out the Americans. The second charge is the claim of superiority. The British West Indians are more hated than those from the other islands because they are more offensive in their assertions of superiority and there are more of them. The third cause is failure to naturalize, and thus not be able to help solve the problem they have created.[23]

Such thinking represented a tension in Harlem over racial hierarchy and internal divisions that coexisted with contemporary efforts at Black political and cultural unity. Watkins-Owens writes of the period from 1900 to 1930:

The African American press conveys ambiguity about Black immigrants. For example, labels such as "alien" and "foreigner" were seldom used in reference to immigrant Harlemites. In most accounts, if a descriptive label is used at all, writers refer to Black immigrants by their nationalities or as "West Indians." . . . In these situations membership in the racial community required neither American citizenship nor cultural conformity.[24]

In *Brown Girl, Brownstones,* Paule Marshall writes of this interwar generation of West Indian immigrants. Selina, the central character, watches as her Barbadian-born parents struggle: her mother and the other "Bajan" women on their street in Brooklyn try to earn enough to buy their houses, fiscal security in "this man country." Her father dallies with different get-rich-quick schemes; takes an African-American mistress; gets involved with a revivalist church in Harlem; and finally drowns falling off of a ship headed "back home." Many of the family's struggles revolve around the "piece of land" he has inherited; the mother sees it as capital to enhance the family's security up north, but Deighton insists that it will provide them with enough to live like kings back home. While these struggles differ from those of native-born African-Americans, they represent im/migrant attempts to make a transnational "home" in negotiation with international structures of capitalism and colonialism, as well as with the racial hierarchy of the United States.

Conflict between im/migrants and native-born workers is an ongoing factor in the history of capitalist development on both sides of the color line. In the case of Black West Indians, race overrode ethnicity in its effect on their lives. Race determined where im/migrants and their children were permitted to live and work, and what political organizations would grant them membership. At the same time, national identity remained important to these early im/migrants, taking the form of voluntary associations, social ties, and active involvement in the politics and culture of their homes.

Between 1932 and 1965, immigration from the Caribbean slowed; between 1932 and 1937, return migration exceeded the number entering the United States.[25] Fewer new immigrants and the difficulty of travel during wartime limited the circulation of Caribbean people between home and metropole. During this period, record companies and traveling calypsonians brought West Indian music to New York. Such Trinidadians as Rufus Gorin, Lionel Belasco, and Wilmouth Houdini popularized Carnival music to mixed audiences of Black and white, im/migrant and native-born people.[26]

Civil rights struggles in New York during the 1940s and 1950s brought people of color together. West Indian immigrants participated in Black politics at the same time that the NAACP consistently called for a reform of the quota system installed by the McCarran-Walter Act of 1952.[27] Adam Clayton Powell supported civil rights within the boundaries of the United States at the same time that he proposed unlimited immigration from the British West Indies.[28] In 1948, West Indian and African-American citizens helped elect the first Black member of the state assembly, Bertram Baker.[29] Immigrants and people of Caribbean descent began to rise to political power through African-American institutions. In the vision of politicians such as Powell, Hulan Jack, and Shirley Chisholm, Black people in New York had common public interests, including the reform of discriminatory immigration laws. Ironically, this reform would complicate such alliances when it brought a new cohort of Caribbean im/migrants into the city after 1965.

Unlike Caribbeans in New York, Native American im/migrants arriving in Minneapolis–St. Paul did not join a large and thriving, if complicated, community of color. Instead, they encountered a small population of Indians in the Twin Cities, living predominantly in inner-city neighborhoods close to communities of Jewish and African-American im/migrants and working-class white native-born Americans.[30] This small native population reflected older patterns of seasonal migration between the several reservations in Minnesota and the neighboring Dakotas and Wisconsin, as well as the wartime migration to urban areas.

During the 1940s, many Indian people had left reservation communities to join the military or work in war plants.[31] After the war, the federal government established relocation centers for Navajo and Hopi people during the difficult winter of 1947, and passed Public Law 474, which instituted a ten-year program to alleviate the poverty on the Navajo and Hopi reservations. Increasingly in the postwar period, Indians' participation in the war effort was used to justify their assimilation into the national family. In this context, the relocation program offered supposedly voluntary assistance to people who wanted to move to the cities.

As Peter Iverson points out, not all Indians came to the Twin Cities or other urban areas in response to BIA policies. Many followed an established pattern of seasonal migration; in addition, many Indian people left the comparative lack of economic opportunities on reservations for the promise of urban areas.[32] Right after the BIA established the Branch of Relocation in 1951, it received more applicants for the program than it could process.[33] Both federal policy and native initiative, then, shaped Indian migration to the cities after World War II.

With increased Indian migration to the area, Native American enclaves grew in the low-income areas of both Minneapolis and St. Paul. Because of its proximity to so many reservations, the Twin Cities area was not chosen as an official federal relocation site; BIA officials chose relocation sites far from the reservations, as if to minimize the chances that the people who relocated would return home.[34] But many Indian people moved to the area from Ojibwa, Dakota, Menominee, and Winnebago lands in Minnesota and Wisconsin. For these im/migrants, the Twin Cities area had long served as a place to trade and get temporary work. As early as 1955, a social service memo found that Indians tended to cluster in south Minneapolis, in the Elliot Park neighborhood.[35] Geographic proximity to reservation communities, the existence of a longstanding Indian community, and the tendency of urban Indians to cluster within the cities, along with the comparative dominance of two tribal groups, the Ojibwas and the Lakotas, distinguish the Twin Cities from other receiving communities during this period.[36]

To the BIA agents and social scientists who administered the termination project, Indian relocation paralleled the arrival of European immigrants in the United States. For this program to succeed, these administrators thought that Indians would have to become assimilated to their new homes, much as their own ancestors had done. The agency that was originally charged with welcoming these new im/migrants in the 1950s had previously been responsible for settling relocated Japanese-Americans in the Twin Cities, away from the coastal ethnic enclaves thought to be so perilous to national security during the war.[37]

The contradiction between the assimilation touted by the termination coalition and the experience of Indian im/migrants in the racialized hierarchy of urban life in the 1950s indicates the flaws of ethnicity theory in explaining the lives of im/migrants of color.[38] In practice, relocation tended to deposit native im/migrants in central city areas without provision for their housing, jobs, or education. In a 1964 address, Superintendent Kent FitzGerald of the New Mexico BIA explained this as a temporary problem of acculturation: "So we find many Indian families living in the poorer parts of the big cities. And this does not bother those who become slum-dwellers nearly as much as it bothers us."[39]

As relocation got under way in 1950, area agents were given quotas to fill, creating a situation in which guidelines were bent and pressure was placed on reservation residents to move. The program often presented idealized and misleading scenarios of urban life in its literature and the sales pitch of the agents. Individuals were pressured to apply to fill quotas. Preparedness for urban living was ignored. Many of those who made the move found the services in their new homes to be non-existent or woefully inadequate.[40]

In the cities, these people faced unfamiliar urban conditions. Dorene Day remembered her family's hasty relocation from Nett Lake in northern Minnesota to Cleveland, Ohio, in the early 1960s. The family had not received any preparation for their move; on their arrival in Cleveland, they were housed in an emergency shelter until the Bureau of Indian Affairs located inner-city housing.[41] The BIA never found adequate employment for either her father or her mother; unfamiliar with the city and urban life, the family experienced economic deprivation and cultural alienation: "My father had four different trades, but in the entire three months we lived in Cleveland, Ohio, the Bureau of Indian Affairs, which had promised him employment, really didn't do much in terms of helping him obtain employment."

After a short time in Cleveland, during which Day, the youngest of eleven children in the family, was nearly abducted from their first-floor apartment window, her father demanded return tickets home. The family returned to Nett Lake. They were not alone: Depending on the source of the estimates, the rate of short-term return ranges from 30 to 90 percent. The family would move again, seeking employment and opportunities for the children, but this time the father stayed behind. "It was because we were relocated that happened. And my father never intended on living in a city to begin with. Because all of the work that he did was seasonal, or in the woods type work. So he never, after that, would live in a city."

A deep conflict lay at the heart of the termination project. While termination was intended to rid the federal government of the Indian problem, hence severing legal ties to Indian nations through the federal trust established by treaty, few provisions were made for Indian people to receive the social services available to other citizens. Bishop Blair Roberts, secretary of the State Commission on Indian Affairs in South Dakota, commented in 1950: "The difficulty in the whole Indian matter is that we don't know who is responsible for what."[42] In practice, then, naturalizing Indians meant literally transforming their status from the semisovereign "nations within" to an urban minority group with few claims to full citizenship.[43]

Like West Indian im/migrants in Harlem, many Indians in the cities wondered what they stood to gain from such "full" citizenship. Rather than assimilating easily into urban life, many found themselves in conditions more resembling the economic and social isolation of inner-city life in the postwar period. In response to the experience of relocation, they developed a pan-Indian identity grounded in their common histories, current experiences, and a resurgence of political activity for indigenous sovereignty.

In the Twin Cities, Indian migrants established close social ties. Like Caribbean people in New York, they initially tried to recreate the specific culture of their homes. In the 1950s, as they experienced the shocks of migration, many Indian people associated with others from their reservation or tribe. Bill Means, an organizer for the American Indian Movement in Minneapolis, recalled:

> I can remember as a young kid, coming to the city to visit relatives, we'd have picnics where it'd be tribal almost, like Sioux, Winnebagos would have their picnics. . . . Some of the other things I can remember as being very tribal in some ways. And even on the streets, most of your friends that you hung together with, at those times, my older brothers and them, was of your own tribe. Very seldom one person was, could move amongst all tribes.

With the increased im/migration of the termination period, such tribal bonds would stretch to accommodate new alliances between Indian people. Based on shared location and conditions of relocation, this collective Indian identity would develop initially in municipal social service programs, and then, when the necessary services failed to appear, would spill over into a vital movement for urban and reservation sovereignty.

PERFORMING IDENTITY: THE URBAN CONTEXT TO 1965

Both Caribbean and American Indian im/migrants were increasingly drawn to identify with one another in the cities, despite differences of tribal, regional, or cultural origin. They participated in existing cross-cultural forms, such as powwow and Carnival, transforming them to suit their particular contemporary needs. Along with a growing sense of solidarity with African-Americans, Caribbean people in New York developed ties to other im/migrants from "back home." And, in Minneapolis, a pan-Indian identity became the basis for a political discourse of local empowerment and opposition to oppressive federal policies.

While many Indians looked for people and social gatherings from back home, they also came together during the 1950s and early 1960s in the powwow, a time-honored site of intertribal celebration and exchange. Powwows were held by early intertribal associations, such as the St. Paul American Indian Club, the Broken Arrow Social Guild, the Upper

Midwest American Indian Center, the American Indian Intertribal Association, and the Urban American Indian Committee, at places such as the YMCA, St. Steven's Church, the St. Paul Dance Club, and Deitsch's Hall in St. Paul, the Waite Community House, the Halle Q. Brown Center, Unity House, and the Japanese-American Community Center in Minneapolis, and, in the summers, at Battle Creek Park, just south of St. Paul. These powwows provided a place for Indians of diverse tribal backgrounds to come together, socialize, and exchange their different cultures.

The Indian people who came to the cities in the 1950s left a reservation community that had experienced a long period of economic and cultural deprivation from the end of the period of colonial conflict in 1890 up through the beginning of World War II. George P. Horse Capture writes:

> Long ago, when my father was a young man, his generation and the previous ones lived through some hard times. They were made to feel ashamed of their Indianness. It was during this period that, in order to protect the children, the Indian people tried to learn the white ways. As a result, many of our customs faded and our language was not passed on.[44]

During the period when federal boarding schools discouraged the use of native languages and many ceremonies were officially outlawed, many reservation powwows had tended to become more socially oriented. Traditional Indian dances mixed with popular Euroamerican styles such as the waltz. Because they were conscious that some traditions were only partially remembered, many Indians during the 1940s and 1950s avoided using sacred bustles or belts, focusing on the more social aspects of powwow culture.[45]

At urban powwows during the 1950s, people came with partial memories of traditions. Jim Clermont, who grew up in the traditionalist Lakota culture at Standing Rock reservation, remembered how urban powwows drew on partially clandestine practices:

> We were banned from doing our dances. Our singing. Because of the white society, that they, you know, they think that it will cause voodoos, and, you know, things like this, when we do our ceremonies. . . . So people just kind of kept hush-hush. You know, but eventually, different organizations started to have these powwows indoors. It finally graduated to becoming more and more. So nowadays you have a powwow right here in the [Minneapolis Indian] Center, then you'll get a lot of young guys singing, dancing.[46]

In February 1955 *The Peace Pipe,* "The Voice of the Indian People of the Twin Cities," commented on a powwow at Deitsch's Hall, urging Indians who attended powwows to remember, or perhaps invent, more elaborate dress to wear to the gatherings: "We thank Otto Thunder for his efforts to stage a powwow. Even though there were but few costumes in evidence, everyone joined in for a good time. If those of you who have costumes would bring them along when you have a dance, we could make a much better showing and draw trade from the outside as many people are interested in seeing the Indian dance."

Many of this first generation of urban Indians were the ones who had left the reservation in the 1940s to serve in the military or seek war work.[47] These adults would have been the generation that Horse Capture refers to, the children whose parents had protected them by not speaking native languages around the house. Their memories of tradition, then, were partial; urban powwows were places for them to gather as Indians, to share memories of a common past.

Through such memories, Indian people in the 1950s began to reinvent intertribal culture. The travels of drum groups such as the Porcupine Singers and the Red Lake Singers spread local Lakota and Ojibwa traditions throughout the upper Midwest and Canada in the late 1950s.[48] The combined forces of urbanization and the proliferation of automobile and bus travel in this period made Indian people much more mobile and likely to travel between reservations and cities. As Jim Clermont of the Porcupine Singers remembered, this new mobility allowed Indian people in the 1950s and 1960s to travel between reservations. The Pine Ridge–based singing group traveled to reservations throughout the United States and Canada, popularizing their drumming and singing style, which previously had been restricted to the districts of the reservation. Reservation communities that had retained parts of repressed traditional practices now became sources for their diffusion. Urban powwows were centers for the performances of such famous drum and singing groups, as well as for the formation of local groups that learned and revised traditional singing styles.

Powwow socializing, with its exchange of memories and invention of a common cultural fabric, brought Indian people in the Twin Cities together. It also had strong political undertones. As Emily Peake, director of the Upper Midwest American Indian Center, said in 1965, "One of our concepts has been that Indian people relate better with other Indian people."[49] In this context of intertribal unity and nascent Indian pride, Indian people began to organize to build an Indian center. According to American Indians, Inc., such a building would "provide a center where all tribes and Indian organizations may gather together to enjoy each other's fellowship and to obtain from each other, as tribes with varying cultures, the best that each tribe has to offer in the way of American

Indian heritage, and to acquaint the public with the values of the Indian's culture in the American scheme of life."[50]

By the mid-1960s, the struggle to create, shape, and run an American Indian Center in Minneapolis would politicize the urban Indian space created by relocation. This struggle would parallel a renewed movement for reservation sovereignty. Together, urban and reservation Indians responded to the termination project by redefining and defending the boundaries of "the nations within."

Similarly, the costume balls of Caribbean Harlem marked the creation and maintenance of a Black ethnic identity. The enormous street festival of Carnival began in the United States in the 1920s, when immigrants from Trinidad and Tobago held private dances in honor of the festivities back home. According to Basch, Schiller, and Blanc, these balls were evidence of im/migrant Anglophilia. A mock coronation of King George VI in Harlem in 1937 "enabled the immigrants to present themselves as Black British subjects, establishing distance from African-Americans through and emphasis on their proximity to a culture still highly revered in the United States, that of the British."[51] In this interpretation, Caribbean costume balls maintained immigrant connections to home, insisting on homeland ties, as opposed to identities recognized in the dominant racial hierarchy only as Black.

But the creation of a West Indian ethnic identity in Harlem need not be interpreted as opposing the emergence of an African-American identity among Caribbean im/migrants. Ethnicity is not a freight train to assimilation, particularly not for im/migrants of color. Nor does ethnicity exclude the development of racial consciousness, as an ample scholarship on white and "not-yet-white ethnics" demonstrates. An emerging scholarship connects im/migration and imperialism, insisting that im/migrant ties to colonized countries generate complex allegiances, both at home and abroad.[52] As Paul Gilroy writes about a slightly different historical context, "The political consciousness of Black settlers and their children draws on histories and memories of struggle beyond Britain's borders."[53]

Indoor costume balls in Harlem did connect im/migrants to their homelands. In the 1920s, for example, these balls very much paralleled contemporary trends in Trinidad. As detailed in Chapter 2, both the colonial administration and the colored middle class favored the decorum of costume balls and calypso tent performances after the Canboulay Riots of the 1880s.[54] The Black working and colored middle classes celebrated Carnival simultaneously. But the middle class, pressured toward Anglicization, were ambivalent about the display and licentiousness they saw in street processions and barracks-yard celebrations until after the Second World War. Colonial and police administration of Carnival continued to suppress the grass-roots Afro-Creole aspects of Carnival in favor of more manageable and commercially profitable forms of celebration throughout the first half of the twentieth century.

During the late 1930s and early 1940s, the grass-roots or Black working class in Trinidad again gained a foothold in the ongoing struggle over Carnival. Steel bands emerged from inner-city neighborhoods such as Laventille, Port of Spain, to challenge the sway of calypso singers as the musical back-beat of Carnival. By their nature large, loud, and mobile, steel bands provided a road music that animated street processions and drew an increasingly diverse crowd of Trinidadians to them.

In Trinidad, this re-creolization of Carnival provided cultural anthems for decolonization and nationalism. In New York, the move of Carnival out onto the streets of Harlem allowed an expanded population of Caribbean immigrants, their American-born children, and their African-American neighbors to participate. Jessie Wattle obtained a permit from City Hall to parade on Lenox Avenue from 110th to 140th Streets in 1947, the same year that the popular Les Amants Ballroom burned down in Port of Spain.[55] Although coincidental, this simultaneous burning and beginning are instructive about the transnational circulation of culture. Errol Hill argues that the burning of Les Amants was part of a larger shift in Carnival that saw the merging of fancy costume balls with popular processions. At the same time, the founding of Carnival in Harlem marked the emergence of a public pan–West Indian identity in New York.

In New York the transformation of Carnival from small homeland balls to a Harlem street festival embodies the multiple tensions of Caribbean immigrant social life in the 1940s and 1950s.[56] At the same time that they struggled alongside African-Americans for equal rights, Caribbean people were emotionally and politically compelled by their home nations' struggles for sovereignty. The dual affinities of this generation were expressed through support for Marcus Garvey and in the writings of pan-Africanist, anticolonialist intellectuals such as Eric Williams, George Padmore, C. L. R. James, and I. T. A. Wallace-Johnson. English-speaking residents of Harlem could read the writings of Padmore, for example, in the African-American press. As they did so, they were simultaneously connected to debates taking place throughout the Black Anglophone world.[57]

The context of common struggle back home brought West Indians in New York closer together. At Carnival in Harlem, they celebrated their common origins along with a pride that paralleled the growth of nationalist sentiment in the Caribbean. Among Anglophone im/migrants, Carnival in Harlem expressed an emergent pan-African consciousness as well as a developing Black ethnicity. Victor Brady, who claims to have led the first steel band in New York at Carnival, felt that his music defied anti-immigrant prejudice. "I played in Labor Day Parade in Harlem in 1959," he recalled, "when they still used to call West Indian people 'monkey' in this country."[58] While contemporary accounts place steel bands at Harlem Carnival in the early 1950s, the presence of such bands in Harlem Carnival, amidst more military colonial-style organizations such as St. Martin's Cadets Civil Defense Unit and the Junior Monarch League Batons, asserted Caribbean grass-roots pride. Although U.S. and British flags flew over Harlem Carnival in 1958, the festival and the nations represented were in the midst of great changes.[59] While the steel band, particularly in 1959, was a specifically Trinidadian form, its public incarnation in New York came to signify a *Caribbean* cultural identity.[60] At once carrying pan-African and pan-Caribbean valences, Carnival practices took on diverse symbolic weights in New York.

Carnival in Harlem ended after the Harlem Riot of 1964 resulted in the banning of public speech and organized demonstrations for two months.[61] This violation of their civil rights certainly indicates that Caribbean-Americans were subject to the same impeded municipal status as their African-American neighbors, regardless of ancestry or naturalization status. This was the effective end of Carnival in Harlem. After 1965, long-term efforts to overturn immigration restriction would culminate in the lifting of the ban on Caribbean immigration in effect since 1924. An influx of new im/migrants from the Caribbean would come to New York, take up residence in Brooklyn, and complicate the politics of this emergent Black ethnic identity.

"A LITTLE INDIAN WORLD": THE POLITICS OF SOCIAL SPACE IN MINNEAPOLIS

American Indian political and cultural mobilization in the Twin Cities differed from Caribbean-American struggles around similar issues in New York. While pan-Indian politics mobilized a reinvigorated cultural identity among Indians of different nations, Indian im/migrants did not have to define themselves so distinctly from another urban minority group in the Twin Cities. Pan-Indian organizations asserted an alternative national romance of native sovereignty, linking reservation and urban communities. Indian activists were aware of the Civil Rights and other social movements, as well as the changing arena of social welfare policy in this period, but the emergence of native institutions in the Twin Cities would come about in dialogue with the "special relationship" between Indian people and the federal government, and the emergence of pan-Indian political and cultural solidarity.

The growing impetus for an Indian center during the 1950s and 1960s seems logical enough today, when the Twin Cities has, in addition to three Indian centers, two survival schools and numerous Indian-run agencies. But efforts to create an urban Indian space were initially met with hostility from the BIA and from social service agencies concerned with "the urban Indian problem." Contending with these forces, Indian im/migrants debated what kinds of spaces were most appropriate to their needs: whether an Indian center would be a specifically native cultural space in the city or facilitate assimilation; how the existence of an Indian center would affect relations with other minority communities and with the dominant white society; and how to obtain funding. As these debates developed during the 1960s, Indian people claimed, for the first time, an urban sovereignty that paralleled their connections to the reservation land base. Concurrent with social programs that emphasized grass-roots definitions of urban community, such as the Model Cities program, this evolving notion of urban sovereignty represented a transformation of what home meant to Indian people in this period.

For social service and BIA administrators in the late 1950s and early 1960s, the idea of an Indian center contradicted the national romance underlying the termination project. An Indian center, wrote Charles F. Wright of the BIA in 1961, would continue the "dependency which binds them to the reservation. . . . This making of a little Indian world which is shut off from the rest of the world is not good, in my opinion; and I think that an Indian center does just that."[62] Just as termination administrators were concerned about Indian connections to their homelands, BIA officials worried about allowing Indian people even a semblance of urban sovereignty.

The struggle for Indian-run and -controlled institutions in the Twin Cities, "a little Indian world," brought into question the assimilationist underpinnings of termination. As one Indian person who was interviewed for a Civil Rights Commission report in 1975 explained it:

> I guess the primary difficulty is the fact that our Indian community would prefer to come in whole. . . . In this community and in this country, people have systematically tried to strip themselves of everything that is unique about them . . . and our people want to come in whole. They don't want to leave

what is unique about them behind at the borders of this community, and yet people want us to become assimilated.[63]

The experience of relocation reveals a stark contradiction between the intended transformation of Indian people from "wards" to "citizens" of the state, on the one hand, and, on the other, their status as urban denizens of color. Public Law 280, established by the termination act in 1954, placed Indian people under the civil and criminal laws of the state. But few municipal, state, or federal agencies were ready to provide for the educational, social, and economic needs of Indians who relocated to cities.[64] "Termination" meant that the BIA took no responsibility for these services until it was forced to do so by the Supreme Court in 1972.[65] This contradiction, in turn, led to a social service vacuum, which was filled by churches, private charitable agencies, and Native American im/migrant organizations.[66] As Nancy Shoemaker points out, such organizations had existed in the Twin Cities since the 1920s; both political organizations that oriented themselves to reservation communities and social organizations that sought to build urban community. Many of these organizations had established relationships with non-Indian charities, both public and private.[67] In the postwar period, charitably funded neighborhood centers such as the Waite Settlement House of South Minneapolis employed such urban Indians as Ada Deer, who as Indian program director on the Menominee reservation had been deeply involved with the struggle against termination. Waite House also hosted meetings for Indian groups such as the Broken Arrow Sewing Circle, the Twin Cities Council of Chippewa Tribes, the Governor's Indian Action Committee, and American Indians, Inc., an urban Indian group founded in 1940.[68]

In a meeting in 1958, the Hennepin Community Welfare Council, composed of nonnative charitable organizations, dismissed the idea of an Indian center: "To some extent the Indian community is torn between these needs, with a strong yearning on the part of some for 'a place of their own' but a realization by others of the need to become socially a part of the larger community."[69] At the same time, many people, both Indian and non-Indian, recognized the importance of agencies specifically responsive to the needs of the Indian community. Supported by a coalition of native and charitable groups, the Upper Midwest Indian Center was founded in 1954 and moved into a storefront in South Minneapolis in 1961.

As the first urban Indian center in the Twin Cities, the Upper Midwest American Indian Center was pulled between assimilation and the implications of creating a specifically Indian social space. This conflict was in part generational; an older generation of urban Indians, such as Frederick Peake, had advocated assimilation and the maintenance of an Indian ethnic identity.[70] A generation later, Emily Peake would advocate an Indian center while disagreeing often and vocally with a new generation of urban activists. The first issue of the center's newsletter, in 1961, characterized it as a nonpolitical, nonsectarian organization. The center's goals included the desire "to assist Indians and their families to become assimilated into the modern urban structure."[71]

The St. Paul Indian Club, founded in 1962, listed in its charter three central goals: to "unite members of different tribes to preserve, maintain, and display the authentic history and culture of the American Indian . . . to work for equal opportunity in employment, housing, and all other benefits to which they are entitled as American citizens,"[72] and to found an Indian center.

Many of the urban Indians, such as Ada Deer and Bill Means, who were involved in the founding of these institutions had been raised on the reservations with grandparents who still often spoke in their native languages and told stories about the better days of large powwows and open religious practices. These children, a "skip generation" in the processes of assimilation and urbanization, came to the cities in the 1950s and 1960s to join urban-dwelling family members. This generation of Indian im/migrants brought with them more substantial memories of language and culture, along with the more recent memories of reservation struggles against termination policy and local poverty.[73]

Although the Upper Midwest American Indian Center (UMAIC) was an important development in facilitating social space for Indian people in the Twin Cities, many Indian people came to see it as a partial solution to larger community needs. Neither the UMAIC nor any other Indian group in the Twin Cities had a building of its own. In 1961 a small group of Indian people began to meet to discuss the founding of an American Indian center with its own building, run and controlled by Indian people alone. The group included Emily Peake, who was closely associated with the UMAIC, and Eddie Benton, a future leader of the American Indian Movement in the Twin Cities. In 1964, this group, The American Indian Center Organizing Committee, published a report calling for an Indian center that would be an Indian-run and -controlled space, linking urban im/migrants and reservation communities:

> It is the forethought that these Indian communities will be rehabilitated and grow through the experience and knowledge gained by American Indians in

the urban society. . . . This is the sincere desire of the proposed Indian Center. Not only will the Center foster fuller Indian citizenship participation in an urban society, but will also encourage the participation of Indian art, culture, customs and tradition. Here we must say that the Center will be an institution between the Indians in the City, between the Indians in the reservation and the City, between reservation life and urban life, between reservation and reservation, between reservation and Washington, D.C.[74]

The language of this statement marks a distance from earlier ideas about social spaces for Indian people in the Twin Cities. Rather than providing a meeting place for Indians and their non-Indian neighbors, or a settlement house atmosphere to help im/migrants assimilate into the Twin Cities community, this concept of the Indian center links reservation and urban Indians. In this report, an idea of pan-Indian sovereignty emerges. This idea would become central to urban Indian politics during the 1960s and 1970s.

Local memory and invention, along with the exigencies of inner-city life, facilitated politicized cultural revival in the Twin Cities during the 1960s. Drawing on the experiences and collective know-how of the "skip generation," along with the increasing frustration of Indian im/migrants with the resources available to them, groups such as the American Indian Movement responded to police brutality, substandard housing, and discrimination against Indian students in the schools. Here the shortsightedness of relocation policy ultimately led to the development of a new Indian vision. Dorene Day came of age during the 1970s. She remembered how closely Indian politics and culture were tied in this period:

The American Indian Movement *was* the community. It wasn't just a bunch of rough guys trying to cause radical problems. It was every age of people. Of Indian people. And that's what I remember. . . . So that when we talk about how the Indian community began, and how Indian people corralled together to address these issues, it was the community. And so that the powwows, when they began, were even some very small celebrations that were a direct result of what kind of battle we won. If we kept some Indian kids out of juvenile because their parents were being harassed by the public school system, because they weren't going to school, because they were being discriminated against. I mean that, in itself, was a little victory. So that those victories, as they got bigger, then the powwows got bigger, to salute those victories. We just wanted to have fun, because there was a real purpose, meaning behind that.[75]

Members of the American Indian Movement during these early days often organized Indian people in bars, bringing them to rallies and powwows to sing. Almost all of the Indian people I spoke to in the Twin Cities, including some who were currently not politically allied with

AIM, credited the movement with bolstering the pride of Minneapolis Indians in their culture and identity. "It was kind of like a renewed Indian pride type of thing that was taking place when we first moved here in the early seventies," explained Norine Smith, who grew up on the Red Lake Reservation, speaking Ojibwa as her first language.[76]

This movement toward cultural sovereignty in the Indian im/migrant community developed in the mid-1960s, at the same time that federal policy makers, trying to respond to urban riots across the nation, looked to grass-roots social movements for new ideas about the inner city. Launched in 1966 as a component of the War on Poverty, the Demonstration Cities and Metropolitan Development Act replaced previous sweeping federal programs such as Urban Renewal with the Model Cities program, designed to coordinate the efforts of local agencies with urban and regional planners.[77] This impetus for community involvement had its origins in U.S. development policy initiatives in the Third World, and the increasing necessity of responding to the Civil Rights Movement in northern cities after 1964. At the same time, native resistance to termination was having an effect. While termination would not be formally abandoned until 1974, the resistance of the Menominee and Klamath nations, along with the increasingly evident expense of a program initially designed to "get the government out of the Indian business," led to the slow abandonment of the aims of termination.[78] Programs such as Model Cities, then, were likely to respond to the community needs articulated by urban pan-Indian organizations—the very thing that relocation was supposed to make unnecessary.

In 1969 the American Indian Center Committee confirmed the development of a pan-Indian identity in the Twin Cities: "It seemed to be the overwhelming agreement among the Indian committee members that the tribal differences of the past are disappearing and that most Indian people are more concerned today with identifying as Indian rather than within a specific tribe."[79] But this emerging pan-Indian identity did not mean that Indian people were in agreement about what kinds of institutions and politics were appropriate for the urban community. While the Upper Midwest American Indian Center, with support from federal poverty programs, had moved into its own building in 1967, many charged that this center was inadequate to the needs of the Indian community. The UMAIC was limited in staff and resources, and "functioned mainly as an information and referral agency for Indians."[80] Representing the American Indian Employment Guidance Center, Gerald Vizenor charged in 1968 that the UMAIC was a conservative group that didn't facilitate contact among Indian groups in the area, and refused to work with non-Indian organizations, particularly African-American ones. Ultimately, because of these disagreements, the UMAIC split off from the Indian and non-Indian organizations working to found an Indian center in the Twin Cities.[81]

Conflict around the founding of the American Indian Center, which ultimately opened its doors in 1975, came from both Indian and non-Indian organizations in the 1960s.[82] These groups balanced the developing pan-Indian identity of the urban community in the Twin Cities with the often ambiguous imperatives of War on Poverty programs developed to respond to and simultaneously to appease an increasingly politicized inner city. A developing notion of local Indian sovereignty claimed "the right to serve the Indian community in a manner in which the Indian community dictates"[83] and asserted strong ties between urban and reservation communities.

Non-Indian agencies wrestled with these various forces. "During these times of urban unrest and crisis," wrote the League of Women Voters in a 1969 report to the United Fund, "all of us who are looked on as part of the established order need to take a hard look at our organizations. . . ."[84] But what did this mean? Programs such as Model Cities attempted to empower local communities by channeling federal funds to grass-roots organizations and to decentralizing social services in the cities by targeting "model neighborhoods" for special, locally designed programs. But it was unclear whether these federal funds were really earmarked for nationalist enterprises or "militant" political organizations. A rubric of assimilation and integration remained from the pre-1964 era of federal policy. Under this framework, it was difficult to reconcile the competing aims of Model Cities programs and the constituencies they were supposed to serve. Politicized social identities in the inner cities could, in this view, only lead to division and difficulty.[85]

Indian organizations, too, wrestled with this issue, but from a slightly different perspective. More politicized groups, such as the American Indian Movement, recognized the need for cooperation with other people of color, even if their needs and perspectives sometimes differed. At the same time that AIM supported the founding of an Indian center, the group was also involved in working with African-American organizations on police-community relations, a central issue in the Model Cities area of South Minneapolis to this day.[86] While such issue-specific coalitions do not exclude the possibility of tension and competition between groups, it was increasingly clear to activists of color as well as social service providers that not all people could be served by the same agencies. Because federal programs such as Model Cities needed, at least on paper, "maximum feasible participation" from the grass roots, they were compelled to listen to the emerging voices of pan-Indian sovereignty.

At the opening ceremony for the Minneapolis Regional Native American Center in 1975, in "A Message to All Peoples" delivered by the urban Indian activist Pat Bellanger, the powwow serves as a central metaphor for the creation of pan-Indian unity in the Twin Cities and the alternative national romance of native sovereignty:

> We are all separate tribes, separate nations, each different from the other. Yet, there comes a time when we must become as one tribe, as one people, as one person with a single goal. Sometimes just to talk to one another, other times to sing together, to share our songs and to join in friendly competition in dancing. Then we sing a good old 'forty-nine song, a social dance of brotherhood, and unity. Then, of course, we cannot forget the courtship songs and dances, where we forget our differences and concentrate on one and other.[87]

"THE KIND OF IDENTITY ALREADY ENJOYED BY OTHER NATIONAL GROUPS IN NEW YORK": THE SOCIAL LOCATION OF CARNIVAL

The massive influx of Caribbean im/migrants to New York after 1965 helped move Carnival from Harlem to Brooklyn. Caribbean im/migrants clustered in the more spacious and cleaner streets of Flatbush and Crown Heights. They rented and purchased residential space as the area was made available to them through the twin forces of antidiscrimination housing regulations and white flight.[88] The avenues and hills of Brooklyn "looked like home," said Carlos Lezama, longtime director of the West Indian–American Carnival Day Association (WIACDA). As the area gradually filled with immigrant residential and commercial enclaves, it became the site for New York Carnival.

Rufus Gorin, a Trinidadian immigrant who had "played mas' " in New York since 1947, attempted to organize a carnival in Brooklyn in 1965. In concert with a small ad hoc committee, he obtained a parade permit from the city in 1967. Along with Lezama, whom he had met in a New York steel band, Gorin was one of the founding members of WIACDA, which today sponsors not only the massive Labor Day Carnival on Eastern Parkway but steel band, calypso, and reggae concerts, costume and music competitions, and a "kiddie karnival" at the Brooklyn Museum.[89]

Photo 3. A Brooklyn poster advertises a Guyanese party on "Labor Day Sunday," the day before Carnival.

The spaciousness of Brooklyn, though much more limited than the neighborhoods of Port of Spain, allowed Carnival costume clubs (mas' bands) and steel bands to flourish in storefronts, alleys, and backyards of blocks. Mas' bands such as Hawks and Borokeet combine the club atmosphere of traditional immigrant associations with work spaces for costume designers and room for the entire band, sometimes numbering thousands of people, to congregate and celebrate at Carnival time. Other bands are smaller, occupying storefronts. Designers make Carnival kings and queens, huge costumes often stories high, wherever they can find room—in apartment basements or alleyways—grumbling about the lack of air and light. Similarly, steel bands have found space in Brooklyn. Some steel band associations have built practice halls behind row houses and tenements; some practice in dance halls and church basements; some rent alley space and "beat pan" until the late hours, becoming a stopping-off place for neighborhood residents walking home from work.

The move to Brooklyn gave im/migrants space to form specifically Caribbean neighborhoods (see photo 3). Flatbush and Crown Heights during the late 1960s and early 1970s were increasingly Black neighborhoods as well. In moving to New York, the post-1965 im/migrant cohort encountered a long-standing and highly developed Black community, along with a smaller population of older Caribbean immigrants. This group of new immigrants experienced racism at some sites that did not correspond with the experience of native-born Blacks: in their dealings with the immigration and naturalization process; in the parallels they drew between U.S. domestic racism and the neocolonial economies that had caused them to leave the Caribbean; in their discoveries that their adjustment to their new country would be mediated by race differently than it was back home.

While the experiences of transnational migration and settlement, along with the politically charged climate created by decolonization and civil rights struggles, provided ample grounds for solidarity between West Indian immigrants and African-Americans, they also created rifts and tensions that are, to some degree, operative in New York politics to this day. The logic of the ethnicity paradigm, in which new immigrants worked hard for a stake in the American dream, worked against Black unity. Of course, this ethnicity paradigm operates on a deeply racialized basis, providing assimilation into a dominant conception of whiteness and upward mobility only on those grounds.

Stories about Carnival's move from Harlem to Brooklyn after 1964 are emblematic of the tensions attendant on this process of identity formation. The mainstream New York press, including the *New York Times,* the *Daily News,* the *New York Post, New York Newsday,* and African-American papers such as the *New York Amsterdam News* and the *Daily Challenge* tend to write the history of Carnival in New York as based on the innovations of Gorin and Lezama, with pre-1969 Harlem history serving as a historical footnote to this colorful narrative of ethnic celebration and pride.[90] Some writers maintain that Carnival moved out of Harlem after a "small disturbance" in 1964, while others link the change in venue to tensions between West Indian celebrants and "dissident elements in the Black Power movement."[91] The *Amsterdam News* recorded a brawl at the West Indian Day Parade in 1961, and speculated in 1978 that Carnival had been thrown out of Harlem, losing its permit because the organizers couldn't control rioting and looting. In a telephone interview in 1992, Carlos Lezama declined to talk about the move, dramatically asserting: "I don't think there is anything to say about that. What I have been through is too terrible."

Certainly the antiriot injunction, effective after the Harlem Riots early in the summer of 1964, foreclosed the possibility of a Labor Day festival that year.[92] Such legal prohibitions would have been familiar to Caribbean immigrants; they had vivid historical memories of struggles over Carnival in the Caribbean, as well as a growing consciousness of police repression of Black culture in the United States and Canada. However, the injunction does not explain why Carnival could not have continued in 1965, as it had done for almost twenty years in Harlem. The

many stories surrounding the end of Carnival in Harlem, though apoc-
ryphal, indicate the difficulties of explaining West Indian im/migrant history along the lines of racial, ethnic, or national loyalties. These difficulties bear on struggles for municipal power and cultural sovereignty.

Although WIACDA obtained a permit to parade in Brooklyn in 1969,
the twenty-five years of celebration since then have seen debates over
whether Carnival should remain there or move to Fifth Avenue, like other
"ethnic parades." But Carnival is not a parade; it does not move down
the Parkway in an orderly procession, and the Labor Day festivities serve
as much to symbolically conclude a week of performance and partying
for the Caribbean community in New York as they do to celebrate an
ethnic identity. Both the form of Carnival and, more broadly, its capacity as an ethnic symbol have been the subjects of much debate in the history of Carnival in Brooklyn.

As early as 1973, Shirley Chisholm, then state representative from Bedford-Stuyvesant, called for Carnival to be moved to grander quarters. "We
want eventually to have our parade moved to Fifth Avenue, like all the
other grand parades, specifically St. Patrick's Day and Columbus Day. We
deserve as big a celebration as the other ethnic groups."[93] Horace Morancie, another West Indian community leader, echoed this idea of Carnival's
role in ethnic entitlement: "It's high time New York's West Indian community of more than one million people was united behind a meaningful
community effort that will help forge for it the kind of identity already enjoyed by other national groups in the New York metropolis."[94] In 1974 a
group that wanted to move Carnival to Fifth Avenue held a separate parade; groups such as the New York Carnival Council, Inc., and the Committee for Concerned West Indian–Americans have put pressure on
WIACDA to move the Carnival as well. WIACDA responded by asserting that Carnival needed to stay in Brooklyn to maintain its cultural identity and community spirit.[95] By 1974, Chisholm had switched her position, advocating Brooklyn as the true home of West Indian Carnival.
"Brooklyn is a great borough," she said, "and I'd like to see it stay the
home of this great parade."[96]

During the 1970s, the mainstream white press emphasized the ethnic
and national aspects of Carnival. A *Daily News* headline in 1976 proclaimed "It's Trinidad in Brooklyn!" at the same time that *New Brooklyn* magazine found that more West Indian people inhabited Brooklyn
than any one Caribbean nation. As Caribbean immigrants migrated to
Brooklyn, attendance at Carnival moved toward one million people. Carnival during the 1970s expanded: WIACDA worked to upgrade the fes-

tival, holding fund-raisers and working with local officials to provide health and maintenance services.

Debates over the location of the festival indicate pressures within the Caribbean community over ethnic identification and municipal recognition during a time of community expansion and redefinition. Advocates of the Fifth Avenue parade saw West Indian people assimilating in a model of urban ethnicity exemplified by the Irish and Italians in their parades; Fifth Avenue, they felt, was the deserved place of a hardworking immigrant population.

At the same time, many in the Caribbean community sought to make political and cultural alliances with African-Americans. In 1972 the editor of the *Antillean Echo,* Neville Butler, was among the founders of the National Organization of West Indian–Americans, a group dedicated to Caribbeans' integration into Black communities while preserving "West Indian cultural traits." In their policy statement, the group emphasized the common origins of people of the African diaspora. "As to relations between Blacks from the Caribbean and Black Americans, the fact to be borne in mind is that it is sheer chance that the ancestors of the one lay his bones in the Caribbean and the ancestors of the other in North America."[97] The short-lived *Antillean Echo,* while written from a distinctly Caribbean perspective, promoted such pan-Black alliances, commenting on the racism of federal immigration policy and debating the representation of West Indians on television at the same time that it reported on events in the transnational Caribbean community in the United States and Canada. Carnival could play a specific role in this construction of Afro-diasporic unity. "When we join the hearts, hands, and resources of all the people of Black America, Africa and the West Indies in a permanent demonstration of our economic and political self-sufficiency and humanity, the 'oneness' we celebrate on the Parkway will be fully justified," commented Horace Morancie in the *New York Amsterdam News.*[98]

Efforts to move Carnival to Fifth Avenue, to earn for West Indian–Americans the recognition accorded to other ethnic groups in New York, continue to the present day. Randy Brewster, the designer of the Culture of Black Creation mas' camp, told me that he feels the Carnival deserves to march down Fifth Avenue, that this would constitute recognition of his culture in New York City. Lezama commented: "It is not fair for us to be living in a place and to be rejected for so long from a place in Manhattan."

At the same time, as Frank Manning points out, Carnival is not an ethnic festival. The tradition resists assimilation at the same time that the community seeks economic and political integration, demanding "full civic, political, and economic rights and opportunities."[99] In looking for these opportunities, the new cohort of immigrants confronted the rapidly changing structure of opportunities in New York during the 1970s and 1980s. While Kasinitz follows William Julius Wilson in arguing for the "declining significance of race" with the emergence of a permanent underclass in the context of deindustrialization, the history of Carnival in the 1980s and 1990s suggests to me that contemporary Caribbean immigrants, as much as their predecessors, consciously confront a profoundly racialized urban landscape.[100]

In 1979 there were several violent incidents at Carnival: muggings, chain snatchings, and one homicide. Rumors flew as to the cause of the violence. Lezama claimed to have received anonymous telephone threats informing him that there would be trouble on Carnival Monday. One potential source of violence, according to these anonymous sources, was the Reverend Herbert Daughtry, who had supposedly planned to lead Black United Front members to confront Hasidic Jews on Eastern Parkway. Daughtry publicly denied these charges.[101] Police arrested a Rastafarian named Noah Robinson for the homicide, and made public their assumption that the shooting must have been over drugs. The *Daily News* explained that the Rastafarians are "a drug cult believed heavily involved in selling marijuana and cocaine."[102] Chain snatchings and muggings were attributed to roving bands of youths, and assertions about organized violence diminished as the WIACDA and the Caribbean community in general attempted to put the event behind them and to recover the public image of Carnival.

In the wake of violence at Carnival, Chief Robert Johnson of the Brooklyn police worked with the WIACDA to impose new restrictions. While this move purportedly responded to the incidents at Carnival in Brooklyn in the 1970s, it paralleled contemporary efforts to contain the Notting Hill Carnival. In London, police raids on the Mangrove Restaurant, a gathering place for panmen as well as multicultural residents of Notting Hill, in 1970 and 1976 and an amplified police presence at Carnival in 1976 resulted in confrontations between the force and Carnival celebrants. According to Abner Cohen, such repression polarized Notting Hill Carnival along lines of race and politics: the Carnival was increasingly seen by whites as dangerous, while Afro-British participants became more involved in a political, pan-African interpretation of the festival.[103]

As of 1980, Brooklyn parade time was officially from 8 A.M. to 6 P.M. Street discos were prohibited, vendors were required to register and obtain a license from WIACDA to sell, and each mas' band had to have its own marshals to keep the parade route clear.[104] The Police Department amplified the force present at Carnival, maintaining a force of about 2,000 throughout the 1980s. In order to contain the revelry to the form of a parade and the time limit of 6 P.M., marchers are met at Grand Army Plaza, the end of the parade route, with a large complement of police, in military formation.

In 1991, the first year I attended Carnival, the force was attired in riot gear, in anticipation of "violence on the Parkway" after a summer of incidents between Black and Jewish residents of Crown Heights. Such efforts to contain Carnival parallel municipal responses in cities such as Rio de Janeiro, where Carnival takes place in an elaborately maintained and monitored "sambadrome," and in London, where Police Chief Robert Mark commented in 1976: "We are not opposed in principle to the concept of an annual festival, which seems to us to be a remarkably happy occasion. But the police would prefer that in future it should be held in a stadium or some other controlled area."[105] But an escalated police presence at Carnival amplifies rather than contains existing social tensions over the festival. While the official rhetoric emphasizes the safety and security such a force provides, it also ensures a hundred small incidents that dramatize the everyday tension felt by an urban minority community toward the occupying forces. For every newspaper photo showing a beat cop festooned in Carnival attire and enjoying the music, there are thousands of unsnapped photo opportunities of minor scuffles, arguments, and ongoing hostility between police and neighborhood.

Many of the people I talked to in Crown Heights have accepted the limitations on the official Carnival celebration. When I asked if the restrictions on Carnival affected the festival, Joyce Quinoma, an official at WIACDA, put it this way: "Well, yes and no. Yes, because it goes on [at] night, we could have gone until we leave, at least nine o'clock at night. But no, because in view of the fact of all that is going on, it's best to be safe then be sorry, like my mother told me. You're better off doing it that way and having peace of mind."[106] Others in the community do object to the restrictions on Carnival. Mighty Sparrow, a calypsonian residing in Brooklyn and Trinidad, wrote the popular Carnival hit "One More Jam, Mr. Officer": "People want to jump up/people want to wail/we come here to mash up/we not in jail." Horace Morancie cited "the destruction of Community Action Agencies and Model Cities Operations, the closing of hospitals serving the poor and staffed in large part by

Caribbean Americans," along with declining Black-Jewish relations in Crown Heights and the unresponsiveness of WIACDA to the West Indian community as possible reasons for problems at Carnival.[107] As early as 1973, Knolly Moses linked police surveillance of Carnival to other governmental apparatuses of repression against Black people. "They are so meticulous in their questioning about the upcoming celebrations," he wrote in the *Antillean Echo,* "that one might think they were working with the immigration authorities."[108] Some link contemporary police and civic repression of Carnival in Brooklyn with events in Caribbean history, such as the Canboulay Riots of the 1880s. In any gathering of over a million people, reasoned Trevor Johns of Basement Recording Studios, some violence will occur. Why, he asked, does crime at Carnival result in official restrictions?

Along with Trevor Johns, I am struck by parallels between contemporary restrictions on Brooklyn Carnival and a hemispheric history of repression. Carnival is a unique festival. But it is difficult to imagine any Euroamerican festival—St. Patrick's Day, for example—being concluded by police dressed in riot gear.[109] These incidents took place in 1979, fourteen years after the Immigration Reform Act allowed for the dramatic increase in immigration from the Caribbean. This reform was very much involved with the politics of labor on the East Coast; the coalition in Congress favoring relaxation of immigration restrictions represented states that would most benefit from an influx of cheap labor. Caribbean immigrants took their place in a newly deindustrializing service economy in New York, Boston, and Miami. And, as Lee Bridges notes, "the policing strategy required to uphold the monetarist economic and social order, in which the new technology and Thatcher/Reaganite policies of enforced inequality combine to produce mass unemployment, growing social polarization and spreading urban decay," required a rearrangement of the urban politics of race and class.[110]

Restrictions on Carnival in the 1980s were very much consonant with this reorganization. In this context, the struggle to represent Carnival and the Caribbean community along ethnic or racial lines was charged with new and contradictory meanings.

EMPOWERMENT AND CONTROVERSY: RACE, PERFORMANCE, AND MEMORY

The histories in this chapter demonstrate the ways in which im/migrants have dealt with hierarchies arranged by race. Both Caribbean and In-

dian im/migrants entered an urban context where public rhetoric and social policy spoke in terms of ethnicity, often obscuring these hierarchies.
I have argued that these im/migrants created performative identities and
social institutions to negotiate the competing claims of an urban ethnicity foisted on them; a color line that is uniquely North American in its
intensity; emergent public policy; anticolonial politics; and their complicated longings for "home." In other words, Carnival and powwows
became places where Caribbean and Indian people spoke about what I
have called here "the political economy of home."

Of course this conversation is, and has always been, uneven. Whatever identities im/migrants created were not as powerful as the ones created for them by national and local institutions. If the ethnicity paradigm represented an illusory offer of assimilation and upward mobility,
how is it that im/migrants of color can and do gain access to municipal
empowerment?

Performative spaces have been key to formulating responses to this
question, not only to the im/migrant communities that use them as sites
of memory, creative invention, and pleasure, but to the broader "receiving communities" of Brooklyn, Minneapolis, the forces of state, and
the ideals of nation. In Brooklyn, police and mayoral initiatives have
joined a long hemispheric history in pinpointing Carnival as a potential
site of social unrest. Carnival has long been a source of grass-roots social upheaval in the Caribbean. But in Brooklyn, this upheaval has been
figured in explicitly racial terms: a Black festival takes over a central ar-
tery in Brooklyn on Labor Day. Conflicts in Crown Heights during the
early 1990s amplified this existing social tension, with a resultant increase in attention by the forces of state to Carnival locations: pan yards,
mas' camps, the street.

In Minneapolis, the establishment of a powwow circuit linking reservation and urban Indian communities was part of an emergent pan-
Indian political community. The struggle against termination on reservations paralleled and informed struggles for municipal empowerment
in urban communities newly swelled by relocation. In both cases, native activists sought political and cultural sovereignty, the "little Indian
world(s)" that the termination project had been designed to extinguish.
In the cities, institutions such as Indian centers and survival schools responded to community needs, providing spaces for gatherings and cultural education.[111]

It is important that urban institutions became economically possible
because of Great Society programs such as the Model Cities program.

As the federal government moved away from such social programs in the 1970s and 1980s, both reservation and urban Indian institutions had to seek financial support elsewhere. After 1981, Indian casinos, "the new buffalo," have emerged as one source of this support. But support from casino revenues has changed the feel of powwows. At the same time that controversy has emerged about the legal rights of Indian nations to operate casinos, Indian people debate the changes that gaming has brought to the powwow circuit.

Contests over im/migrant performances in Crown Heights, Minneapolis, and the newly lush reservation powwows linked to urban performances by the powwow circuit point to the ways in which Caribbean and Indian people are dealing with the ethnicity paradigms that hail them as urban denizens with an unequal share of resources and power. The abandonment of social programs after the mid-1970s left inner-city communities to shift for themselves in the rapidly deindustrializing, increasingly racially divided economic climate of the times.

SMALL SOVEREIGNTIES AND INVENTED TRADITIONS: THE POWWOW CIRCUIT

As the first generation of postwar migrants to the cities practiced the "popular arts of memory,"[112] they mobilized to create educational and cultural centers that could teach language, dance, singing, and drumming. Their children would grow up in a culture rich with reinvented and remembered traditions. Hokie Clermont remembered the constant presence of drumming and singing in his life long before he formed the popular drum group known as The Boyz: "The way I was taught was that my father just brought me around the drum, brought me, like, just sat me down on his lap when he was singing. That's the way, that's how all the generations kind of learn how to" (see photo 4).[113] Similarly, Dorene Day talks about the ways her children, powwow contemporaries of Hokie's, have been raised in this revitalized Indian culture.

> When they were very small infants and I had cradle boards for all of them, they would be in the cradle board and I would take them to the powwow, and they would hear the sounds and they would feel the vibrations, and they would have, you know, this concept in their mind and that's what that feels like. And so, you know, their initiation was a little different than mine, because mine was a little more sparse.

Photo 4. At the Heart of the Earth Survival School Powwow, young men lean into the circle around the drum. At larger powwows, women stand in the second or third ring around the circle, singing along.

Powwows provide a bridge between different Indian cultures, and between urban and reservation settings. Bill Means commented: "I think the powwow allows us to recreate what we left. In the urban area. Bring a lot of people together for that feeling of just being Indian. . . . You can dance, meet some of your old friends. The powwow has become that link, to our homeland and to the past for the urban area."

Urban powwows in the late 1970s and early 1980s became regular events, adding to the roster of annual summer powwows on the reservations. Annual powwows such as the AIM Gathering of Nations powwow on Labor Day weekend, the Heart of the Earth Survival School Powwow, the Indian Health Board Powwow, and the recent "Down the Red Road" New Year's Sobriety Powwow are listed in *The Circle* newspaper, along with smaller local powwows, such as a Women of Nations powwow to support American Indian Women Concerned with the Issue of Violence against Women and a one-day powwow welcoming the National Indian Education Association Silver Anniversary.

As Indian institutions sponsored powwows, the form of the powwow itself changed. Contest powwows, a tradition on some reservations, reward the excellence of dancers, drummers, and singers with gifts, and, increasingly in urban powwows, with cash. Traditional powwows provide gifts for all drummers and dancers who attend, but offer no cash or prizes. After the Indian Gaming Regulatory Act legalized reservation casinos in 1988, the dramatic increase in available revenues has allowed some people to travel the powwow circuit continuously, supporting themselves on the fat cash prizes offered at contest powwows. Contest powwows are sources of revenue for Indian institutions, too. They generate funds that can be used to finance a specific community imperative, or simply the day-to-day life of a survival school or community center.

Both urban and reservation powwows have stabilized with the development of urban Indian institutions and the great profusion of casinos after 1981. On almost any weekend during the winter and every weekend during the summer there is a powwow in the Twin Cities area or on a Minnesota reservation to go to. Because these are stable and recurring events, people plan travel around them. The Heart of the Earth School and the Red School House both have programs that transport student dancers, drummers, and powwow royalty to powwows as far away as New Mexico. One Ojibwa man I talked to at a summer powwow at the Mille Lacs band casino in Hinckley talked about the importance of powwows in his progress down the red road to sobriety. Like Caribbean people making it their business to get to the Parkway to jump up on Labor Day, he puts powwows at the head of his agenda in the summers, arranges with his boss to take every summer Friday off. A Cherokee woman from Indiana at the Mdewaketon Dakota powwow in August talked about driving each weekend with her family to powwows as far away as Montana and Connecticut.[114]

Indian people travel great distances to get to powwows, both winter and summer. The grand entries on Friday night and Sunday afternoon are smaller than those on Saturday, when everyone has had enough time to drive the distance required. Once there, dancers dress in vans if it's warm enough outside, and in the crowded bathrooms of the Indian Center if it's cold. Drum groups bring their drums inside and set up chairs and amplifying systems. The Indian people who come to watch and visit are busy, as well. "You see how single-minded you have to be to be Indian these days?" one woman says, pointing to the numerous video cameras and tape recorders that people hold up to chronicle the powwow. As each drum group takes its turn, people cluster around with small tape recorders held high in the air. These tapes will be the music played at campsites around the powwow grounds or in the car on the way home.

Powwow culture is a mobile, transnational circuit, bringing Indian people from sovereign reservations and reserves to cities throughout the

United States and Canada. Like Carnival, it is a "changing same," a place where a diasporan community meets, catches up, learns the newest songs and dances, and disperses again. Such changes are not without their attendant tensions. The popularity and glamour of contest powwows, for example, create conflicts for many Indian people about tradition and the role of money. But this powwow culture is and has been entwined with the development of a pan-Indian identity in the postrelocation era.

IM/MIGRANT PERFORMANCE AND THE
POLITICS OF RACE IN CROWN HEIGHTS

When you roll into the Carnival, anything could happen.
                    Wyclef Jean, "Anything Can Happen"

In the early 1990s, some pan players and mas' camps began to revive the tradition of j'ouvert, the early-morning festive procession that starts off Carnival Monday. Historically a site for the most African, repressed elements of Trinidadian culture, j'ouvert in Brooklyn comes out of some of the rebel pan yards and "ole mas'" camps in East Flatbush. As John Szwed and Roger Abrahams note, nighttime has traditionally been the location for the components of Caribbean life most threatening to the plantation and colonial hierarchy.[115]

Rebel pan yards and ole mas' camps are two grass-roots traditions that originated in Trinidad. Both protested the denial of working-class Black Carnival roots: rebel pan yards in the 1960s rejected the middle class "college boy" movement that promoted the steel drum as a symbol of nationalist unity. Similarly, ole mas' costumes are black and white and claim a direct continuity to African juju, rejecting the lavish colors of middle-class costume balls.[116]

Responding to limitations on Carnival hours and the heavy police presence restricting access to the procession on Eastern Parkway, j'ouvert is an unregulated Carnival parade. A member of the Juju Mas' Camp, which dresses in the black-and-white costumes of ole mas', told me that his costume band did not always make it to the Parkway for Carnival Monday, because the police sometimes turned them back. Nonetheless, he said, j'ouvert and ole mas' are the heart of traditional Carnival, the most important aspects; worth missing the official parade for.

The year I attended j'ouvert, Metro Steel Orchestra had just won an unprecedented third straight victory at the steel band contest behind the

Brooklyn Museum on Saturday night. Crowds of pan players, fans, and friends thronged the pan yard; the steel drums were standing out in the street in their wheeled metal racks. About 4 A.M. we began to wheel the pans up Flatbush Avenue. Metro played their winning song again and again, while Clive Bradley, their arranger, dashed along the metal racks from pan to pan, smiling and crowing. An added percussion section kept road march time on brake drums. As we proceeded up Flatbush, we met a city bus, which had to pull over to the side, and several cars, which did the same. At Utica Avenue the band turned east to meet other j'ouvert celebrants and play yet again their victorious "Panorama" composition. A group of police noted our passing and directed traffic as the sun came up.

Leslie Palmer has described j'ouvert in London this way:

> The place was Trinidad where I come from and all of we does get that feeling in the morning of the 1st day of the Carnival. I find you does only get that feeling when the pan on the road; so when we living in another country and we attempt to put the pan on the road—is the same feeling we looking to get for man to feel free with himself and get in tune with them rhythms that come through the bamboo and forge demself in steel clashing steel to shock you into the rhythmic excellence of Blackness that does make you hair stand up when the tune-bum call from Africa.[117]

The resurgence of j'ouvert indicates, on one level, the continuity of the struggle over grass-roots cultural forms between the Caribbean and Brooklyn. In a metropolitan context, however, the increased policing of Carnival which has led to the popularity of j'ouvert may represent a shift in West Indian ethnic identity. The experiences of both legal and illegal immigration, as well as the alienation of being Black in a white-dominated society, may, as Nancy Foner points out, transform "vague feelings of common ethnicity into a more articulated cultural and political consciousness," thus responding to top-down pressures on racial definition by imagining grounds for community coherence.[118]

In both the Black and white press during the 1980s, Carnival was interpreted variously as an expression of "Black unity" and of emergent ethnic identity. Jesse Jackson declared his candidacy for president at Carnival in 1987—although, as Kasinitz notes, at an awkward appearance three years earlier he had accidentally snubbed West Indian community leaders on the assumption that "All o' we is one" means that all Black people are the same.[119] New York newspapers featured interviews with African-Americans on the Parkway talking about the pan-African roots of Carnival, as well as the traditional "ethnic parade" angle on the colorful procession.[120]

Because of the specific history of Crown Heights, as well as because of their access to white privilege, the Hasidim have had what many feel is undue influence in local struggles over schools, police attention, and control over federal grants for urban development.[121] The incidents that came to be called "Crown Heights" amplified deep existing tensions between Hasidic and Black residents of the area over access to everything from housing stock to municipal funding and power. In this sense, the conflict in Crown Heights is part of a larger conflict between Blacks and Jews that comes about as a component of postwar racial formation in U.S. cities. Jews have gained access to white privilege and used it, while Blacks, regardless of their ethnic or national origins, have not.

At the same time that this conflict clearly comes about because of the dynamics of racial formation, the stories told on both sides of the issue both complicate and refine this understanding. The Hasidic community considers itself separate from the mainstream American Jewish community. Jacob Goldstein, an active member of the Hasidic community who works for the Department of Housing and serves on Community Board 9 in Crown Heights, repeatedly drew a distinction between Hasidic Jewry and assimilated American Jews—those he called "Park Avenue Jews." This alienation from other Jews, along with the focus on daily life in the Lubavitch community, leads to an intensely closed cultural identification, perhaps parallel to that of the Caribbean community in New York during the period of the costume balls in Harlem. At the same time, Hasidic Jews, having immigrated from Eastern Europe only as a response to the Holocaust, identify culturally as an embattled minority. Conflicts in Crown Heights, from the murder of Israel Turner in 1975 to the more recent events of 1991, evoke memories of *Kristallnacht* and other violent incidents of Nazi anti-Semitism.[122]

Goldstein told me a common Lubavitch story about relationships between Blacks and Hasidim in Crown Heights. "We all get along," he said, "our children play together. But I won't let my children go into the houses of their Black friends, or of any non-Jewish friends, for that matter. Not because of race, but because they might eat something that isn't kosher."[123]

The ways the Hasidim in Crown Heights identify themselves, as Jews, as an embattled religious minority, erases the social process of whiteness. This does not mean that the Hasidic community does not benefit from white skin privilege; their ample clout with police and city officials indicates the contrary.[124] And protestations about kosher foods seem disingenuous in light of the difficult racial history of Crown Heights, Brooklyn, and New York City in general. But I think it is important to recognize that, subjectively, the Hasidim do not think of themselves as assimilating into white America, or into a more or less powerful Jewish establishment.

Similarly, the politics of racial identity on the other side of what Anna Deavere Smith has called "fires in the mirror" turn on culture and nationality as well as skin color.[125] I opened this book by describing the reaction a group of West Indian–American women had to hearing that one of the lawyers for the Hasidim had stated that Caribbean people in Crown Heights were not "really American"—an immediate assertion that Jews were not "really American," either.

A portion of this exchange reveals a lack of knowledge about Jews consonant with Goldstein's certainty that the Black families on his street could not possibly learn to respect the dietary laws of their children's friends. But the concerns raised about citizenship and claims to home reflect the deep uneasiness of im/migrants of color in the United States. Correctly, they perceive that access to citizenship, to becoming American and having the right to bury their dead here, is limited, restricted on a racialized basis. At the same time, they resent the entitlement of the Hasidim. Many people in mas' camps and pan yards complain of Hasidim double parking and blocking traffic on side streets, of the extra police protection the Hasidic community received during the weekly procession to the cemetery.

In this charged context, Carnival 1994 fell on Erev Rosh Hashanah, the beginning of the Jewish High Holidays. Tension between the two communities mounted, as Police Commissioner Ray Kelly asked Carlos Lezama if he would consider moving the Carnival to Sunday. Rabbi Joseph Spielman of the Crown Heights Jewish Community Council requested and got the city to cordon off a corridor of Crown Heights to facilitate access for Hasidic visitors in town for the High Holidays. This plan was roundly condemned by the New York chapter of the American Civil Liberties Union as creating ethnic separatism. Rumors accumulated on both sides: anti-Semitic Carnival revelers wanted to urinate on synagogues; Hasidim planned to harass West Indian women as they made their way down the Parkway. According to the *Village Voice*, several meetings between Lezama and Rabbi Spielman and some open town meetings only amplified fears on both sides of this conflict.[126]

At the same time the conflict between Lubavitch and WIACDA officials was taking place, the Brooklyn police, operating under Mayor Rudy Giuliani's newly implemented "quality of life" campaign, began to move against pan yards and mas' camps. They raided late-night rehearsals and parties in the name of neighborhood quiet and order. Cecil Mitchell of Hawks International, one of the two most popular mas' camps in Brooklyn, reported that membership in Hawks, as well as attendance at parties, dwindled because of police intimidation. And, not surprisingly, j'ouvert was a target of this campaign of intimidation.

Such harassment, it should be clear, is not new. In addition to the long history of repression of Carnival forms in the Caribbean, Brooklyn police have been active in monitoring and restricting Carnival activities, both on and off the Parkway. In August 1992 I interviewed Sergeant Frank Caramonica of Brooklyn's 67th precinct. Before the restrictions were imposed on Carnival hours, he told me, Carnival in the 1970s had gone from being a festive occasion to incorporating a "criminal element." Pan yards were raided because some of them were occupied by "squatters" who didn't belong there; in other cases, neighbors had asked that the noise from practice be kept down late at night.

In the context of Crown Heights history, police repression of Carnival is likely to be read in the frame of ongoing Black-Jewish conflicts. Noel reports that the mood before Labor Day "can be summed up as 'Fuck dem Jew-bwoi.' It has come to that. 'We will not stand for nonsense,' vowed Kevin 'Fuzzy' Davis, the designer for Borokeete U.S.A. mas' camp. 'We will be off the parkway at six, without any confrontation. If it's forced upon us then everything *t'un ole mas*.'"[127]

Such an interpretation falls victim as much to structural anti-Semitism as it does to racism. Repression of Carnival historically takes place as a component of Euroamerican subjugation, in the Caribbean or in New York. In contemporary Crown Heights, Jews become the veil under which the operations of regional and international capital continue unimpeded. This is not to absolve Jews in general or the Hasidim in Crown Heights in particular from local responsibility. Rather, my intent is to argue for a longer historic view of conflicts such as the one in Crown Heights. Tensions between Blacks and Jews, between Hasidim and Caribbean people, take place in a context of struggles for local power and economic mobility. And these conflicts, in turn, operate in a racialized urban and regional political economy.

In its multiple incarnations in New York, Carnival has been a place where West Indian people create themselves: as foreign nationals, as proud citizens of newly decolonized nations, as striving new immigrants, and as Black people. The various incarnations of Carnival in Harlem and Brooklyn, at dance halls, on Eastern Parkway, and on quiet side streets in the early-morning hours have both responded to and created definitions of race, ethnicity, and nation. Caribbean and Caribbean-American people come to Carnival from all over the East Coast and Canada; some travel from the Caribbean to "jump up" on Eastern Parkway on Labor Day weekend. At Carnival in Brooklyn today, old friends from the Caribbean encounter one another, Caribbean-American children who have never been back home discover a sense of place, and African-American neighbors come to see and participate in the Culture of Black Creation, brought to Brooklyn by the ongoing circulation of capital, labor, and culture.

Carnival has also been a place where the forces of state and capital, the Immigration and Naturalization Service, police, municipal regulations, candidates for office, and corporate ad campaigns attempt to inscribe Caribbean people: as dangerous inner-city denizens or potentially upstanding citizens. This dialectic between grass-roots imagination and colonial administration has long informed the creative strategies of Afro-Atlantic culture. While Carnival "refuses to speak in one voice," everyone who "jumps up" on the Parkway is involved in a broad politics of diasporan denizenship, where im/migrants stake a claim to their homelands abroad and to their rights in the countries where, perforce, they live and work. The multiple narratives of this diasporan denizenship challenge racialized discourses of citizenship and assimilation. They provide a context for ongoing struggles against municipal and hemispheric colonialism, in their equally myriad forms.

When mas' bands celebrate "fancy Africa" or proclaim loudly that "Columbus lied," they stake a claim to history for the denizens of the continuing diaspora in this hemisphere. Carnival has always maintained the links of memory between the exigencies of the present and memories of the past. And in maintaining these links, Carnival has been a site for the articulation of identities not yet recognized or authorized by official institutions.

Throughout the history of Carnival in New York, Caribbean and African-American people have debated the possibilities for unity between them. As politicians and the media recognized the demographic

power of "Black Brooklyn" in the 1990s, local activists and community leaders negotiated the fissures of ethnicity and nation. At the same
time that Caribbean people are pressured to assimilate in a model of
ethnicity designed to describe the experiences of European immigrants
at the turn of the last century, they struggle alongside African-Americans for access to dwindling municipal services, for entrance to a de-
pressed job market, for places in a public educational system that is
underfunded and constantly under attack. At the same time that Carnival has been increasingly identified by participants, police, and media
as a Black festival, it has become larger and larger. Thus the very agencies that enforce national and municipal initiatives designed to blame
urban underdevelopment on the people who benefit least from it may
well function to help Caribbean and African-American people to recognize common enemies and goals. Certainly the popular arts of memory so central to Carnival are already engaged in writing an account
that resists the daily exigencies of life in a city so stratified by race and
by class.

CONCLUSION

Unlike Caribbean Carnival in Brooklyn, contemporary powwows have
not been the sites of municipal repression and sanction, in part because
powwows are held indoors and make their much more explicitly politicized statements through the microphone of the powwow MC or guest
speakers. Indian people in the Twin Cities have developed semi-autonomous
institutions that facilitate their culture. While Caribbean people have newspapers and community centers as well, the massive jubilance of a Black
street festival is not well received in a city and a nation that see Black
people as dangerous people.

    This distinction speaks to another level of race and history that dis-
tinguishes mainstream, white reception of Carnival and powwow. While
both Afro-Atlantic and Indian cultures have been continuously appropriated by the mass culture industry, they have been appropriated in different ways. White culture has continuously drawn on Black cultural
forms as at once exotic and threatening, whereas Indian cultures are seen
as the last vestiges of a dying race, as a truly American heritage. While
both Caribbean and Native American populations have been inscribed
into U.S. racial hierarchies in the process of their migrations to the cities,
these hierarchies have a different place for each of them. As Caribbean
people are increasingly identified as Black people, their culture is a part

of an inner-city culture widely exoticized and dismissed. Pan-Indian resurgence, on the other hand, is seen as a vestige of a more whole, authentic culture that was necessarily displaced by American civilization. Current claims for sovereignty are not necessarily acceptable as part of this package, and urban Indians are dismissed as partial bearers of invented traditions. But powwows are nonetheless appealing for their resonance with a lost American West.

I have argued that Indian and Caribbean im/migrants responded to racialized policies and circumstances, creating and modifying existing cultural identities to facilitate resistance and multiple alliances. At the same time, in the ongoing dialectic of racial formation, the distribution of municipal goods and services and the racialized narratives that rationalize this distribution attempt to take on these newly forged identities and alliances. As Caribbean people have increasingly identified themselves as Black *and* Caribbean, they have been criminalized by both the New York press and the police force. Through this criminalization, Rastafarianism, for example, can be identified with Third World drug lords and fundamentalists: a historical rhyme with white frontier beliefs that the Ghost Dance religion justified the massacre of believers. Caribbean immigrants, particularly English-speaking West Indians, are pressured to adhere to a dying ethnicity model and succeed, proving once and for all that race is no barrier in this country. But formidable economic and social barriers against their success are constantly under construction. Similarly, as Indian people in Minnesota have gained a unified and powerful political voice through institutions such as the American Indian Movement, counternarratives about excessive Indian entitlement to run casinos and fish in waters long guaranteed them by treaty have also gained local credence.[128]

Indian and Afro-diasporic people are separated by racial categories and cultural distance. But in other places, their common experiences of colonial and municipal administrations bring them together. At recent powwows, a newly cross-cultural form has begun to appear. Reflecting the inner-city lives of a new generation of urban Indians, Indian rappers such as Litefoot bring the bass-heavy collage sound of rap together with the concerns of contemporary Indian people. Just as Caribbean people in New York "jump up" as "fancy Indians," in partial testimony to the Caribs and Arawaks who successfully eluded colonial rule, Native American rap narrates the mixed heritage of resistance in the Western Hemisphere. Cultural forms and stories cross, imitate, and rearticulate identity.

While the mass culture industry, along with the colonial technologies of museums and anthropologists, constantly exploits and appropriates Afro-diasporic and Indian cultures, they are also sites of reinterpretation and resistance. Randy Brewster, the well-known costume maker who runs the Culture of Black Creation mas' camp, once showed me a picture from one of his trips to the Smithsonian. The picture showed him standing between one of his fancy Indian costumes and an Indian wearing a full Blackfoot headdress and bustle. Two years later, Johnny Smith, a culture instructor at the Heart of the Earth Survival School in Minneapolis, argued that Indian people never lost their dance and songs. "I got hidden friends at the Smithsonian," he said, "I know what's in there from the 1870s. And I use it in my work here."

CHAPTER 5

Sounds of Brooklyn

Pan Yards as Im/migrant Social Spaces

RUM AND COCA-COLA

This chapter explores the steel band movement in its im/migrant incarnation in New York. Like the main story told by this book, the history of the steel drum involves the transnational circulation of capital, culture, and people. As Caribbean im/migrants came north after World War II in search of economic opportunity, they brought their cultural practices with them, often discovering that some forms, such as calypso, had preceded their arrival in metropolitan centers. Im/migration transforms the meaning of a social art such as the steel drum. In this chapter, I look at the steel band in contemporary Brooklyn, and attempt to understand its significance to Caribbean im/migrants, who are hailed by multiple names in their adopted city: as Black people, foreign nationals, "new immigrants," "the largest ethnic group in New York,"[1] and as members of the African diaspora.

The steel drum, or pan, as the instrument and its music are called in the Caribbean, originated in Port of Spain, Trinidad, during World War II, when residents of Laventille, a working-class neighborhood, began to use the oil drums left at the U.S. refueling station in Trinidad to make percussive instruments. The steel drum was a direct descendant of Afro-Trinidadian percussive forms such as Shango drumming and the tamboo–bamboo stick band. The music of both Afro- and Indo-Trinidadian Carnival had invariably been at odds with colonial power throughout Trinidadian history. Along with parading, it was often banned as a threat to the municipal order.[2] After specific Carnival practices were banned, often because of their close connection with the most African strands of Creole society, newly resistant "re-creolized" forms surfaced. These forms often appeared in areas of Port of Spain associated with Black, grass-roots society; they were also associated with the tradition of j'ouvert, in which unofficial and socially unacceptable components of Carnival would take to the streets early in the day, before official festival hours.[3] The steel drum also incorporated some East Indian influences, reflecting the multiethnic nature of Trinidad's working class. The tassa drum, played at the Muslim festival of Hosay, was an influence on the development of the steel drum.[4]

The history of the steel drum begins at j'ouvert at the turn of the twentieth century, when the controversial tamboo-bamboo bands began to integrate tin pans and kitchen utensils. During the 1930s, bands such as Alexander's Ragtime Band added brake drums and metal containers, as well as pieces of umbrellas to keep time during their marching. Members of the "saga boy" subculture in Port of Spain transformed oil drums during the 1940s into the only acoustic instrument invented in the twentieth century. Early steel bands such as Desperados were a key part of this subculture. Their predominantly male members wore zoot suits, listened to American jazz, and were often supported by women who, like the mother and daughter in "Rum and Coca-Cola," got their cash by "working for the Yankee dollar"—entertaining GIs stationed at the base in Port of Spain. The steel drum, then, developed alongside the transnational migrations of both capital and workers.[5] And, as the song points out, such migrations transform not only the geographic but the gendered location of culture.

Steel band music came to North America as a result of the circulation of capital, workers, and culture around the Western Hemisphere during the postwar period. Changes in U.S. immigration policy after 1965 favored increased immigration from the Caribbean, Asia, and Latin America to fill largely service-sector jobs. Unlike economic development during the "great wave" of immigration at the turn of the century, postindustrial employment in retail, domestic labor, and light industrial work favored the employment of women as a potentially docile labor force.[6] As U.S.-dominated corporations and development agencies extended their reach south and east to newly decolonized Caribbean islands, citizens of these new nations fled the economic ravages of neocolonialism, migrating north in search of work.[7]

At the same time that steel band music was traveling north, popularized by tourism and the increasingly multinational configuration of both capital and culture, Caribbean im/migrants in New York were figuring out how to implement their cultural practices in a new social geography. Panman Rudy King recalled going from his new home in New York to the oil refineries in Newark to find steel drums.[8] Once they had made the drums and learned the tunes, early New York pan players strung the drums around their necks and marched in Harlem Carnival, and organized themselves into small ensembles to perform at parties and weddings. Just as the migration of working-class Afro-Trinidadians from rural to urban areas had triggered transformations in the social arts of Carnival during the 1870s and 1940s,[9] international migration between the United States and Trinidad would bring changes to the meaning and practice of the steel band movement.

Im/migrants from the eastern Caribbean, where the steel drum had become a crucial element of Carnival by the 1950s, celebrated Carnival in Harlem during the 1940s and 1950s as a marker of their longing for an increasingly commonly imagined Caribbean homeland. At the same time, they were also seen, by native whites and African-Americans, as Black people. For im/migrants from the Caribbean, issues of class and color are more complex than the solidly enforced line separating Black and white in this country. Jim Crow, then, was a striking, sometimes confusing social fact.[10] King told of his experiences on tour on the college circuit in the 1950s:

> Those were some rough days, because you couldn't go in restaurants to eat and all this. There were a lot of problems on the road with this Black and white business, you know. Anyway, we didn't have too much problem, because I didn't know the difference, I used to just walk anyplace and if then they tell me that, then I say I didn't know any better. But I figure what happen is that I'm spending money, so I just used to walk into a place and get whatever. I didn't realize how serious it was.

Caribbean im/migrants entered a charged arena of negotiations about the social meaning of race in this period.

In Trinidad, along with other Carnival forms such as masquerade and calypso, the steel band is a component of diverse narratives of race and national pride, ethnic solidarity, and memories of a variously imagined homeland. During decolonization, Eric Williams's People's National Movement appropriated the steel band as a symbol of cultural autonomy to mobilize Afro-Trinidadian grass-roots political backing.[11] During the late 1950s and early 1960s, the steel band movement was transformed by national and corporate support. No longer identified as an inner-city cultural form associated with the "saga boy" culture in Laventille and with the waves of labor unrest in the oilfields during the Great Depression, the instrument was recognized as a uniquely Caribbean musical innovation.[12] "College boy" bands, made up of middle-class players who had grown up being warned to stay out of the pan yards, became common in Trinidad. The late 1950s and early 1960s were, according to Les Slater of the Trinidad and Tobago Folk Arts Society, a kind of golden age of pan, with tremendous technical innovations by such musicians as Ellie Manette, Junior Pouchet, Winston "Spree" Simon, and Bertie Marshall, as well as expanding participation by economically and racially diverse components of Trinidadian society.[13]

The steel band accompanied Trinidadians and other im/migrants from the eastern Caribbean north in their postcolonial diaspora. Just as the steel band movement in Trinidad developed in relation to issues of decolonization and national identity, the steel band movement in Brooklyn negotiates both the conflicts of cultural formation in diaspora and those of local urban politics.[14] A form fraught with national symbolism for Trinidadians, the steel band has nevertheless begun to attract players in Brooklyn from Caribbean nations without a steel band tradition, as well as some young African-American players. To some degree, steel bands and other Carnival forms in New York may become more Africanized, more of a "Black thing," as Indo- and Afro-Trinidadians move to separate neighborhoods.[15]

In the urban metropolitan context, the ongoing im/migrant production of identity and place proposes some alternatives to the ways U.S. cities have traditionally dealt with im/migrant communities. Ethnicity theory, as scholarly theory and municipal practice, has failed to take into account the centrality of race. But North American ideas of race have often failed to encompass complex formation of identities within constructs of "Blackness" and "whiteness." This has prevented our understanding of urban, as well as international, politics.

Caribbean im/migrants are pulled between a model of ethnic empowerment that is offered to them as a "model minority" and the equally cogent demands of their position as Black im/migrants in a two-tiered racial hierarchy with an increasingly anti-immigrant bias. As im/migrants, they are confronted with a model of assimilation that offers to swap economic success for cultural identity. As Afro-diasporic people, however, they see the failure of this model to negotiate racial hierarchy. In neighborhoods such as Crown Heights, they hear and become involved with the narratives of contemporary African-American culture. Their responses to these dilemmas suggest the creation of complex identities that straddle claims of state and nation, ethnicity and race.

This chapter, along with the one that follows, focuses on the "changing same" of im/migrant popular cultures as a way to understand the inner history of im/migration. In both chapters, I explore incidents that embody the tensions between cultural memory and social change. The experience of im/migration generates its aftershocks: the dreams and visions of urban diaspora. These visions suggest new interpretations of identity, citizenship, nation. Adapting to im/migration means that people have an acute sense of what is being lost and created; what can be salvaged, whether meaning inheres in form, or whether meaning continues to speak through the voices of invented traditions. Very often, I found, these issues are expressed in social conflicts that take place over gender and generation.

My focus on gender and generation in these chapters comes out of my increasing conviction that these are the terrains on which im/migrants struggle for their right to be citizens *and* denizens: to be entitled with respect to the dominant nation, as well as to their stake in narratives of homeland, exile, and return. Tradition and cultural survival are intimately involved with and implicated in the category of youth and the practices of young people. Because of their dual socialization, young people are particularly important in the cultural process of im/migration. Gender roles, similarly, are one of the charged spaces in which culture is both transformed and reproduced.

Notions of respectability and reputation have informed approaches to the study of Caribbean culture since Peter Wilson's influential article was published in 1969. Respectability is the domain of women and older or married men, and covers socially sanctioned notions of success: performance in church, home, and workplace. Reputation, on the other hand, is the domain of younger, unmarried men and covers often forbidden or disdained innovations in grass-roots culture, such as the steel drum.[16] The steel band movement developed in Trinidad during the 1940s among young men involved in the kinds of activities that engender *reputation* in the peer group and wider society, but not *respectability* in terms of dominant ideas of success. Much like African- and Mexican-American zootsuiters of the same period, panmen flourished in the half-light of the cultural underground, flaunting respectability and officially imposed wartime restrictions.[17] Stephen Stuempfle writes: "Playing on the streets during the war years was a form of open defiance in which the panmen expressed their resentment of the ban on carnival."[18] And, indeed, both zoot-suiters and saga boys often found themselves in direct conflict with representatives of respectable authority, through street fights, arrests, and frequent raids on their neighborhoods.

One way of explaining the relative absence of women from such subcultures is that their active participation is precluded by the violence of conflicts between representatives of respectability and reputation. Often, as well, there is a gendering of roles within the subculture. The "saga boy" subculture, for instance, was organized around the labor of female prostitutes, who supported their pan-playing boyfriends by "working for the Yankee dollar" at Trinidad's two U.S. bases during the war.[19] Some scholars argue that more women got involved with the steel band movement as it moved into the respectable spheres of Trinidadian middle class life during the 1950s.[20] However, a Trinidadian pan player living in Brooklyn remembered growing up around "rebel" pan yards, where her mother played. She remembered the rebel yards as always having more women in them than respectable, middle-class bands. Nonetheless, the official history of the steel band through the 1950s is almost exclusively male. Women's participation, as in many other grass-roots subcultural forms, seems by all accounts marginal until pan's acceptance as a middle-class, respectable cultural practice.[21]

Im/migration profoundly transforms cultural priorities, among them gender roles. Acts of Americanizing or resisting Americanization, struggling for economic mobility, maintaining family ties and connections to newly distant homelands call on im/migrant men and women to adopt new attitudes and activities.[22] Further, for Afro-Caribbean im/migrants, gender roles in the new society are complicated by changes in the social meaning of race.[23] As the social categories that govern notions of respectability and reputation change, so do established ideas of propriety and deviance. Appropriate actions for "good Trinidadian women" may change in the context of Caribbean neighborhoods in Brooklyn along with developing ideas in the community about social identity, ethnicity, and race. In its im/migrant incarnation in Brooklyn, the steel band movement struggles with these transformations.

A NIGHT OUT

We are Western, yet have to separate what is ours from
what is Western, a very difficult task.

> C. L. R. James, "The Mighty Sparrow"

March 1993. A "Sounds of Brooklyn" series held at Brooklyn College features an evening dedicated to the steel drum. The evening begins with a symposium honoring the famous steel drum tuner Ellie Manette, and moves on to performances by two Brooklyn steel bands and two solo players. Manette is widely credited as the innovator who first tuned the notes of a scale onto a steel drum, moving the instrument towards its current level of acoustic richness and sophistication.

The program takes place on a raw night in March, and the lecture hall is not half filled by the appointed time for the beginning of the symposium. Manette's Brooklyn appearance brings out a few pan aficionados; members of the Trinidad/Tobago Folk Arts Society, a group of first-generation im/migrants dedicated to documenting and recording their culture, who cosponsored the event; some of the players from the bands and their families; some ethnomusicologists; and some interested people, both Black and white, from the ethnically mixed neighborhood of East Flatbush.

The two solo performers, Boogsie Sharpe and Arddin Herbert, represent important phases in the development of the steel band, or pan, in Trinidad and in New York. Both men work as solo performers and also as composers and arrangers. Sharpe is widely known as the first jazz-pan fusion arranger. He works as arranger for bands in both Trinidad and Brooklyn, and is well known and popular in both places. Arddin Herbert is the musical director and arranger at the Caribbean-American Steel Youth Movement (CASYM) and a music student at Brooklyn College—the first student there to create a major focusing on the steel drum. The leadership of CASYM recruited Herbert in Trinidad and offered him a partial scholarship to come to the United States, lead the band, and study music. A half-generation younger than Sharpe, Herbert is intimately involved with the urban life and dual cultural identity of West Indian–American youth in Brooklyn. The piece he composed for CASYM to play at the concert, Crown Heights Symphony, reflects his involvement with and concern for daily life in the Caribbean neighborhoods of New York.

Manette, who is now a professor of music at West Virginia University in Wheeling, is introduced with some flourish by Les Slater, president of the Trinidad/Tobago Folk Arts Society, and by Ray Allen, a folklorist at Brooklyn College. He begins to talk about the history of steel drums in Trinidad and about his own work, in both pan yards in Trinidad and the acoustical engineering laboratories of the university. His lecture focuses primarily on his work to refine the tuning of the steel drum further, and to gain recognition for the instrument in academic music circles. Like many older im/migrants who have been in the States a long time and are not involved in the steel band scene in Brooklyn, Manette sees the future of pan in its potential recognition as a serious musical form. Many others in the Brooklyn steel band community think differently; they see the steel drum as a link to "back home" as well as a way to create leisure and educational space in New York.

As Manette continues speaking about his current work on tuning the steel drum, I look around the audience. A row of women in their thirties and forties catches my attention, partly because a row of women together is rare at steel band events and partly because of the way they are acting. In an auditorium of attentive listeners, they shift uneasily, whisper back and forth to one another, and, when they notice me looking over at them, raise their eyebrows at me, gesturing their annoyance at what is happening on the stage.

Finally, during the question-and-answer period, one of the women speaks up. All of this talk about furthering the art form was well and good, she said, "but what about the children? What are you doing for our children here in Brooklyn?"

The woman who spoke, I later found out, was a founding member of the Caribbean-American Steel Youth Movement and the mother of three daughters. "Anything to keep them in here," she told me, gesturing around the yard outside the church where CASYM practices, where parents and friends of players were busy putting together the metal stands that hold steel drums and players for outdoor performances, "rather than out there." She swept her hand out, pointing toward Nostrand Avenue and the other streets that are just outside the entrance to the church parking lot that CASYM uses for practice.

"Out there" means the streets of Flatbush, with their high rates of unemployment, teen pregnancy, and crime. Like many parents, she wants something quite different for her three daughters "in here," in the world she and the community of CASYM have staked out and tried to make safe through their creativity and hard work. This distinction between inside and outside raises the question of where home, for Caribbean people in Brooklyn, is to be found, and what role im/migrant institutions such as the steel band play in making this home. Her question to Manette places the epic narrative of pan's development on the more dicey terrain of everyday life.

Along with the majority of the Caribbean im/migrant community in New York, steel bands moved from Harlem to Brooklyn after 1969. The two steel bands present at the Brooklyn College concert, Sonatas and CASYM, both originate in Brooklyn, and, it can be argued, are as much

Photo 5. Players at Metro Steel's pan yard in Flatbush practice and socialize before the evening practice session.

Brooklyn institutions as they are Caribbean ones. Each band has a home base, a pan yard (see photo 5). Located in the yard inside urban blocks or in schoolyards, church basements, or parking lots, pan yards are the spaces where the steel drum is made and taught, and where steel bands practice all summer for Panorama, the competition that is part of the massive West Indian–American Day Carnival in Brooklyn. All of the metropolitan area pan yards are now located in Brooklyn, with the exception of the Harlem All-Stars. Panorama, along with the other musical and dramatic events that accompany Labor Day on the Parkway, is held at the big outdoor stage behind the Brooklyn Museum.

People in the pan yards, along with organizations such as the Caribbean American Steelband Association (CASA) and the Trinidad and Tobago Folk Arts Society, attempt to manage and direct the cultural and social life of the art form away from "home." For Manette, as for Slater and many members of the Trinidad and Tobago Folk Arts Society, recollections of pan's "golden age" emphasize individual accomplishments during pan's formative years, and call for the recognition of these accomplishments in recorded history. "I don't go to the pan yards here," Slater explained in an interview, "because I really have no interest in it. . . . I am not going to be part of that whole crowd that gets involved in Panorama. All that is an excuse to party. . . . What I am doing, the Folk Arts Institute, is so much more important, so much more important, it's not funny." As Manette works to continue the technical evolution of the steel drum as a "serious" acoustical instrument, Slater and the Folk Arts Society work to document the history and development of pan.

In order for pan to be recognized as a "serious" music, a lineage must be produced for the instrument that aligns it with other narratives that are familiar to the history of Western "high" art.[24] Such a lineage creates heroes as well as a distanced memory of a classical age when this history was formed. Pan originates in the traditional limiting of African-derived percussion in Caribbean history, the literal dumping of First World trash in the Third World, and the transformation of this trash into music. To build an epic from such heroic beginnings, many histories of pan add great men such as Manette, as well as earlier innovators such as Neville Jules, Winston "Spree" Simon, and Tony Williams. Such tales of origin are often in conflict: interviews with pan historians and important figures in the development of the steel drum often feature a routine denunciation of other stories and narrators. Various figures and events become more and less important depending on who is telling the story.

Epic stories about the steel band tend to emphasize individual innovation over collective artistic developments. Heroic individuals and specific technological breakthroughs take precedence over community expression. As Rudy King put it, "Everybody, you know, different guys put in their little piece in it, so you can't give credit to no one man and say, 'He invented it.' "

In contrast to the emphasis on Manette as a pan pioneer, people in the pan yards in Brooklyn often stress the collective origin of the steel drum. During one of my first evenings at a Brooklyn pan yard, I asked a woman who was sitting on the bench next to me, listening to the band practice, where the mallets that pan is played with came from. I had in mind a quick trip to a local music store, or perhaps a hardware store for the wood and rubber that are used to beat pan. "Oh," she responded, "we made those in slavery days."

While this story perhaps tells, as much as anything else, how a Caribbean im/migrant in New York responds to the presence of a Euro-american ethnographer in the yard, this woman's recourse to grass-roots memory is telling and very common in the vocabulary used by those involved with pan to explain the history of their music. Stories told about the origin of pan and other carnival forms commonly range in their historical breadth to include events from the African diaspora in the Caribbean, emancipation from slavery, national independence. Like all stories of the steel drum, these narratives carry a heroic charge. But in contrast to the narrative of pan as a serious instrument, their focus, like that of the women at the concert, often emphasizes the role of music in the history and daily life of a people. Such present-oriented stories challenge the solid march of the epic, allowing for a more flexible interpretation of culture and community.[25]

Caribbean im/migrants tell various stories concerning pan's origin and affiliations. In some interpretations, pan is an urban art form, belonging to the residents of Laventille, whether they live in Port of Spain, Brooklyn, or Toronto. For others, it is a national symbol of a proudly independent homeland, taking on a particular force and appeal for those living in the economic exile of contemporary neocolonialism. Some, both in the Caribbean and in North American diaspora, take this further. The panman Victor Brady sees the steel drum as part of a pan-Caribbean culture: "Trinidad invented it," he said, "but it's like the Wright Brothers invented the plane at Kitty Hawk. It's part of the Caribbean cultural chain." Others see pan and Caribbean culture in general as part of the huge African diaspora that connects jazz to pan, rap to reggae in dance hall and go-go, and that gestures toward solidarity among African peoples around and across the Atlantic. Trevor Johns is a second-generation Trinidadian immigrant who plays pan, has an engineering degree from Columbia, and runs the progressive Basement Recording Studios, which aims to provide musical technology free of charge to the African-American and Afro-Caribbean community in Brooklyn. He said: "I wouldn't even break it down in terms of Caribbean. I think what you see happening, especially in our community, is African."

The more academic concerns of Slater and Manette for the preservation of pan's history and its future formal development correspond to what Timothy Brennan calls the "traditional aesthetic conflicts" of exile and nationalism: "artistic iconoclasm and communal assent, the unique vision and the collective truth."[26] In an im/migrant context, these aesthetic poles are charged with social and political meaning. Concern for the documented past and recognized future of the art form is not relegated solely to academics; each pan yard has its own historians and promoters, all with visions of the instrument's future and versions of its story. A younger generation of pan players hears the international success of Caribbean artists such as the Mighty Sparrow, Shabba Ranks, and the jazz pan composer Boogsie Sharpe as inspiration. These younger players dream of taking pan in new directions in rock and jazz music, and they think about how these developments may affect the ways pan is taught, in England and North America as well as back home in the Caribbean. In many of my interviews with players, the subject of Andy

Narel, a white pan player whose jazz-inspired albums had begun to get some airplay on New York album-oriented radio stations, comes up as a way to talk about the future of pan as a crossover art form as well as complicated issues of race, ethnicity, and culture.

On the other hand, the attempt to bring the steel band "up" to the level of European music by treating it as a serious music inevitably involves a hierarchy that has social as well as musical implications. Categories of "high art" and academic knowledge exist in both the Caribbean and North America in a deeply racialized context.[27] Dan Simon, a Vincentian calypsonian and sociologist, views the same period that others see as the golden age of pan as a time of conflict between local innovation and colonial hierarchy. "Most of the sounds played during that period of time was, like I say, the classics from abroad. That was how you were measured because your masters, the people in authority, the government and everybody was European, white. . . . The matter of playing the native sounds did not get accepted for a long time." Performative politics mirror colonial hierarchies here; part of pan's ascendance to its golden age involved the arrangement of Western classical music for the steel band.

Such colonial hierarchies, in a metropolitan context, can translate into the racial and ethnic hierarchies that organize access to municipal empowerment. At a performance by the Trinidadian steel band Desperados in Brooklyn in 1993, a speaker from one of the concert's sponsors, the *New York Daily News,* lauded the ability of the band members to play complex classical pieces without reading music. At the same time, he suggested that the predominantly West Indian–American audience was noteworthy for its "strong family values and a good work ethic." This ideology of West Indians as a model minority of color has been used to buttress flagging paradigms of assimilation and ethnicity theory, as well as to bolster the neoconservative racial agenda aimed at undercutting years of incremental civil rights reform.[28] The construction of a golden age narrative of the steel band's ascendance to high art parallels the attempt, in the U.S. urban context, to elide the complexities of Caribbean social and economic identity into a paradigm specifically generated to explain the gradual melting of "white ethnics" into "Americans." In other words, epic stories about high art can obscure the operation of local power.[29]

During decolonization, Eric Williams and other Trinidadian nationalist leaders turned to the traditionally African in Caribbean society to provide a cultural context for political liberation. Stories about the steel band emphasized the Caribbean and imagined African village as a social unit, and looked to what Robert Hill terms "internal maronnage" in places such as Laventille to provide inspiration.[30] As in other postcolonial settings, this recourse to Afro-Trinidadian forms to provide such narrative coherence challenges racialized and classed colonial hierarchies. Williams's emphasis on the steel bands, along with the call of other postcolonial intellectuals to valorize the African in Caribbean culture, inverts the traditional hierarchies of colonial society, resulting in what Donald Hill calls a "re-afrocreolized culture."[31] The contradiction, as the work of Partha Chatterjee points out, is that the Trinidadian state, seeking a source for national pride, solidarity, and sovereignty, generated a story that valorized the invention of the steel drum in Western, hierarchical terms. A form of community expression, with its diverse genius and cultural resonance, was, then, valued only insofar as it fitted into categories of high art and individual accomplishment. Further, of course, the emphasis on African roots in a complex, multiethnic society leads to problematic new hierarchies after decolonization.[32]

The problem raised by the row of women at the concert is not that this process demeans some kind of authentic, nonwestern spirit existing in the art form[33] but that this idea about pan will always suppress the emergence of a truly popular, locally useful democratic culture. This problem is amplified in an im/migrant location such as Brooklyn, where the challenge of cultural politics lies in connecting popular creativity with the actual sources of municipal power.

For Earl Alleyne, currently chairman of the board of CASYM and former business manager of PanTrinbago–New York, issues of nation and culture are as pressing in Brooklyn as they were for Trinidadian cultural nationalists twenty years ago. "Pan in Trinidad brought tranquillity to the nation," he said, in a conversation outside the church basement where the band was practicing for Panorama. "And it can do the same thing in Brooklyn." The cultural politics of the steel band movement in Brooklyn revolve around ideas of art form and nation, race and ethnicity. Such issues touch on the practices of daily life, on gender identity, memory, and the forms of popular culture.[34] In turn, these issues have an important effect on im/migrant ideas about home and the stories they tell about exile and return: to neighborhood or nation, island or region, united past or future coalition.

"WE'RE AN AMERICAN BAND"

The dominant culture talks of the white world, corporate America holds up those principles with the ties and
the WASP values, and all the, you know, "work hard"
and "pull yourself up with your boot string." That exists, but then for me as an individual, see, I can leave
there, and this is my pan and my calypso and a group
of my old friends who identify with the same things I
identify with—that I think plays a role. The other one
provides the bread, means of survival and meeting your
responsibilities. But if a person had the chance to have
another, most of the Caribbean people would choose
the subculture. Why? Because that's the culture they
maintain their sanity with.

Dan Simon, 1991

I'm like this American-Trinidadian woman that's playing an instrument that probably not half the world
knows about. And then the other half of me is like this
Brooklyn woman, that's something that everyone
knows.

Player, BWIA Sonatas, 1992

The steel band movement in Brooklyn is pulled along several axes. For
one, the steel drum is an important symbol of home. Many Trinidadian
immigrants wear necklaces with the shape of Trinidad and a replica of
a steel drum in gold strung from them. Copies of Ancil Neil's celebra-
tory history of Desperados in Laventille circulate during the Labor Day
festivities, as do pamphlets variously explaining the history of pan as
African, Caribbean, and Trinidadian. These practices suggest the symbolic richness of pan in a diasporan context.[35]

Pan in Brooklyn straddles two homelands, in the Caribbean and New
York; it provides a continuity with home at the same time that it acts as
a force in shaping the culture of the urban diaspora. A pan player and
student at Brooklyn College who has grown up in Brooklyn and has never
been to the Caribbean commented: "Being that you are away from what
you would consider your homeland, you can be away and feel like you're
still there. Pan, the calypso music, makes you feel like you're still at home,
even though you're away from what you would call your home."

For second-generation im/migrants, pan offers a primary experience of Caribbeanness. It has a different meaning for many first-generation im/migrants, who see pan yards as "little Laventilles," direct replicas of specific places in Trinidad. One young woman, the second-generation daughter of a Trinidadian father and a Grenadian mother, said, "I consider Grenada, Trinidad, and Brooklyn as part of me." Young Caribbean-Americans identify, sometimes simultaneously, with North American constructions of race, Caribbean ideas of nation, and Brooklyn-based exigencies of class, gender, and neighborhood.

In an im/migrant context, pan yards take on a different meaning than they had back home. Judy Henry, a Trinidadian-born woman who never played pan back home, comes to the pan yard with her boyfriend, Jerry LeGendre, every night after her full-time job in a day-care center. Her connection with Metro Steel began in 1991, after she left her Indo-Trinidadian husband and started seeing Jerry. A light-skinned woman who is proud of her French grandmother, she worried at first about her slide down the Caribbean continuum of race and class. Jerry, dark-skinned, is proudly involved with the Afro-Trinidadian culture of pan. In the summer of 1991, Henry told me that she felt isolated in Brooklyn, from other Trinidadians as well as the African-American community there. "I stay very much by myself," she said. In the summer of 1993, in contrast, she spoke of the connections she had made, particularly to other women, in the pan yards. These are contacts she probably would not have made at home. In Brooklyn, the convergence of racial and national ideologies produces new connections between people, even as it continues to separate them.

Pan yards themselves represent a broad range of responses to the experience of im/migration, as well as to generations of Afro-Caribbean life in New York. Some are like small-scale versions of yards in Laventille: they retain the names of bands in Trinidad; maintain a fairly patriarchal social organization, where older men, many of them friends from home, run the finances of the yard and use it as a meeting and socializing place; and even import players from Trinidad to perform in the Panorama competition. Others, such as CASYM and Sonatas, focus on the importance of teaching Caribbean culture and values to young people. Some of their players were born in the Caribbean and immigrated with their parents or to attend school in the United States, while others were born in Brooklyn but maintain a dual sense of identity through their immersion in both African-American and Afro-Caribbean urban cultures. And some yards, among them the three-year Panorama winner Metro, a notable exclusion from the evening's program at Brooklyn

College, combine the functions of im/migrant and neighborhood social center, teaching pan to children at the same time that they host both local people on their way home from work in the evening and serious pan players who come up from the Caribbean as often as possible to attend Brooklyn Carnival.[36]

No pan yard embodies a single kind of im/migrant identity, but people in each yard make a number of choices. The community of each pan yard is composed of the members of the steel band, its players, arrangers, and leaders; the organization of the steel band, which is often made up of former players, or of people who do not play pan at all but are interested in the continuation of the music in New York; and by the community of listeners, supporters, friends, and parents that forms the immediate audience and constituency for each yard. Their choices concern how the band will be run, who will arrange and teach the music, whether or not the pan yard will be strictly devoted to making and playing the steel drum, and who will be involved in the life of the band.

Pan yard geography sometimes shifts according to available space and local sponsorship. As of the summer of 1993, four of the Brooklyn pan yards (Metro, Pan Rebels, Moods Pan Groove, and CASYM) were southeast of Eastern Parkway, in the heavily Caribbean areas of Crown Heights and Flatbush. Sonatas was a few blocks north and west of the Parkway, between Crown Heights, Bedford-Stuyvesant, and Clinton Hill. Metro II, or Despers USA, has a pan yard on Fulton Street in central Bedford-Stuyvesant. Except for Sonatas, which has a privately owned practice space behind row houses, all practice in alleys, backyards, or basements owned by other institutions (see map).

CASYM focuses on education and, according to Alleyne, is the only steel band in Brooklyn to receive funding from state sources.[37] Founded in 1983, CASYM had its start five years earlier as an attempt to found an African-American soccer team to play in the Five Borough Soccer League. The team drew mainly English-speaking Caribbean youths, who were familiar with the game from home. Many of them had been having trouble in school. As the team developed, parents got to know one another, and recognized the need to sponsor cultural as well as educational activities oriented around their common Caribbean culture. "We believe in developing the child totally," Alleyne emphasized. "We use pan to attract them."

CASYM's motto, "Education a must," reveals the organization's commitment to getting Caribbean children through high school and supporting their efforts in higher education. The band offers small scholar-

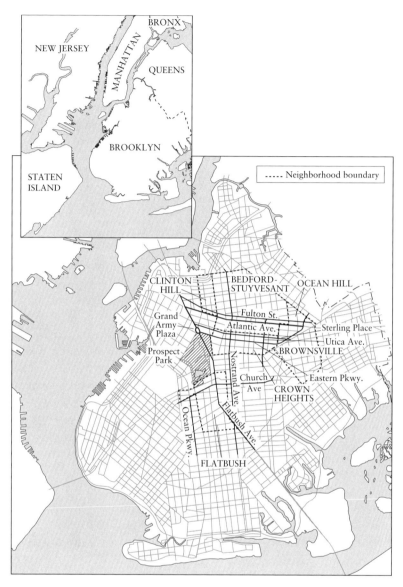

Brooklyn neighborhoods

ships to its alumni; as of 1993, ten CASYM players were attending Brooklyn Technical College. In contrast to other pan yards, where the focus is on learning the piece for performance in Panorama, at CASYM Arddin Herbert works on teaching the players about the music they are playing. The church basement, with its blackboards and murky acoustics, serves as a practice room for the band, while parents congregate in the lot outside the church to socialize, look after children too young to play pan, build the stands for Panorama, and sometimes raise money by selling food and soda. Because CASYM emphasizes pan as a vehicle for family and community, Findlay feels that Manette should have been speaking at Brooklyn College without charge, as a community service. Similarly, Alleyne paraphrases an African proverb, echoing Eric Williams's reliance on the steel band to build the nation, when he explains CASYM's views on education by saying that it takes a whole village to raise one child. "The basic code is to make sure that we build a type of community."

Alleyne talks of the steel band bringing "tranquillity to the nation" of Trinidad by uniting the people around their common culture and history and by symbolizing national creativity and cohesion. In his vision and the vision of CASYM, pan can do the same thing for Caribbean people of diverse national origins in Brooklyn. CASYM functions like an extended family, like a village, and generates the cultural forms and social cohesion that have the power to unify Caribbean Brooklyn. This interpretation of pan's history and future translates the nationalist narrative of the steel drum into a vision of local autonomy and community control that is consistent with progressive Black urban politics in the decades after 1968, when the conflict over community control of education took place in nearby Ocean Hill–Brownsville. CASYM emphasizes economic self-sufficiency and the development of corporations to foster cultural and social sovereignty. "The only concern is liberty," Alleyne told me. "And in order for us to develop, we have to pass that stage . . . we have to develop corporations. Like capitalist corporations." Rather than maintaining a traditional "pan side" where the yard is the center of the organization, CASYM attempts to use pan, as well as other cultural forms such as sports and dance, to create an alternative nationality in Brooklyn.

CASYM's approach to pan as an im/migrant cultural form takes the idea of nationality into the realm of urban politics, consistent with the dual imaginings of citizenship existing among Caribbean people in Brooklyn, as well as the increasing racialization of urban politics after 1968.[38] The rhetoric of community control has been deployed by Black progressives to suggest the reclaiming of urban politics by the African-American majority. However, in the case of CASYM, the confluence of nationalistic discourse with state funds and the discourse of *ethnic* rather than racial empowerment suggests that the rhetoric of community control may have traditional as well as progressive valences. CASYM's interpretation of the steel band movement has been rewarded with some support and interest on the part of commercial sponsors such as the *Daily News,* as well as state funding for Caribbean cultural activities in the wake of the violence in Crown Heights in 1991. As the only pan yard to receive this kind of commercial and state support, CASYM is under some pressure from American sponsors to act as a traditional ethnic organization, and to use its funding to help to cool out the largely Afro-Caribbean neighborhoods of Flatbush and Crown Heights. This pressure parallels that on steel bands in Trinidad to support the People's National Movement (PNM) in return for the corporate sponsorship advance by Eric Williams, and to downplay alliances with the trade union and Black Power movements.[39] At the same time, as a group of politically aware Caribbean im/migrants who increasingly identify themselves as Black people in a U.S. context, the organization will contend with such notions of ethnic assimilation and mobility as they strive for economic security and political enfranchisement.

The second band, Sonatas, is also focused on education. Maintaining a traditional structure, the band is administered by a board of Trinidadian men who live near one another and near the pan yard. Sonatas is known as one of the better run, more disciplined bands in Brooklyn. "We run a tighter ship," a board member explained. "I'm not saying anything against the other bands, but things that they allowed, I would not have allowed here." The band is also marked by some regional distinction, first because their initial arranger and tuner were both from southern Trinidad rather than Port of Spain, and also because their location, in northern Crown Heights, bordering on Bedford-Stuyvesant, sets them apart from most of the other Brooklyn bands.

Sonatas started in a community center, then moved to Fulton Street, and now enjoys a roofed pan yard in back of a block of row houses on Sterling Place. Players contributed labor and money for the construction of the pan yard; Sonata's former captain lives next door. Access to Sonatas' backyard pan house is strictly limited to players and band members. Some of the men who are involved with the band will drink beer from a refrigerator that is stocked with cold drinks, but Sonatas' pan yard is not known for its sociality. "It comes back to discipline," a board member explained. "No one comes here and makes noise in front of the building, the neighbors wouldn't have to call the cops. Having everything run as a tighter ship, keep the good relations with the community."

Sonatas enjoyed sponsorship from British West Indian Airways from 1983 through the summer of 1992. Citing financial limitations, BWIA stopped funding Sonatas in 1993. Around this same time, the corporation began sponsorship negotiations with CASYM.[40]

Where CASYM uses pan to lure kids away from other forms of urban leisure and toward education and upward mobility, the board of Sonatas is interested in maintaining Caribbean culture in Brooklyn. "We try to keep the kids here," Sonatas board members explained. "Get their parents to bring them in, and keep the culture alive." Some players commute from as far away as the Bronx and Staten Island; others walk down the street from neighboring row houses and apartment buildings. Younger players see the steel band as an important part of their lives: one young woman came back to Brooklyn to play in Panorama the year she spent away at college in Virginia. She explained: "We're not actually from Trinidad, and we wasn't born there, but we play to keep that culture alive, just as long as we can."[41]

Along with passing their culture on to the younger generation, the board of Sonatas, possibly because the band is located in what they call "a mixed community," less homogeneously West Indian, more African-American and Latino, emphasizes good relations with their neighbors. The band plays at block parties and contributes food and trophies to local events. "Here," a board member told me, "you have to worry about a neighbor, if they don't like the music, you might practice too late, and it might get on their nerves, they want to sleep and they can't sleep, it's kind of tense. Back in the Caribbean . . . music could be right around the corner and it's no problem. Here it's tense."

Where Alleyne sees the possibility of a Brooklyn-based nation that uses pan to ensure the success of the West Indian community here, Sonatas' claims to the urban public sphere are somewhat more modest. By trying to run a pan yard in a disciplined manner and to ease relations with neighbors, Sonatas creates a context for the maintenance of cultural ties to home. For the older, first-generation im/migrants who run the band, this provides continuity and meaning, as well as an affordable way of maintaining a nation-based cultural identity. Younger im/migrants, who come north to diminished economic prospects and a racially stratified job market, use their involvement in the steel band to create meaning as well. A thirty-year-old tenor player who came to New York from Trinidad four years ago talked about how diminished his life feels when the main steel band season is over in Brooklyn. He works at a big hotel and plays in Sonatas' small "stage side" during the winter, he said, but only during the summer season does he feel truly alive. And clearly, the second-generation players who commute from far boroughs, from college out of state, or, like one young woman, take three buses across Brooklyn to get to practice every night are taking part in the formation of an im/migrant identity.

These identity formations are not easily reducible along lines of class or nationality. The board's concern for its relationship with the mixed neighborhood surrounding it indicates a careful negotiation with the social landscape of contemporary urban Brooklyn. At the same time that the band provides a link to an imagined or remembered homeland, its players and administrators are actively involved in creating a culture in diaspora. While not all of Sonatas' neighbors enjoy pan practice or sleep through it easily, the band becomes an important fixture in the life of local people, both im/migrant and native-born.

The administration of Sonatas, which is composed entirely of first-generation im/migrants, maintains the band's integrity and momentum. At the same time, this structure may militate against the band's success in Brooklyn. It is important to point out here, consistent with the earlier discussion of the steel band movement in Trinidad, that what the board sees as a "traditional" steel band actually resembles the second-generation, golden age pan yard, with its concern for education and order, emphasis on discipline, and disapproval of partying and disorder. In part, this is due to concerns about keeping the neighbors up at night. But the board of Sonatas remembers "tradition" selectively; its understanding of the pan yards is part history and part imagination.[42] And this selective memory casts both past and present in a partial and limited frame.[43]

A young woman who had been a five-year member of the organization's stage side as well as its summer road side had inventive ambitions for Sonatas. A long-term veteran and a talented player, she often teaches other players and demonstrates the parts during practice sessions; both the administration and the musical director rely on her skills and experience. Like other young players, she has aspirations for the future of pan. Where some players take the instrument into a rock context and others plan to reinvent pan back home in Trinidad, this woman hopes that Sonatas may be able to cross over to a broader audience, using the jazz style of the band's arranger, "Professor" Ken Philmore, to attract audiences unfamiliar with the steel band sound, and drawing on the current marketing of "that international stuff, you know, world music, so to speak," that has allowed Andy Narel some success on album-oriented radio stations. "You would personally like to know that your culture progressed because of the unity of your people," she said. "Which, boy, is going to take a while. I mean, I love Andy Narel, he's white, but it's what he has done for the invention of the pan."

In order to realize some of these ideas, the band needs a place to practice that has better acoustics than the low-roofed yard, as well as money for demo tapes and sessions. This project would call for a different approach to Sonatas' finances, in terms of revenues from both the stage side and the BWIA sponsorship. But these plans met with little enthusiasm from Sonatas' board, and she eventually abandoned her ideas about management and musical production. "Either it's because I'm young, or because I'm a woman," she explained. "It's one of the two. I don't think it's because I'm a woman. I just think that it takes time, you know, to make that change. They're still thinking the old way. Do things the old way. We gotta get modern, you know."

It is unclear whether Sonatas' intractability resulted in their loss of sponsorship, or if this woman's ideas about commercial crossover would have been viable. In both contexts, the band as an im/migrant institution confronts metropolitan assumptions about race and ethnicity. Did BWIA move to sponsor CASYM because state support made it look more viable as an ethnic institution? If so, what could Sonatas have done to compete? Would the band have been able to get a recording contract? For Sonatas to cross over to a mixed-race American audience would involve negotiations with a music industry that has historically managed to package the products of Black creativity with white performing faces.

What is clearer is that the board's interpretation of tradition maintains a cultural form at the expense of some innovation by its members. In part, this is a gendered negotiation. Gendered divisions can point to the tensions within pan yards. And in fact, this woman has backed off some of her dreams of managing the band. "It's a man's thing," she said. "It was always a man's thing, they think it's always going to be a man's thing."

Because of the very discipline that holds the band together, Sonatas sometimes loses players who are looking for a different environment in which to practice pan. One talented thirteen-year-old player, who commutes to practice from the Bronx every night during the summer, moved from the more regulated atmosphere of Sonatas to play at Metro during the summer of 1993. Metro is a more free atmosphere, he told me, more challenging for him as a player. In addition, coming to Metro at night allows him to walk around Flatbush, which he feels is like a second home. "In Brooklyn, if you're West Indian, it has everything you need," he said. He has visited Trinidad five times, and, though he was born in New York and has lived there all his life, considers himself to be West Indian.

Metro Steel has managed to win Panorama an unprecedented three years in a row. Clive Bradley, whose adaptations of calypsos for pan have made him one of the most successful and popular pan arrangers in both Trinidad and Brooklyn, has been the band's arranger and musical director all three of its winning years. Because of this success, Metro is arguably the most popular band in Brooklyn.

Run by a board that is divided between older immigrants who no longer play pan and younger immigrants and second-generation Brooklyn natives, Metro is plagued by internal corruption and disorganization. Apart from the owner of the Roti Shack's permission to practice in the alley behind the small shop and a small amount of money for T-shirts at Panorama, Metro has no sponsorship. In contrast to the educational orientation and strictly controlled environments at CASYM and Sonatas, Metro Steel functions more as neighborhood social space. But for Metro Steel and its followers, the neighborhood includes both Brooklyn and Trinidad.

Metro Steel began in New York in 1975 as an offshoot of the popular Trinidad band Desperados. In 1990, Despers New York, as it was known, split into two bands: Metro Steel and Metro II, or Despers USA. The band currently known as Metro moved east down Flatbush Avenue to its present location in central Flatbush, while Metro II stayed on Atlantic Avenue, north of Crown Heights. According to Tony Josephs, who has been captain of Metro Steel since 1988, the split was the result of differences in attitude among the players and followers of the band. Older immigrants wanted the band to be a place where they could relax and see friends from home; primarily, for those associated with Desperados, from Port of Spain and Laventille. "Despers USA," Josephs explained, "they're more like a whole bunch of brothers doing something. They grew up together, from Trinidad, and with me being a leader from outside, it was a friction. . . . I was born there, same place that they were from, but I grew up here all my life, I came here when I was a little baby. . . . If you go down there now, that's Laventille. Despers USA, they want to keep that tradition."

After the split with Metro II, Josephs and others around the pan yard wanted the band to act as something other than a traditional Trinidadian social space. Like members of CASYM and Sonatas, they saw the band becoming a site for the education of younger im/migrants. "We used to have a lot of kids running around the yard. And when we broke off from Metro, they had all the experienced players, old experienced players. There were these kids running around the yard, and I said, 'You're always running around here. Learn to play!'" New players at Metro learn the parts from older players. This is a more haphazard system than that at CASYM or Sonatas. Potentially, it can discourage women from playing pan, though Metro has quite a few women throughout the band, including some active tenor players. Some players don't get to play in competitions because of the tendency for older, more experienced players to show up in the last few weeks of the summer, on vacation from jobs in Brooklyn, New Jersey, Trinidad, or St. Vincent.

Because of its disorder and reputation for being a party band, Metro Steel is one of the bands that some CASYM parents strive to keep their daughters out of. A woman who plays with Sonatas recalled the earlier days of pan's image as a dangerous inner-city pursuit in Trinidad when she talked about the band: "Metro, they have a really good pan yard as far as acoustics are concerned. But they are in an area that attracts violence. . . . That would be like a typical steel band, as far as, like 1960s or something."

Despite the suspicions that some parents have about Metro's environment, Metro does attract young men and women from the neighborhood right around the yard, and from elsewhere. Young kids such as Jamaal King hang out at the pan yard and learn to play slowly, starting by knocking around on the less complicated bass pans when more serious players aren't using them. The kids Jamaal runs with at school don't play pan because, he says, they are scared to learn, but since they moved to Brooklyn from Trinidad three years ago, his parents bring him to the yard when they come by. He is proud to play in the "best band in Brooklyn."

On any night during the summer, the street in front of the alley leading to the yard is crowded with Metro's ensemble of fans, family, and players. People who know each other from back home, as well as neighbors on their way to and from work, gather to talk and listen to the music; a stand run by the band sells rum and mixers. The split between Metro and Despers USA is not total and clear-cut; many of the board members of Metro, as well as of the Caribbean American Steelband Association, of which it is a part, are old panmen and pan yard hands from Laventille.

During the summer, men such as Jerry Legendre, a jeweler from Port of Spain, make it their business to be at the pan yard every night. They are concerned with making the pan yard safe, facilitating important details such as local sponsorship and maintenance of the drums, and above all, with keeping the band playing and successful. He is often at the pan yard until well past midnight. Legendre sees the yard as his primary commitment in New York; his identity is very much involved with the daily workings of the band.

For Tony Josephs, the comparative anarchy at Metro reflects the complexity of Caribbean life and culture in the States. "Hell, we've got some of everything here," he said. "We've even got Jesse [a white player who lives in Flatbush]. We've got two white girls. We're an American band." What Josephs means, I think, is not an assimilatory idea of an American pan yard. The comparative anarchy at Metro Steel reflects the complexity of this most recent Caribbean diaspora in Brooklyn. In some sense, pan yards become small spaces that are spoken of in terms as large as those of nations. Metro Steel combines the social spaces of neighborhoods in Brooklyn and different Caribbean homelands with a nationalist nostalgia symbolized by the steel drum.

WOMEN AT THE DRUM

It is common to see women in Brooklyn pan yards playing the less difficult, less prominent parts on alto and bass pan. Few women play the complex solos required for tenor pan. A bass player at Sonatas commented: "I love to see a woman play a tenor pan. For me, you've got to have real patience to get all these notes, get the right phrasing and the right tuning. And see, because everybody thinks it's a male thing, you always see males playing tenor pan. But to see a girl do that, she could do it just as well as a male." Another woman player told of a friend, a woman who played tenor pan for fifteen years, who left a band when the arranger mistakenly assumed that incorrect playing in the tenor section was hers and asked her not to play.

Along with young and inexperienced players, women are often displaced in the week or so before Panorama, when more experienced players come to practice and compete. In addition, women sometimes are harassed or ignored at pan practice. One woman told of watching an arranger change a part he had written for a section of the band that was mainly composed of women, because he thought the music was too hard for them. "He is saying, 'Oh, but they will never play this,' and I said, 'Give it to them as a challenge.' . . . I said, 'How will you know what they can do unless you try it out?' "

The question of gender in the pan yards points to the ways im/migrant social spaces do and do not respond to local needs. For Caribbean women in Brooklyn, the struggle for equality in the pan yards enters into the ways they think about their identity. Where many of the people involved with pan in Brooklyn talked about national, racial, and ethnic identity and pride, some women also spoke of the conflicting obligations that arise with such identities. Some called the academic narratives of Manette and Slater into question, while younger women often questioned Afrocentric narratives and the place of both Caribbean and African-American women in them. "Yes," one student said, "I admire those men who try to make things better, but they're not doing shit for me. They don't give a shit for me and all my other Black sisters. We have to do it ourselves, and of course it would have to be that way."

The role of gender in the yards complicates the use of the steel band as a symbol of national or racial pride. In the metropolitan context, young men and women are under different pressures than they are at home. Maintaining a connection to the Caribbean becomes a purposive act away from home, as young people experience the daily exigencies of a differently segregated society in New York. At the same time, young women may find greater access to a feminism that describes their lives as women; gay Caribbean-Americans encounter a more open, flourishing subculture than the one back home. Their demands on the pan yards, the ways they make meaning and express their identities there, change along with im/migration. These different interpretations of pan in its im/migrant incarnation indicate that the relationship between this popular form and legitimating discourses of state and capital is changing as Caribbean people migrate north to metropolitan centers.

CHAPTER 6

Gender and Generation
Down the Red Road

COLONIAL OPTICS: THE PHOTO OPPORTUNITY

July 1994. Powwow at the Mille Lacs Band Ojibwa Casino in Hinckley, Minnesota. The powwow is taking place in a new open-air amphitheater right next to the casino. There are a band shell, a stage, and rows of benches that climb a small incline up to a row of concession stands. On other weekends, this arena features country singers and comedians, open-air entertainment for casino patrons. The powwow MC jokes about how much money his wife has lost already, but encourages people to go try their luck at the machines next door anyway.

Admission to both the casino and the powwow is free; you have to pay only to eat or to gamble. The only thing separating the two places is a specially marked-off parking lot for powwow participants. Here vans and older cars cluster, from as far away as Oklahoma, Louisiana, and Oregon; as close as the nations of Leech Lake, Red Lake, White Earth, and Mille Lacs in northern Minnesota.

A steady stream of people crosses over between these two worlds. People from the powwow take breaks at the glowing slots and cheap buffet of the casino. People up here to gamble wander into the powwow, sometimes accidentally, lost; sometimes to get a breath of fresh air and watch the dancers.

Sunday morning of a weekend-long powwow. Few people have left yet, because the final rounds and judging of important events, such as the Grass Dance, Fancy Dance, and Jingle Dress Dance, have not yet taken place. Casino powwows offer prize purses fattened by this new source of revenue for some Indian bands.

I have been waiting to interview the current Comanche tribal princess, Karel Ann Coffey, who waited up late last night and most of this morning for her contest dance event, Women's Southern Style Straight. The dancing and drumming went on until past one in the morning; they picked up again just after noon.

Finally, Coffey's event takes place. One of the drums does a lighter, southern-style song to accompany this dance. About ten young women, fewer than for traditional northern events such as Jingle Dress and Women's Fancy Shawl, move into the circle. They dance slowly, dipping gracefully around the circle. Faster powwow dances, such as fancy dancing, originated in North Dakota, while slower dances permeated northern powwow culture from their original base in Oklahoma. Southern straight dancing, though, is slower than any dances now commonly performed at powwows in the north.[1]

After the Southern Straight, we meet at the edge of the circle where the dance competitions are taking place. Together with Coffey's friend and traveling companion, DaLynn Alley, Little Miss Shawnee Nation, we walk up the slightly dusty incline away from the circle of drum groups, dancers, and spectators.

The two young women, aged eighteen and eleven, respectively, are dressed in carefully crafted traditional outfits. Each has a long, fringed buckskin dress, beautifully beaded jewelry, feather headbands. These represent long hours of work and dedication for powwow royalty. Coffey, currently Comanche tribal princess, has held five titles in five years. She is carefully made up, her hair held back in a long braid.

As we walk up the incline, looking for a place to sit and talk, an older white man comes up, seemingly out of nowhere. Without looking at us, he quickly puts his arm around Coffey. A second: he poses. Someone (his wife?) snaps a picture, and he is gone without a word. Rewinding, the woman comes up to us. "Did you make that, honey?" she asks, friendly. "So lovely." She leans to finger Coffey's skirt. The couple leave, headed for the casino.

Being a powwow princess makes a young woman used to this kind of attention. Coffey spoke during our interview in the confident public voice of one used to talking to curious media. Alley, though younger, is also a veteran of royalty competitions, and she acts in local television commercials in her native Oklahoma. When I asked her if the incident with the camera had bothered her at all, Coffey responded with practiced charm: "If people see us, and they think it's beautiful, then good. Come on, come talk to me, and see what I am, not just on my outside, but on my inside. An Indian princess isn't just her looks, it's her mentality. It took her a lot to get where she is. And it's good that people recognize that. As far as people putting their arms around me, they better be good looking!"[2]

As Johnny Smith, who teaches at Heart of the Earth Survival School in Minneapolis, points out, powwow royalty function as goodwill ambassadors between their Indian culture and a sometimes rapaciously curious white public.[3] This idea of royalty as ambassadors between two worlds points to their importance as symbolic figures that represent different, but related, ideas in distinct contexts.

This chapter explores postcolonial inventions such as the figure of the powwow princess. These figures serve not only as goodwill ambassadors, translating alterity into a language that tourists can understand, but as powerful symbols and actors in the landscape of contemporary Indian culture. Like the powwow grounds at Hinckley, this culture is crucially intersected by the myriad processes of national and international capitalist culture. At the same time, Indian people draw on an arsenal of memory and reinvented traditions to negotiate their positions as dual citizens of Indian and U.S. nations and cultures.

In this ongoing negotiation, young women such as Coffey and Alley play an important role. Young Indian people draw on the cultural narratives conveyed to them by elders, role models and teachers, to make sense of their experiences, to create something that sustains them. As denizens of hybrid social contexts on reservations and in cities, they must mediate the everyday occurrences of racism and sexism, modifying the stories and practices that shape their identity as they go.

Rayna Green argues that "in order for anyone to play Indian successfully, real Indians have to be dead."[4] Certainly the way the photo-snapping couple treated the Comanche tribal princess was closer to the playful way one might treat a cigar-store Indian or a cardboard cutout of Ronald Reagan than a typical interaction with a stranger. A 500-year history of displacement, administration, migration, and appropriation prepared all of us for that photo opportunity. The optics of colonialism here operate as a mirror in which living young women look like dead artifacts. Product of a stray tourist moment, the photo will become a relic of a dying culture rather than a moment in a long powwow weekend of many in years of creative invention, retention, and struggle.

In the Americas, the myth of the Indian princess is an ancient interloper between Euroamerican ideas of culture and gender and the indigenous peoples they confronted and colonized, desired and feared. As
George P. Horse Capture writes, "the concept of royalty was first introduced by immigrants, who brought European beliefs with them and
gained favor calling the daughters of Indian leaders 'princesses.' "[5] The
tourist/photographer well may have been prepared for this moment by
the luscious Indian maiden offering him Land o' Lakes butter each morning; by the beguiling, if halting, words of Indian princesses in a thousand
Western films and TV series; by the much mythologized interventions of
Sacajawea and Pocahontas on behalf of their equally mythical Euroamerican companions. But these young people, the subjects of the
tourist moment, will remember the weekend quite differently.

For the young people who participate in powwows, the optics of colonialism is an assumption. Racism and sexism would condition their lives,
regardless of their choice to pursue royalty crowns or advanced degrees.
Young women, for example, use the role of powwow princess to negotiate their dual identities: as young Indian people with a claim to a specific
history and culture and as minorities in a nation that sees them as culturally extinct and calls on them to assimilate.

As im/migrants within a nation that has consistently displaced them,
these young people operate within the claims and restrictions of at least
two institutional logics, both of which operate through discourses of
race, ethnicity, and gender. They are socialized and reared in contemporary pan-Indian culture as well as the dominant culture. Contemporary
Indian people move between an "Indian country" of reservations and
urban enclaves and a dominant culture that seeks to transform and assimilate them as national citizens.

At the same time that powwow princesses suggest an iconography of
conquest, they also play a role, along with dancers and drummers, powwow bums and campers, in the massive pan-Indian political and cultural
revival that began in cities as a response to the culturally genocidal programs of termination and relocation in the 1950s and 1960s. Contemporary native youths are the children and grandchildren of this revival.
As such, they inherit transformative pan-Indian responses to urbanization. Because of the centrality of gender and sexuality to colonialism, the
princess figure retains some of the hierarchical meanings encoded in the
mythologized, colonialist form. But at the same time, actual young
women who hold the title of powwow royalty use the form against itself, to define and practice their complex identities.

Powwows are im/migrant institutions that pass on the political and cultural project of renewal; as such, they are key sites of generational transmission and conflict. In a sense, the figure of the powwow princess indicates the reach of the mass media, and the way it can simultaneously represent and silence cultural and historical difference. But powwow princesses themselves circulate through an alternative media network: powwow circuits and their native-authored iconography.

INVENTED TRADITIONS: "HEARTBEAT OF THE NATION"

This chapter looks at the "invented traditions" of contemporary pow-wow culture.[6] Powwows are places where Indian elders speak about his-torical continuity with the past. At the powwows, Indian youths find a place to hang out and express themselves: as denizens of reservations and urban Indian communities, and as the "seventh generation" that will rise to inherit a legacy of pride and continuity with the past. The con-temporary pan-Indian institutions that host powwows are a direct re-sponse to the history of relocation and urbanization in the post-1945 period. These survival schools, social service agencies, and Indian cen-ters emerged in the 1970s as native responses to the oppressive policies of the termination period, when federal policy sought to resolve the "In-dian problem" once and for all, by assimilating Indians into the national family, compelling them to accept "full citizenship" by abandoning their lands and cultures.

Control over the education and socialization of Indian youth has long been a central arena of conflict between Indian people and the federal government. Federal boarding schools preceded relocation during the post–World War II period. With relocation, urban im/migrants struggled to assert some control over their children's education. Nationally, native legal activists worked for the passage of the Indian Child Welfare Law in 1974, which prioritizes native culture in the placement of Indian chil-dren. Also in 1974, Title IV of the Indian Education Act amended the 1936 Johnson-O'Malley Act to provide for bilingual and bicultural ed-ucation, allowing for the opening of native survival schools, such as the Heart of the Earth School and the Red School House in the Twin Cities. Urban activists worked to found Indian institutions. These institutions, in turn, sponsor powwows as places for people to converge, socialize, and educate their children.

Powwows, then, were reinvented in urban communities as spaces to celebrate the struggle for native self-determination. Native im/migrants reached back in time and partially created, partially remembered "traditional" festivals. Powwows were a logical place for such invention, because they have been spaces of intercultural meeting and exchange since before Native Americans' contact with Europeans. In a quite traditional manner, then, they provide a place for negotiations between the new and the familiar.[7]

Eric Hobsbawm argues that such invention has been the cornerstone of contemporary nationalist traditions, including flags, anthems, and holidays. Powwow royalty march in the Grand Entry at the front of the procession, right behind Indian veterans and flag bearers. The procession goes as follows:

First the eagle staff is carried into the circle, followed by American, Canadian, state, and tribal flags. Then the title holders from tribal pageants and the Miss Indian Nations candidates enter. This is also where veterans enter. Other invited dignitaries are next, followed by the men: traditional dancers first, then grass dancers and fancy dancers. Women come next: traditional dancers, fancy shawl dancers, and jingle dancers. They're followed by junior boys, then junior girls, in the same order as the adults, and fancy dancers, and the little girls, traditional and fancy shawl dancers.[8]

The order of the Grand Entry reveals a great deal about the hierarchies operative in contemporary Indian culture. The sacred symbol, the eagle staff, comes first, followed by flags representing both the official nation and Indian sovereignty. Right behind them come powwow royalty and military veterans; dignitaries, then dancers, ranked by gender, age, and the order in which their dance event was invented. The oldest dances are the Traditional, Grass Dance, and then Fancy Shawl Dance.[9] The Jingle Dress Dance was invented in the late nineteenth century. Finally come the fancy dancers, whose rapid footwork and athletic pyrotechnics have come about recently, with the reinvention of powwow culture in the 1960s and 1970s. Here, marching in a Grand Entry widely held to have been invented at Buffalo Bill's Wild West Show, are the categories that organize contemporary powwow culture. As the dancers move into the circle, they move to the beat of the drum, the "heartbeat of the Indian nations."[10]

Such "invented traditions" offer the inventors a link to a long past and a response to the exigencies of the current situation. Through them, contemporary native people negotiate what George Lipsitz calls a "dangerous crossroads," a place that "encompasses both danger and opportunities" and that calls for "new forms of social theory capable of explaining new connections between culture and politics, as well as for new forms of cultural criticism suited to seeing beyond the surface content of cultural expressions to understand and analyze their conditions of production."[11] Native interpretations of contemporary powwows offer exactly this kind of im/migrant social theory.

Like Indian veterans of U.S. foreign wars, powwow royalty straddle national identification. Both veterans and royalty are dually honored. On the one hand, they march first because their participation in U.S. nationalist projects makes them identifiable symbols of national pride. Some observers have mistakenly attributed the honoring of veterans to an excess of patriotic sentiment among Indian people. But powwow participants use the vocabulary of national symbols to create other meanings, to contest the optics of colonialism. And using the dominant national imagery, of soldiers, princesses, and even cowboys, may suggest as much that Indian people claim their original sovereignty, their participation in their own projects of warfare, governance, and domestic life, as that they are paying tribute to U.S. national hegemony.[12] The invented traditions of the official nation, then, are appropriated by the "nations within" to claim a much contested sovereignty.

But all social forms are refracted through the pervasive optics of colonialism. Homi Bhabha calls the use of colonial forms by colonized peoples "mimicry." Rereading Frantz Fanon, he suggests that this use of colonial hierarchies and symbols "almost but not quite—suggests that the fetishized colonial culture is potentially and strategically an insurgent counter-appeal."[13] In mimicry, he argues, the colonized come close to subverting imperial ambition. Certainly the racial logic of colonialism is undermined by the adoption of imperial signifiers in an antiimperialist performance such as the powwow. But this is a dangerous game. Imperial forms depend for their power on complicated constructs of race, gender, caste, and class. And fragments of these forms can detonate unexpectedly, like land mines from some abandoned struggle for imperial control, the results no less damaging for being residual and accidental.

Aware of these contradictions, Indian people debate their own continuous invention of tradition. With a stake in their creation and insistence on a long history that links contemporary pan-Indian revival to both the long struggle against colonization and a proud precolonial past, Indian people define the best interpretation and practice of this history multiply. These debates are divided by gender and generation, more rarely, in the 1990s, by Indian nation, reservation, and band.

PRACTICING TRADITION:
CONTEST AND TRADITIONAL POWWOWS

Urban powwows, held during the winter months in Indian centers and schools, as well as in rented spaces at local colleges, civic centers, and the state fairgrounds, are a component of a more extensive powwow circuit that expands in the summer to include weekend-long powwows on reservations and at casinos throughout the nation (see photo 6).[14] A Cherokee woman from Indiana told me at the Shakopee Mdwaketon Dakota Community Twenty-fifth Anniversary Powwow that she and her family travel every weekend of the summer to powwows as far away as Montana and Connecticut.[15] Like many contemporary Indian people, they travel the powwow circuit in the summer to see friends, watch grandchildren and other relatives dance and drum, and see the country. While most of the Minnesota summer powwows I went to were, by my license plate count, attended primarily by residents of the upper Midwest, about 15 percent of the attendees came from outside the immediate area.

The powwow circuit has developed and expanded since the 1950s, when the combined forces of urbanization and the proliferation of automobile and bus travel made Indian people much more mobile and likely to travel between reservations and cities. The diffusion of Plains Indian dance songs through the travels of groups such as the Porcupine Singers changed local styles, as did the crossover form of rock 'n' roll, newly accessible over local airwaves.[16] A new style of singing and songwriting that used identifiable words to make songs easier to learn became popular at powwows. Now that amplifiers allowed audiences to hear small sounds, there was no longer any need for singers to be loud and clear and powwow grounds to be small and quiet. George Horse Capture writes: "Unlike the Sioux songs of long ago whose words told a story of honor or bravery, today's songs in this category tell no logical story, but like the Beach Boys, urge one to 'dance, dance, dance.' "[17]

Pan-Indian cultural revival changed powwows. A powwow circuit that links Indian people in southern New Mexico with those in eastern Canada has allowed new forms to permeate Indian country. As song lyrics have become more dance-oriented, dances have become faster and flashier. The traditional Grass Dance, which moved from Oklahoma to the northern plains with the last great diffusion of pan-Indian culture in the late nineteenth century, was revived and reinvented in the 1940s to include faster, more athletic moves and brighter costumes with fringes often made from a psychedelic array of bright yarns.[18] At large pow-

Photo 6. A parking lot serves as a dressing room for a family that has driven up from Indiana for the Mdwakanton Dakota Powwow, Prior Lake, Minnesota, August 1994.

wows in the 1970s, the pace of the Grass Dance, Fancy Dance, and Fancy Shawl Dance picked up.

As Indian-run agencies, centers, and schools replaced small community groups and white social welfare agencies as the central institutions in urban Indian life, they began to sponsor larger powwows. A central innovation in powwow culture in the late 1960s, contest powwows offer cash prizes to top dancers and drum groups.[19] The distinction between these contest and "traditional" powwows, which offer small gifts to all participants, is the single most controversial issue among the people I spoke to. Particularly the people currently in their thirties and forties, who remember the struggle to organize Indian institutions along with pieces of the stories and languages of their grandparents, often worry about the effects of cash in the contemporary powwow circuit. They often feel that their urban children take the size and flash of contest powwows for granted. These two visions, while not always divided strictly along generational lines, point to tensions in contemporary Indian culture about how the past is remembered and what kinds of bargains are to be struck between traditional practices and the capitalistic values of the dominant culture.

The contrast between traditional and contest powwows involves the story of Indian revival in the cities. Sometimes staged in urban arenas,

Photo 7. An Indian band newly wealthy with casino money provides golf carts as well as volunteer drivers from neighboring communities to escort powwow contestants from parking lot to powwow grounds. Prior Lake, Minnesota, August 1994.

traditional powwows more often take place during the summer on reservations. They now tend to be smaller, the costumes less elaborate, with fewer invited drum groups and fewer categories of dance events. Contest powwows are held in the winter at Indian centers and schools, as well as in the huge rented spaces of civic arenas. In the summers, bands with casinos sponsor lucrative contest powwows; some reservations now also sponsor contest powwows (see photo 7). In large part, contest powwows are a product of the success of Indian people in generating and maintaining their own institutions. The increasing size of contest cash purses at powwows sponsored by bands with casinos also exemplifies a particular use of the partial legal sovereignty of native nations. At the same time that a revived powwow circuit links urban and rural Indians to a constantly maintained and recreated past, contest powwows offer a new means of facilitating participation, extending the ability of Indian people to travel, and furthering the development of contemporary pan-Indian culture.

Many of the adults I spoke to were ambivalent about the effects of the contest powwow on Indian traditions and values. They supported

the idea of contest powwows because of their ability to attract participants and revenue, but many questioned this expansion of commercialism into native culture. The owner of a mobile frybread and coffee operation told me at the AIM Gathering of Nations, an annual traditional
powwow at Fort Snelling, St. Paul, that in the four years he has been in
business, he has come to prefer contest powwows, simply because they
are better attended and provide revenue from more hungry patrons.[20]

Many people, though, felt that contest powwows were suspect; that
when commercialism intersected with culture, culture was the loser.
Quite a few people said that they attend contest powwows but dance
only in traditional powwows. At the Mdewakanton Dakota Anniversary Contest Powwow, one man said, "I support what's going on here,
there's a lot of spiritual stuff, but I won't compete."[21]

A neighborhood activist who played a central role in organizing and
implementing the People of Philips neighborhood powwow in inner-city
Minneapolis saw the cash orientation of the contest powwows directly
at odds with the spiritual, social, and political aims of such gatherings:

> It brings out the evilness in people. It brings out greed, it brings out hostility,
> it gets a lot of back stabbing, gets a lot of animosity toward one another. You
> know, when a powwow's supposed to be there to renew old friendships, make
> new friends, trying to have the culture survive. But if you get a contest pow-
> wow, like say you have two top grass dancers. And they want that thousand
> dollars. You know damn well that they're going to throw a lot of animosity
> toward one another, get the other one to quit. Or get the other one to flub up
> somehow, where the other one will take the points. So I don't really believe
> in contests. And I don't attend contest powwows.[22]

Many people expressed their ambivalence about contest powwows in
terms of concern for what their children would learn at powwows.
Dorene Day explained it in terms of her respect for traditional forms and
concern about what cash and competition do to native values:

> I guess there's some conflicts within my own value system with that. On one
> hand, we should realize the things that are valuable and meaningful to us to bet-
> ter our conditions. In other words, if the Heart of the Earth School has a con-
> test powwow to increase the funding so that they can provide quality and cul-
> turally appropriate education for Indian children, then that's a good thing. But,
> on the other hand, in a general view, that is the powwow with the monetary
> value placed into it, that is really not our value. . . . And one of the things that I
> do, is that I bring my children to both. And I allow them to participate in a con-
> test powwow, I encourage them to participate in a traditional powwow, where
> money isn't involved, because they certainly are different powwows.

Johnny Smith, who has been teaching Indian music and dance since the 1960s, saw no conflict between traditional values and contest powwows. Acknowledging that contest powwows are a fairly recent innovation, he said that they are consistent with traditional Indian games and competitions. A teacher of urban Indian youth, Smith sees tradition as continuous, whatever the ways in which it is currently expressed. He dismissed the concerns of his contemporaries as overly finicky, not committed enough to the reality of traditional practices. "People who are always looking down at powwows are not the powwow people, otherwise why are they putting down what belongs to them? . . . Where were these people at when our culture almost died out? Besides," he added, "the people who can't dance at contest powwows are the ones who can't take the competition."

Smith's view allows for ongoing transformations in form and practice. In his view, it is what Indian people do, in struggling to maintain a dynamic culture, that is traditional. Because contest powwows are vital at the current time to Indian culture, they *become* tradition. This vitality, Smith argued, speaks for itself; contest powwows attract the most vibrant costumes, the best dancers, the drum group with the best sound. On this point, Day concurred:

> Well, the contest ones are glitzier, they're more exciting. You know, they're probably more famous drums that will come. . . . For example, my son is a singer, so if he idolizes Stony Park or Black Lodge, and Black Lodge will be there, yeah, he should have the opportunity to hear, and physically go up to that drum and hear that drum sing, and that's gonna be good for him, if those are his idols, you know.

The star-system aspect facilitated by contest powwows keeps Day's son interested, helps him to progress as a musician and a powwow participant. This kind of mass culture appeal is, on one level, distinct from and threatening to the grass-roots powwow form. The mass culture industry can eviscerate the communal appeal of popular forms or co-opt them from native peoples, as the history of rodeos clearly shows.[23] At the same time, powwow culture has long been entangled with colonial power and commercial capital. Exactly how distinct are categories of tradition and invention here?

The fluidity and dynamism among these categories are, in part, what has allowed Indian culture to survive five hundred years of genocidal warfare, so that it is around to be revived in postwar U.S. cities. Concerns about the effects of contest powwows on contemporary Indian life, however, are also important. Questions about forms and practices, traditions and inventions are inherently political questions. They ask how people will learn to be Indians; who will have the power to teach them these skills; how they will resist the considerable pressures to cave in to assimilation; how they will combat the force of the widespread racism that would silence them.

"POWWOW BUMS!" GENERATION AND TRADITION

In part, contest powwows grow out of an established tradition of giving food and money to participants in powwows, particularly those who have traveled to attend. In cities, contest powwows evolved as fund-raisers for such institutions as survival schools. But the prizes of contest powwows now facilitate another development in powwow culture: partial economic autonomy for the participants. An Indian administrator whose agency sponsors contest powwows was ambivalent about the idea of a group of people who are able to support themselves on the money they make on the powwow circuit. "That's all they do," she commented, looking at the record of prize-winning drummers and dancers, "is go to powwows." She expressed deep ambivalence about letting her daughter, who was just finishing college, go on the powwow circuit and become a "powwow bum" for a summer. For her, the middle-class status she has struggled to achieve is threatened by the values of the powwow circuit. "I'm a real workaholic, so it's real hard for me to think somebody just wants to go do that."[24]

The administrator's concern about contest powwows combines a definition of Indian traditions as outside a cash-oriented economy with a focus on the class mobility that she has achieved through hard work and discipline. Contest powwows, for her, provide a distraction from the focus that her daughters and other Indian young people need to succeed in a competitive economy that places them, as people of color, at the bottom. Traditions, in this view, are part of a past that should be preserved by hardworking urban citizens as they struggle for upward mobility. It was easier for this particular woman to show me carefully beaded leggings and dresses made by her daughters than it was for her to think of them as "powwow bums," even for one summer.

The neighborhood activist who was strongly opposed to contest powwows worried about the ways Indian young people are exploited by cultural exhibitions that pay them to demonstrate their drum and dance skills to non-Indian audiences. Contest powwows and paid exhibitions, to her, are a long way from the communal solidarity and exchange offered by powwows. Both she and another woman spoke of their own ex-

periences at contest powwows in terms of losing themselves and their spir-
ituality in their concern for winning and performing well. Both were able
to "make that transition back through myself,"[25] to separate their Indian
values from feelings of competition and nervousness, but both worried
that the engagement with contests threatened the power of tradition in
the lives of young Indians. For these women, contest powwows challenge
the values that have allowed them to become powerful community figures.
While they are not preoccupied with upward mobility in the same sense
that the administrator is, their concerns about tradition focus on the use
of values to negotiate the complex work of urban Indian life.

How do young Indian dancers and drummers deal with the dual pressures of competition and tradition present at contest powwows and commercial exhibitions? For one thing, many of the younger generation of
Indian people I spoke to had a different view of Indian institutions than
the generation that so clearly remembers the rapid change and struggle
associated with urbanization. For them, a survival school is an option
that removes them from racist teachers and name-calling white peers;
cultural programs at school help them travel to powwows and maintain
drum and dance skills that most of them remembered learning as soon
as they could walk; and the cash prizes of contest powwows and cultural
exhibitions facilitate, rather than inhibit, their participation in a vast and
exciting powwow circuit. Urban Indians of this generation, like their
inner-city contemporaries in Brooklyn and across the nation, confront a
city profoundly stratified by race and class. Their negotiations with this
landscape use and reinvent the traditions and institutions that have been
passed down to them through the active struggles of their elders.

For The Boyz drum group, drugs and violence are much more of a
problem than the commercialization of contest powwows. The cash
prizes available to them through the contest powwow circuit supplement
the money they get from part-time jobs and from Indian institutions that
facilitate their continual travel and performance. Being powwow bums
for the ten- to twenty-year-old members of The Boyz constitutes a choice
to work hard at the drum, to perform at powwows, and to follow the
"red road" of sobriety and respect for tradition.

> Either you choose the drum, and you choose to follow that route, to be
> straight and sober and be respectful, or, we figure, you choose the other road,
> and you choose to do whatever you want. Don't gotta answer to nobody,
> don't have to answer to the drum, you don't have to think about, "well, if I
> use [drugs], what are the people on the drum gonna think," because they

aren't gonna be there. So it really is a big decision, almost a life decision. It is a life decision.[26]

The members of The Boyz expressed a lifetime commitment to their decisions about the drum. The two oldest members, at eighteen and twenty, expected their relationship to the drum to survive and even supersede the demands of marriage and family, work and school. Where adults expressed ambivalence about Indian cultural exhibitions, the Boyz see their participation in the Mystic Lake Dance Troop as allowing them to travel and to maintain their connection to each other, to the drum, and to a life of traveling and performing on the powwow circuit.

Both young men and young women can be called powwow bums. While I do not have statistics to show how many of these people actually support themselves by summers on the powwow circuit, almost everyone I spoke to under the age of twenty-five talked with admiration about legendary drum groups and dancers who were able to travel endlessly on their winnings. These heroes were much more likely to be men, but young women as well spoke to me about the pleasures of the powwow circuit, including far-flung circles of friends and "snagging" or cruising those of the opposite sex.

The translations made between generations are sometimes mutually unrecognizable. Where the adults concerned about commodification and appropriation clearly remembered the struggle for Indian institutions in Minneapolis, the younger generation had a much less clear vision of their recent history, one that did not correlate with the careful accounts of their elders. Most of the younger people I spoke to identified the importance of drumming and dancing in their lives and the role of these forms in the life of contemporary Indian nations. They expressed a passionate commitment and connection to their culture, and a deep appreciation of the survival schools and other institutions that facilitated their strong identity as Indian people. But few knew the derivation of these forms or clearly understood the history of survival schools and Indian centers. When I asked the younger dancers, powwow royalty, and drum group members I spoke to about the history of powwows in Minneapolis, they were vague. A group of girls at Heart of the Earth School thought that the jingle dress, a nineteenth-century Ojibwa invention, was probably invented before white people came to the Americas; a powwow princess at South High School could identify powwows only as "very old"; some drum group members knew that veterans' songs went back even before their fathers' generation, but did not say more than that about the songs' history.

Countering, in some ways, the very legitimate concerns of adult Indians about the younger generations, Angela McRobbie writes: "Youth cultures, in whatever shape they take, represent to me a staking out of an investment in society. It is in this sense that they are political."[27] What young urban Indians stake out is a place for themselves to be Indian, to claim an identity. In the baggy pants of b-boy and b-girl chic, Indian teenagers ally themselves with an urban youth culture that is crucially in dialogue with the commodification and exploitation that young people of color confront. They cut their hair into the high-top fades popularized by African-American youth, wear the below-hip baggy pants and team jackets of urban notoriety, and insist that they listen to homemade tapes of famous drum groups and store-bought tapes of rap with equal enthusiasm. At a time when their elders in the American Indian Movement are organizing against the use of Indian mascots and team names, young Indian men often sport Redskins football jackets with defiant flair at powwows, and sometimes at political rallies held to protest the appropriation of native culture and naming practices. Young Indians, then, inherit a hybrid social context of tradition and invention, the moving engine of urban cultural crossover. Their use of these forms is both conscious and dynamic.

Their practices are made possible by the creation of Indian institutions, but at the same time, they are not always in harmony with what their elders imagined for them. While they do not always know dates and time lines, young Indians identify the significance of the cultural forms they do practice. Young girls who can't explain a linear history of dance understand the story of the jingle dress, its healing power, and feel the difference between the Jingle Dress Dance and the newer Fancy Dance. The same young woman who had trouble placing the dance forms in time spoke about the significance of different kinds of dances: "Jingle, it's not as free as you are when you're a fancy dancer. Jingle . . . it's kind of like a spiritual dance, but not really. Jingle, you have to do certain things, we have to be really light on our feet. And when you hit the floor, you have to be slow, not stomping on the ground."[28]

Contest powwows facilitate some of the connections that this generation of Indians makes between their experiences as urban minority youth and their connection to a native past that they recognize as both ancient and sustaining. The Mdewakanton Dakota Anniversary Powwow featured performances by both Dixie Harris, a native country singer, and

Litefoot, an Indian rap artist from Oklahoma. After a long day of contest and intertribal dancing, "specials" and drumming, the affluent Mdewakanton band provided entertainment for their guests. Dixie Harris entertained a generation whose musical tastes were nurtured in the rural Midwest, and Litefoot performed the next night for young Indians whose daily experiences as urban youths have familiarized them with hip-hop and whose historical heritage has prepared them to hear him "teach" them about their history as he sings of the Trail of Tears.

This combination of traditional forms with non-Indian popular styles is not new. The adult generation's current preference for country music was different from the taste of *their* parents, who often danced waltzes and fox trots along with grass and traditional dances at small reservation powwows during the 1930s. And it was this older generation, who learned to manage the fancy footwork of popular dance, who conveyed memories of language and tradition to their children and grandchildren, making contemporary Indian revival possible.

The political act of creating, struggling for, and maintaining an Indian culture does not look the same from generation to generation. The experiences of young people, and particularly of young people of color, often do not reduce along the lines of the ideologies held by their elders or by chronicles like this one. What people with one experience of fighting for economic and cultural survival see as threatening, another generation embraces. Not all practices are equal, and no individual is exempted from the intersections of pleasure and danger so deeply inscribed in the history of popular culture. But invented traditions establish their links to the past through practice and memory.

Contemporary contest powwows, with their large winnings and their ability to draw people from around the country to dance, drum, and socialize, are a part of this ongoing invention of Indian tradition. The Boyz talked about the concurrence of identity, politics, and pleasure: "The way we feel is that the drum is the heartbeat of our people. Without the drum, there wouldn't be anything, there'd be no dances, the dancers wouldn't be able to dance. People wouldn't be able to have a good time, you know, people wouldn't be able to powwow. So it's a big part, you know, of us."

SINGLE MOTHERS, PRINCESSES, AND WOMEN AT THE DRUM: GENDER AND TRADITION

When she started to attend Pow Wows in L.A. she
observed the different traditional and non-traditional

singers. Some women stood and sat behind the drum,
while others sat and played at the drum with the men.
In L.A. most of the male groups excluded the women.
She imagined herself singing and playing at the drum,
but knew it would never happen.

Arlene Bowman, 1994

Arlene Bowman's important film, *Song Journey*, tells of her desire to play
the drum, and of her search for other women on the northern Plains who
want to play drum and do the Fancy and Grass dances. In northern powwow culture, these are traditionally male activities; in Oklahoma, mixed
drum groups, where women both sing and play the drum, are quite common. In the north, women stand behind the drum and sing or hold small
tape recorders in the air to record the music, but they do not sit at the
drum or play it. According to Johnny Smith, it was a woman, Thunder-
bird Lady, who brought the drum to the Indian people. And, he explained, when women sit at the drum, it is because they need to take it
back from men to purify it, because men have abused the sacred trust of
the heartbeat of the nation.

As she traveled the powwow circuit in the northern United States and
Canada, Bowman met Indian women who were forming all-women
drum groups, participating in mixed groups, and learning the athletic
steps required to do the Fancy and Grass dances. She also encountered
resistance from some Indian men, who felt that to breach traditionally
defined gender roles was to challenge Indian cultural solidarity.

At a screening and discussion of *Song Journey* at the Walker Art Institute in Minneapolis, the predominantly native audience talked about
confluences of colonialism and sexism. One man questioned the exclusion of women from the drum, wondering if this was truly Indian tradition, or whether it was a holdover from the imposition of Euroamerican
gender roles onto native life. After the discussion was officially over, a
group of Indian women approached Bowman. They told her that they
had formed an all-women's drum group in Minnesota, and that they
practiced and played together. But, they added, one or two powwow
MCs had requested that they stay away from powwows. Out of respect,
they did.

At powwows, Indian people tell histories that unsettle the monolithic
unity of empire and nation. The women in the drum group did not want
to disrupt this unsettling and its importance in contemporary Indian life.
More even than the politics of intergenerational conflict, the politics of

gender and tradition underscore and illuminate the precarious balanc-
ing acts of anticolonial discourse.

As with generational transmission, the questions raised around issues
of gender concern power and cultural reproduction. Like the Thunder-
bird Lady, who gave the drum to Indian people, women's traditional
roles are charged with sacred power and secular restriction. Urban Indians in Minneapolis come from different nations, each with a different
system of power and gender. Because contemporary Indian revival is not
static, nor is it a "last gasp" of a dying culture, traditional conceptions
of gender are reinvented to sustain contemporary conditions.

Urban Indian women often occupy powerful roles, heading social service agencies and schools, working as activists and politicians. While unemployment among Indian people is high, more Indian women than men
hold down jobs, particularly in cities. Many Indian families, particularly
urban families, are headed by women.[29] The disparity between genders
creates tension, both for the preservation and practice of tradition and
for gender relations in general. Just as migration to the cities has come
about because of racialized federal policy and opportunity structures, all
urban Indians deal with the ways in which the state and mass media create common distinctions between people on the basis of race and gender.

Unlike the issue of traditional and contest powwows, which nearly
everyone I interviewed talked to me about at one point or another, gender issues did not come up in direct connection to the history of powwows. People talked about gender, when they talked about it at all, as
an issue in the ongoing reproduction of Indian culture and tradition.
Many of the women and men I talked to felt that grounds already exist
within contemporary Indian culture for navigating relations between the
genders, and that these changing traditions were sufficient. Some, like
Bowman, insisted that gender must be the terrain on which contemporary Indian traditions are reinvented, so that Indian women can claim
experiences long denied them. Others felt that the key to maintaining a
strong Indian nation was to reclaim a sense of traditional gender roles,
and to preserve these.

Ann Stoler emphasizes the importance of "internal frontiers": boundaries within colonial categories of race and class that determine citizenship through the reproductive offices of the family.[30] Her work points to
the importance of these colonial frontiers in delimiting European ideas
of gender in the metropole. Discourses of gender and sexuality, then, are
cornerstones of nation-building. The kinds of families that are allowed
inclusion into contemporary Indian revival reveal a great deal about the

ways different notions of this revival invent tradition and contest the multiple legacies of colonialism.

In one view, protecting Indian families constitutes a defense of Indian people and traditions. Emphasizing the importance of men teaching their sons to play the drum, Jim Clermont decried the high percentage of single women heading Indian households. "A lot of 'em, they come from a single parent. Mainly their mothers. So they don't have the teaching of the drum, or the cultural or the spiritual aspect."

Echoing much mainstream neoconservative rhetoric about gender and family, Clermont stressed the importance of male role models for young men. In contrast to Bowman's call for transformed and integrated drum groups, this view stressed the maintenance of tradition through gender separation. I was struck by how much Clermont's view of single parents resounded with contemporary claims that social welfare must be implemented through an enforced revision of "traditional values," as well as with traditional Lakota ideas of gender separation and hierarchy. A traditionalist, Clermont sees the continued health of Indian nations as reliant on a specific idea of the family: one with two parents and a strong male role model for young boys. This vision perpetuates a historically specific vision of the family, and undercuts the powerful role women play in contemporary Indian life.

The Miss Oglala Nation contest, held in September on Pine Ridge Reservation in South Dakota, upholds this sense of traditional values in its selection of tribal princesses. Tribal princesses differ from powwow princesses, who tend to represent local institutions such as the survival schools or national ones such as the NCAI. Contestants for the Miss Oglala Nation title are judged on their costumes, their ability to stand up in public, their cultural talents, and their cooking. "It's not so much a beauty contest," explained Fern Mousseaux of the Oglala Nation Powwow Committee, "but their style of maintaining culture. How long ago the women were the backbone of the culture."[31] In addition to their skills and talents, Miss Oglala Nation contestants must be enrolled members of the Pine Ridge band, and they have to sign a contract stating that they are not going to "cohabitate" with a man. Past royalty, Mousseaux said, have lived with men, showing no respect and upsetting the elders.

The vision of family and gender upheld by Clermont and by the Oglala Nation Powwow Committee seeks to maintain Indian culture through preserving a notion of tradition that emphasizes family values and the virtues of a woman's proper role. This vision contrasts with some of the constraints of contemporary Indian life, for most people live in cities at least some of the time. In cities, women have become community and family leaders for complex reasons, involving the exigencies of federal policy, labor markets, im/migration, and their impact on the emotional economies of family life. Having watched some of the single mothers whom Clermont holds responsible for a decline in tradition stay up late after a full day's work to sew grass dance outfits and bead leggings and still get up early enough to drive two or three hours to make Grand Entry, I had trouble accepting his view of the inextricability of cultural preservation and family values. Discourses of family and gender are crucially formed in dialogue with colonial power. To accept one version of "family values" as natural and traditional excludes other constructions of family relationships, as well as of gender relations.

For example, Miss Indian South High School talked about her desire to compete in the Miss Indian World Pageant, but she was uncertain if she would qualify. While both of her parents are Indian, she does not meet the standards of blood quantum to qualify for enrollment in any reservation. Though she has relatives she visits on reservations, she would not be able to compete for the many tribal princess titles that require enrollment. The princess competition at South High, she explained, emphasizes a different idea of tradition. Contestants are nominated on the basis of their knowledge of Indian tradition and dance, and must meet a minimum grade point average to be chosen. This notion of tradition, clearly reinvented in historical context, accommodates both the hybrid nature of urban life and the legacy of migration and intermarriage that have resulted in a population of mixed ancestry, many of whom are culturally Indian but not able to enroll by the standards established by Indian nations. This notion of tradition, clearly reinvented in historical context, accommodates both the hybrid nature of urban life and the legacy of migration and intermarriage that have resulted in a population of mixed ancestry, many of whom are culturally Indian but not able to enroll by the standards established by the federal government or Indian nations.[32]

Just as Caribbean-American youths in Brooklyn find a sense of a home they may never have seen in the pan yards and roti shops of Flatbush, urban Indians come together around traditions that they shape and reinvent by their presence. Cultural forms that look one way at home, on the reservation or back in the Caribbean, change their shape and significance in the context of im/migration and diasporic community. *Song Journey* stresses the respect for Indian traditions that leads young women to desire a more firsthand encounter with them. A Navajo raised in Phoenix, Bowman points out that her experience growing up in the Southwest gives her no traditional access to the Ojibwa dance drum, only one that comes about through urbanization and the ensuing pan-Indian revival. Other members of the urban Indian community emphasize how crucial cultural change is to survival.

In April 1994, the Minnesota Indian AIDS Task Force invited a group of powwow masters of ceremonies to an educational meeting. The idea of the meeting was to get the MCs to use their role as statesmen at pow-wows, and encourage them to educate the Indian community about AIDS prevention and safe sex. At the meeting, Task Force members, many of whom are HIV positive, spoke about the dislocations that traditional values had caused in their lives. Many felt that they could not return to their reservations because of homophobia and a general fear of AIDS. One man spoke of being asked to leave a pipe ceremony, and how he felt about being ejected from this important, and healing, traditional prac-tice. Another movingly compared Indian and gay subcultures. Both groups, he pointed out, live in cities, find each other there through a net-work of neighborhood and alternative institutions; both travel around the nation to see each other. HIV, he added, can travel along the same circuits. He invoked historical memory in comparing his experiences in the gay and Indian communities, and urged the MCs to take this com-parison seriously. "I don't have many living gay friends anymore," he said. "This is a disease that can devastate us like smallpox did."

The powwow MCs, who at this particular meeting were all men from reservations in northern Minnesota and Wisconsin, reacted differently to this information. The fault lines separating them from the slightly younger, urban, predominantly gay Indian people there were based on generation and attitudes toward sexuality. At the meeting, the discussion took on the invention of tradition, as well as concerns about sexuality, gender, and monogamy. One MC suggested that he could use his role as speaker at powwows to promote safe sex through monogamy and abstinence. An-other wondered about how MCs could talk about sexuality, because of the diversity of national traditions represented at any one powwow. One man invoked Christian teachings, arguing that homosexuality is forbid-den by the Bible, and should find no voice at powwows at all. Receptive to the message that the Task Force was promoting, another MC argued with the idea that powwows promote any specific tradition:

> The language I use is not a traditional language, it's a language we can all un-derstand, with respect to my Lakota brothers, my Winnebago brothers.

The question of where the discussion of AIDS/HIV fits into powwow culture addresses the hierarchies operative in contemporary native life. Clearly, some in the Indian community reject gay people on grounds of tradition, whereas others allow a place for them, arguing that homophobia is just one more aspect of colonialism. At the American Indian Movement Down the Red Road Alcoholthon/Powwow on New Year's Eve, 1993, MC Dickie Graves echoed the MC at the Task Force meeting: "There's a lot of controversy over the word 'tradition.' What we see here is a whole lot of people and a whole lot of traditions." At this powwow, Graves talked during the Grand Entry about the importance and diversity of veterans. Along with the veterans of foreign wars, marching right behind the flag bearers, he honored the warriors of the American Indian Movement, those fighting alcoholism, and those fighting HIV/AIDS. All these, he announced, are part of the struggle for Indian survival.

CONCLUSION: COLONIAL OPTICS, POSTCOLONIAL OPTIONS

The Indian Princess is a cultural myth that emanates from the myopia of cultural contact and the myriad oppressions of colonial control. The princess comes from nowhere in precontact history, but becomes a standard feature at the powwow, a hybrid of postcolonial performances. Winning a Princess title represents fluency in various conceptions of tradition. It can also represent popularity for young women who are crucially involved in the economies of sexuality and dating. Some of the princesses I talked to emphasized this aspect of holding a title, and explained that other girls were jealous of them, while boys tended to be more solicitous of their attention. Some young women I talked to at powwows did not hold titles, but wished that they did. And some mothers, when their daughters cried over a lost title or crowed over a new one, questioned the similarity of princess pageants to beauty contests, wondering what exactly this particular invention of tradition is preserving.

In her analysis of girls' magazines and dance culture, McRobbie suggests that contemporary femininity is fluid; that young women may assert power through practices that look to their feminist elders to be dangerously engaged with patriarchy and cultural commodification.[33] Young Indian women confront a dangerous field of race and gender hierarchies. On one level, the princess as a myth looks like an engagement with mythologies that have sponsored generations of degradation for native women. As Tricia Rose insists, however, it is also crucial that young women, particularly young women of color, stake out a place in public to speak and be heard.[34]

After the photo opportunity passed, Coffey and Alley, the Comanche Tribal Princess and Junior Miss Shawnee Nation, resumed their conversation with me. Coffey wants to attend law school; she sees her experience as a princess, in addition to getting her dates and travel and attention, as setting her up for a career of defending the rights of her people.

> I think that being a princess allows you to see all different sorts of people and meet different people and the way things are. Being a lawyer is kind of out of the rank of being a princess, but still it is very helpful in that area. You talk in public, meet Indian people, get to see what kind of people I like, you get to hear about different tribes and their problems.
>
> Now with water rights, tribal sovereignty, and our own religious freedom. They take it away from us. And I'm not gonna allow that to happen for my children. And I have the right to do it, and my children have the rights to do it, and same with my grandchildren.

The position of Indian princess, reinvented in the contemporary pow-wow circuit, here allows a young Indian woman to speak in a voice that simultaneously claims tradition and insists on the struggle for justice. Coffey speaks in a voice that is at once feminine, claiming the rights for her children and grandchildren, and feminist, aspiring to work as a lawyer for her people. The position she outlines straddles claims of tradition and the exigencies of the present, using the culture that Indian people have brought together in this most recent revival to protect the self-determination of future generations.

Political Economies of Home

Citizenship and Denizenship

GENDER, CITIZENSHIP, AND THE IDEA OF HOME

My focus on gender and generation in the last two chapters comes out of the idea that these are the terrains on which im/migrant peoples struggle for their right to be both citizens and denizens of their adoptive places. Conversely, as Caren Kaplan argues, "One's citizenship and placement in relationship to nation-states and geopolitics formulate one's experience of gender when the threat of deportation, the lack of a passport, or subaltern status within the nation as an indigenous 'native' place limits on or obstruct mobility and modes of survival."[1]

The national romance written by federal policy has always drawn on gendered metaphors to write im/migrants into the national family, often as subordinate members.[2] The image of a pregnant Mexican woman surreptitiously crossing the border to enable her child to claim citizenship has become a common one in the contemporary rhetoric of immigration restriction. Like her mythical sister, the inner-city welfare queen, the image of the uncoupled, undocumented woman as an unmarried yet procreative peril to the national family system has bolstered support for federal immigration reform as well as state initiatives such as Proposition 187. Gender, then, has been figured in dominant narratives of Americanization and attaining citizenship, as well as im/migrant efforts to create home.

In the family romance, the "marriage plot" is a key narrative of Americanization.[3] As K. Tsianina Lomawaima writes, Indian girls at federal boarding schools received "training in dispossession under the guise of domesticity."[4] Much the same might be said for Indian im/migrants to cities during the 1950s and 1960s. The federal government offered inclusion into the national family at the cost of land claims and cultural identity. The national romance, then, promises the domestication of the im/migrant into the national family. But in this Americanization narrative, the problem is the children: what past will they remember, and how will they learn to be citizens of what nation? Just as women must be disciplined to raise good American citizens, young second-generation im/migrants are a focal point for both dominant notions of assimilation and community hopes for adaptation and survival in an urban setting.[5]

But the experience of relocation transforms relations between genders and generations in im/migrant communities.[6] In the pan yards of Brooklyn as well as the powwow grounds of Minnesota, young men and women struggle to define both ethnic and gendered identities, often at the cost of some misunderstanding from older generations. Where their elders often hark back to gender patterns that seemed stable in the context of remembered homelands, young im/migrants continue to invent themselves as gendered denizens of urban communities with complex claims to both prior and current locations. These struggles over appropriate roles for genders and generations reflect tensions among im/migrants over how to adapt to a new social context. As Paul Gilroy argues, conflicts over gender roles often express the daily ravages of racial division.[7] Just as powwow princesses and steel drum players work to create a place for themselves within im/migrant subcultures, these young men and women are also defining new meanings for long-established concepts of citizenship and Americanization.

IM/MIGRATION HISTORY: CONCEPTUALIZING DENIZENSHIP

Boundaries are violent things. That is, they are imaginary lines, drawn on a map or written on the doors of offices in the university or the State Department. Imaginary or not, boundaries are maintained by regimes of implicit or explicit terror.[8] To cross one risks violent attention from the authorities: the Immigration and Naturalization Service, for example, newly working in coalition with local police forces.[9] In what Leslie Silko aptly calls "the Border Patrol state," people of color are disproportionately targeted for suspicion of illicit border crossings.[10] Many people are detained or harassed at the border; many people suffer in trying to cross the border secretly, and some do not make it across this most violent of intersections. Between 1993 and 1996, 1,185 undocumented persons died trying to cross the U.S.-Mexico border.[11]

Crucial to the comparison I am drawing in this book is the argument that the disciplinary boundaries drawn by academic rhetoric support the violence taking place at geopolitical borders. Academic rhetoric disseminates distinctions and parallels among migrants and immigrants, refugees and exiles, legitimate and illegitimate reasons to cross national borders at specific times. Kaplan writes of the necessity to examine the conceptual boundaries that separate our understandings of immigrants and migrants, refugees and exiles. These terms, she argues, are laden with assumptions about intention and ability to assimilate, reasons for leaving, motivations for staying.[12] Such assumptions, in turn, are embedded in the ways that policy decisions get discussed and made. Immigrants *overwhelm* our national economy, taking jobs away from native-born Americans; refugees *deserve* safe harbor from an array of political and natural disasters. Try switching the italicized verbs and you can hear how deeply these assumptions are embedded in our language.[13] Because language is so important to the ways we understand and enforce borders, I want to make an argument in this final section for two terms that appear throughout this book: im/migration and denizenship.

Recent work on transnationalism has begun to challenge some long-standing assumptions about im/migration, acknowledging the deep connections many people who leave their homelands maintain over time and distance. Scholarship on transnational migration has challenged traditional notions about assimilation and undermined the popular reductionism of push and pull factors. The concept of transnationalism challenges the assertions of many commentators that the United States is being flooded by hordes of people seeking to overwhelm its national culture and traditions.[14] But the diffusion of the word "transnationalism"—a neologism roughly concurrent with the emergence of NAFTA as a political strategy and George Bush's proclaiming of a "new world order"—overemphasizes what is new about transnational connections, either from the perspective of "transmigrants" themselves or from the standpoint of global economics.[15]

Cristina Blanc-Szanton, Nina Glick Schiller, and Linda Basch define transnationalism as:

the processes by which immigrants forge and sustain multi-stranded social relations that link together their societies of origin and settlement. We call these processes transnationalism to emphasize that many immigrants today build social fields that cross geographic, cultural and political borders. Immigrants who develop and maintain multiple relationships—familial, economic, social, organizational, religious and political—that span borders we call "transmigrants." An essential element of transnationalism is the multiplicity of involvements that transmigrants sustain in both home and host societies.[16]

The writers here work to correct some of the assumptions of immigration policy and historiography: that immigrants make a clean break in coming from home to the host nation, and that they intend to assimilate, making the new country home. Kaplan discusses "the commonplace belief that immigrants *intend* to assimilate: they leave their homes without reluctance and they face a new situation with an eagerness to become as much part of the nation or community as possible."[17] Basch and her colleagues describe how their research on post-1965 Caribbean and Filipino communities in the United States forced them to challenge such scholarly assumptions. The growing literature on "transnationalism" takes apart simple and misguided connections between immigration, intention or ability to assimilate, and voluntary migration. This is a crucial development, particularly in terms of immigrants of color, who are often denied the socioeconomic mobility that facilitates assimilation.[18]

Basch and her colleagues historicize transnationalism by describing a break with previous national forms in the recent past. Now, they argue, a nation-state is likely to incorporate within its boundaries citizens and denizens who "remain socially, politically, culturally and often economically part of the nation-state of their ancestors."[19] Michael Kearney thoughtfully links this historic break in the ability of capital to partition the universe into First and Third Worlds with the decline of master narratives associated in Western intellectual history with the "crisis in representation" and the postmodern condition.[20] But how new are such dual loyalties and such skepticism regarding the "grand truths" authored by the modernist project?

As early as 1944, Eric Williams's classic *Capitalism and Slavery* turned modernist narratives of economic progress upside down by asserting that the forced transatlantic migration of African peoples facilitated the Industrial Revolution.[21] Williams laid the groundwork for claims of a transatlantic Black modernism. His important argument undermined the idea that modernization crossed the Atlantic in one (westerly) direction. Similarly, recent scholarship on the "great wave" of European immigrants, the ones who are now assumed most likely to assimilate and leave the past behind, documents the ongoing importance of homeland ties in influencing the social and political lives of immigrants in the United States. This work contradicts generations of scholarly assumptions about the one direction of progress across the Atlantic.[22] In her important work on Black political thought, Gayle Plummer demonstrates that native-born African-Americans often formulated their opinions on U.S. foreign policy through a complex tug-of-war involving various geographic and political affinities, such as: their loyalty to the United States; concern for domestic civil rights, and affective and organizational ties to Afro-diasporic and colonized peoples throughout the world.[23] An emergent scholarship traces the rich history of transatlantic connections between workers in Europe, Africa, and the Americas.[24] Similarly, critical work in Asian-American studies has demonstrated that generations of Asians have crossed the Pacific, and that these im/migrants have maintained close connections with their homelands, in part as a means of dealing with the exigencies of racialized U.S. law.[25] Drawing on such scholarship, we have to conclude that transnationalism has been ongoing, disguised by the rhetorical boundaries drawn by state policies and academic disciplines.[26] Crossing back and forth over oceans, im/migrants have created hybrid identities at the same time that they have labored to build the physical infrastructure of the nation and often occupied its geopolitical borders and internally administered frontiers as denizens rather than citizens. The marginal status of im/migrants has been particularly harsh for women; legislation against prostitution had the effects throughout the twentieth century of forcing Asian and other im/migrant women into the legal gray area of denizenship.[27]

That transnationalism is not so new does not contradict the importance of the work of scholars engaged in redefining it. Certainly the increased circulation of people between First and Third Worlds in the postwar period is an important shift. And, as the empire "comes home," racialized ideas of national community have been called into question. These are crucial transitions. But to assume that they are monolithic or new obliterates historical parallels.

For example, in analyzing the recent wave of nativism that has resulted in Save Our State initiatives and Proposition 187 in California, Patricia Zavella writes: "What is new about the fin de siècle nativism is that white supremacy has been undermined by global economic restructuring, which has created tremendous wealth while increasing the vulnerability of white citizens."[28] Whenever I read this quote, I think of the *nineteenth* century fin de siècle: pressure from native-born Euroamericans, including labor unions, to restrict Asian immigration, and the fear of the migration of cheap Black laborers from the South to industrial cities that resulted in tacit national support for the terrorism of Jim Crow. "The vulnerability of white citizens," in other words, has long had tremendous ideological capital.[29] Proposition 187 represents a *resurgence* of popular nativism; a reassertion of faith in the nation at a moment when state policy reaches out to affirm the new ascendance of global interdependence. Supporters of such initiatives long, on the one hand, for a national coherence that has always been artificially produced and maintained, often at the expense of the rights of im/migrant workers. Rhetoric of restriction and exclusion, from the nineteenth to the twenty-first century, draw on gendered metaphors of contagion from figurative unwed women contaminating the national family. On the other hand, new initiatives innovate, integrating im/migrants into the regime of an increasingly militarized "Border Patrol state" in Leslie Silko's suggestive term.[30] The success of Proposition 187 *does* suggest a historic change, in the role of state bureaucracies and professionals in policing denizens and citizens in ever more draconian measures.[31] But if we ignore the continuities between anti-im/migrant initiatives over time, it is much easier to miss the rearrangements taking place among state, national, and transnational powers.

Moreover, by ignoring compulsory migration *within* national boundaries, the rhetoric of transnationalism adds to the tendency of immigration historiography to unintentionally reify the nation as a political unit. What about people who are compelled by public policy or economic circumstances to move without crossing national borders? Further, what if those who are compelled to migrate think of themselves, as many Indian peoples historically have done, as residing in a "nation within" the one outlined by official geopolitical boundaries; or, as has historically been the case with African-Americans, if they have struggled for access to the citizenship rights that are supposed to be a part of belonging to a nation?[32]

Silko points out that the violence of the U.S.-Mexico border disrupts older patterns of migration and connection between indigenous peoples of what are now called North and South America. For her, "the Border Patrol state," with its infrared technology and racialized rhetoric of citizen and alien, is only the most recent manifestation of Manifest Destiny and the long conflict over the Americas. The ongoing migrations of Indian peoples predate the arrival of Europeans on this continent; their forced migrations across the empires and nation-states carved out in this hemisphere have been a crucial component of Euroamerican hegemony here since colonial times.[33] Crossing between the United States and Mexico, Native Americans become suspected of being "alien," despite their long-term claims to the land and their comparatively recent access to citizenship rights.[34] But this does not happen only on the geographic border.

In rediscovering Indian "civil rights" in the wake of World War II, academics and policy makers treated Native Americans living in the United States as if they were refugees from primitive nations. The rhetoric of federal termination and relocation policies drew on the extant rhetoric of immigration and ethnicity to position Indians as "new immigrants" to urban areas, requiring assistance to assimilate into the American way of life. At the same time, both traditionalists and younger activists argued that Indian people *were* crossing an international boundary when they were compelled to leave sovereign Indian lands for cities. Different definitions of native identity and nationhood, then, shaped the conflict over the political status of Indian people in the postwar period. And during the postwar period, many women rose to leadership positions within the urban Indian community. Similarly, in her study of African-American women migrants to California during the 1940s, Gretchen Lemke-Santangelo demonstrates that these im/migrant women challenged both gender and race relations in struggling for civil rights and fair labor practices.[35] In the ongoing process of racial formation, such conflicts are crucial to projects of local resistance.

If immigration history excludes migrants who cross such internal boundaries, we will have trouble understanding the process of racial and gender formation that divides different groups of im/migrants. If we don't attend to the ways people define themselves, it will be harder to understand the ways Native American migrants, for example, did and did not identify with the struggles of the African-Americans who lived near them in the postwar inner cities. Lacking the language to discuss the hybridity of im/migrant identity, we may ignore the crucial study of "new immigrants" from Asia and the Americas because they don't seem to fit into older paradigms of ethnicity and Americanization. And we may miss out entirely on the parallels and dissimilarities between these groups of people. In their compilation of immigration and ethnic history syllabi, for example, Donna Gabaccia and James Grossman noted that most history courses rely on sociological literature to cover the post-1965 immigrant cohort. Only one course included any study of Native American migrations, though a few looked at the migrations of African-Americans, Euroamericans from the Southern United States, and the urbanization of Mexican-Americans after 1848.[36] Alternately, an im/migration historiography can attend to the work of cultural and new labor historians in documenting the construction of racial and ethnic identities; we can look to critical work in literary, cultural, and postcolonial studies to understand the ways the nation itself is rhetorically produced, and gains its definition, at its margins.

Hailed by assimilation-oriented social agencies as "new immigrants" to such cities as Minneapolis, American Indians responded to relocation by emphasizing their connections to the land base, pointing out parallels and contrasts to urban African-American social movements, and aligning their struggles with a developing internationalist sensibility among indigenous people of the "Fourth World." Similarly, Caribbean im/migrants to New York City invented identities to negotiate the municipal and racial hierarchies so clearly at stake in Crown Heights, as well as the global ones that compel them to leave their homelands in search of employment. These are stories about race and identity as much as they are about immigration and Americanization. An im/migration historiography can place the creation of identity at the center of an analysis of migratory histories of this hemisphere.[37]

For instance: once when I was teaching Kathy Peiss's important study of immigrant women and mass culture in an immigration history course, an African-American student wondered why Peiss did not include African-American migrant women.[38] The Italian and Jewish immigrants Peiss writes about worked on the shop floor with African-American migrants; these im/migrant women struggled to have the economic and social rights to enjoy entertainment such as movies, amusement parks, and dance halls during their leisure hours.[39] They were, of course, separated by the ongoing depredations of capital and the continual production of the mythical yet powerful category of "whiteness": bosses paid Italian, Jewish, and African-American workers different wages; Jewish and Italian unions excluded African-Americans. All these women lived together in the same city, segregated by neighborhood. The production of these racialized and gendered distinctions is crucial grounds for study, as are the times and places where these differences are less important than the common interest of these different women in a livable wage, a safe workplace, a good time in the evening.

I mention this incident not so much to take Peiss to task for the exclusion. Not every study can do everything. But I want to suggest that the disciplinary assumptions of immigration and ethnic history can often blind us to the way social identity works to enable and disarm solidarity. In 1972 Roy Simon Bryce-Laporte noted the "double invisibility" of black immigrants: as new arrivals and as denizens of color, immigrants from Africa and the Caribbean don't fit into established paradigms of social policy and immigration history.[40] This is also true for migrants within the nation-state: while their experiences often parallel those of immigrants, the focus on "Americanization" in traditional immigration historiography has excluded them from comparison in scholarly work as well as, perhaps more important, in teaching.[41] Perhaps because immigration history originates with the Chicago School's focus on the assimilation of the immigrants who later became known as "white ethnics," the discipline, even as it has changed its questions, has maintained that focus.[42]

Cindy Hahamovitch's *Fruits of Their Labor: Atlantic Coast Farmworkers and the Making of Migrant Poverty* looks at African-American and Italian im/migrant laborers as different members of the same group of workers. Without reducing the complexities of race and ethnicity, Hahamovitch deftly analyzes the gendered and racialized practices of the state and of growers.[43] Migrant farm workers, she points out, were excluded from the Wagner Act in 1935. This exclusion radically diminished their power to organize and bargain collectively. Inclusion in the collective bargaining of national unions has been crucial to domestic farmworker unions, such as the United Farmworkers (UFW) and the Farm Laborers Organizing Committee (FLOC). But as these unions and many other groups of people are figuring out, the increasing mobility of capital necessitates organizing across the borders inscribed on maps and in political rhetoric.[44] For Hahamovitch, im/migrant workers threaten the collective bargaining power of migrant workers: bracero and H2 programs supply cheap "labor from abroad at taxpayer expense."[45] While this is indisputable, it is also true that no laws restrict the ability of capital to migrate across borders, seeking cheaper labor and fewer environmental restrictions. As long as this is true, people will migrate in search of work as well as the often mythical benefits of democratic citizenship.

An im/migration history offers us the chance to write stories without replicating the disciplinary and rhetorical borders of the nation-state: to acknowledge that internal frontiers of race, class, and neighborhood often separate people as much as geopolitical borders do; and that im/migrants have a long history of spanning and contesting whatever boundaries confront them. The inter- and intradisciplinary innovation implicit in im/migration history gives us a map of the world, suggesting counternarratives of place and identity, denizenship and home. Such innovation allows us to understand the implications of a long-term, global transnationalism as well as the process of racial formation within national borders.

The violence of current debates over citizenship indicates that the traditional liberal basis of rights to membership in the nation-state is changing. Democratic representation does not work well in the many nations where im/migrant denizens who are long-term residents cannot participate in the political process. As Tomas Hammar points out, this system of nonrepresentation disproportionately disenfranchises working people, since most im/migrants are workers.[46] Noting this, David Jacobson argues that the tremendous geographic mobility of the post–World War II period will likely result in the ascendance of human rights over citizenship rights.[47] This rhetoric of human rights suggests the comparative powerlessness of nongovernmental organizations in the post–World War II period. At the same time, though, it opens up the possibility for redefining access to the rights and privileges previously limited to a racialized membership of the nation-state.

True democracy means the political enfranchisement and municipal empowerment of denizens as well as citizens. To develop such a democracy, public policy must be able to read and respond to the various voices in which people make claims on the state. Imagining a meaningful public sphere, then, means paying attention to the claims made by denizens on the nations they inhabit. These claims are written everywhere: in performance, local politics, and popular memory.

Notes

CHAPTER 1. IM/MIGRATION, RACE, AND
POPULAR MEMORY IN CARIBBEAN BROOKLYN AND
AMERICAN INDIAN MINNEAPOLIS

Joe Austin, Tony Dreyfus, Pat Kaluza, Frieda Knobloch, Jason Loviglio, and Steve Ziliak read and edited this chapter. A portion of it was presented at the Young Americanists Conference at Harvard University in January 1998. Much of the thinking here was developed in seminar conversations with Patrick Alexander, Sharon Deaubreau, Jeff Flagg, Natalie Gould, Andrea Kabwasa, Mike Kimaid, Victoria Lees, Lori Liggitt, Kristin McKeown, Julio Rodriguez, Keith Scheurman, and Matt Young. I had helpful research assistance from Dave Haus.

1. In August 1991 a car driven by Yosef Lifsh, a Lubavitch Hasid, went out of control in Crown Heights and fatally injured a seven-year-old Guyanese-American boy, Gavin Cato. Lifsh was part of a motorcade that was returning from escorting the Lubavitch leader, Rebbe Menahem Schneerson, on his weekly visit to his wife's grave in a cemetery in Queens. Several hours later, a crowd of Black youths surrounded a Hasidic yeshiva student, Yankel Rosenbaum, and stabbed him to death. These incidents together became a focal point for deeply rooted social and economic tension among the predominantly Caribbean Black community and the largely Hasidic Jewish community in Crown Heights. (See *New York Newsday*, September 3, 1991; *Village Voice*, September 3, 1911.)

2. As of the 1990 census, 18.5% of Black people in New York County were foreign-born. Of these, 33.1% were naturalized, while 66.8% reported that they were "not a citizen." This figure compares to 42% foreign-born among Hispanics,

with 28.9% naturalized and 71% not, and 19% foreign-born whites, of whom 48% were naturalized and 51% were not. Among all im/migrants to New York since 1965, 50.7% of those entering the country between 1965 and 1979 were naturalized, while only 15.7% of those entering between 1980 and 1990 became citizens (*U.S. Census Reports*, 1960–1990).

3. Irma Watkins-Owens reports that fraternal and benevolent associations providing health and funeral benefits have long been a component of Afro-Caribbean and African-American im/migrant society in New York (*Blood Relations*, 65).

4. Asians were ineligible for citizenship from the Exclusion Act of 1882 until the McCarran-Walter Act in 1954.

5. Hongo, "America Singing."

6. The cosmology of Haitian vodou sees the dead as having access to Ginen, or Africa. See Brown, *Mama Lola*. See also Ng, *Bone*, on the disruption of Chinese-American burial traditions as a result of "paper" identities taken on to satisfy anti-Chinese immigration regulations in California.

7. Benedict Anderson's now classic *Imagined Communities* is of course the source of this phrase. But many critics have extended both the site of the community and the source of the imaginings beyond Anderson's formulations. See especially Homi Bhabha, "Introduction: Narrating the Nation" and "Dissemi-Nation: Time, Narrative, and the Margins of the Modern Nation," both in his *Nation and Narration;* and Partha Chatterjee's useful postcolonial counter to Anderson in *Nationalist Thought.*

8. Counting illegal immigrants is, of course, a dicey business: how does the state account for those most likely to elude its technologies?

9. Yellow Bird and Milun, "Interrupted Journeys," 20.

10. Roach, *Cities of the Dead*, 38.

11. Lowe, *Immigrant Acts*, 2

12. Gilroy, *Black Atlantic*, 37.

13. Nora, "Between Memory and History."

14. Hall, "Culture, Community, Nation."

15. Noel, "Politics of Carnival."

16. It is estimated, for example, that about half of the Cherokee people died as a result of removal during the 1838 Trail of Tears. See Stiffarm and Lane, "Demography of Native North America"; Thornton, "Cherokee Population Losses."

17. See Thomas, "Pan-Indianism."

18. Roach, *Cities of the Dead*, 4.

19. Ibid., xi.

20. See Bederman, *Manliness and Civilization;* Lott, *Love and Theft;* Rosaldo, *Culture and Truth;* Green, "Pocahontas Perplex."

21. See my "Teaching Crown Heights"; Slotkin, "Buffalo Bill's 'Wild West'"; Moses, *Wild West Shows.*

22. Winokur, *American Laughter*, 10.

23. See Powers, *War Dance.*

24. Gilroy, *Black Atlantic*, 102.

25. Ibid., 37.

26. In 1966, before the decolonization of the British West Indies, the number of immigrants admitted from the United Kingdom who intended to make

New York their place of residence was similar to the number of Dominicans and Haitians. By 1991, New York had the highest immigrant admissions for Jamaicans, Guyanese, and Dominicans (statistics were not available for Trinidad and Tobago) (U.S. Department of Justice, Immigration and Naturalization Service, *Annual Reports,* 1963–1991).

27. See Patricia Williams, *Alchemy of Race and Rights.* For an example of the way im/migrant urban social movements reimagine history in the case of the relationship between Garveyism and Rastafarianism, see Nelson, "Rastafarians and Ethiopianism."

28. Goldberg, *Racist Culture.*

29. Balibar writes about this contradiction:

> This fiction, however, also derives its effectiveness from everyday practices, relations which immediately structure the "life" of individuals. And, most importantly ... the race community dissolves social inequalities in an even more ambivalent "similarity"; it ethnicizes the social difference which is an expression of irreconcilable antagonisms by lending it the form of a division between the "genuinely" and the "falsely" national. ("Fictive Identity," 167)

30. Hall, "New Ethnicities," 162.

31. The heading for this section, "Stories That Could Be True," comes from the title of William Stafford's collected poems. The same book includes the lovely and applicable phrase: "We owe the rain/a pat on the back—barefoot, it has walked/with us with its silver passport all over the world" (5–6).

32. Johannes Fabian argues in *Time and the Other* that in struggling to create a discourse of expertise, ethnographic practice forces a distance from the world of the "informants," thus creating them as the objects rather than the subjects of our accounts. For Fabian, the separation between researchers and the researched creates the "denial of coevalness," a deep rift between the social spaces each inhabits.

Interviewers and informants inhabit different systems of time: the *Times* reporter and photographer were on an overnight deadline; I was on the somewhat more lenient but also exacting schedule of dissertation research.

33. The article that came out of this encounter does a good basic job of interviewing the public figures involved in West Indian–American Day Carnival and in the Caribbean community in general. It makes some very general speculations about the climate in Crown Heights, and actually quotes Randy Brewster very briefly. My point here is not necessarily to criticize journalists but rather to point to the collective problematic in the representation of social experience by "official discourses," such as the *New York Times* and academic dissertations. See *New York Times,* August 30, 1991, B1, B3.

34. Traditional practices of "salvage anthropology" (Marcus and Fischer, *Anthropology as Cultural Critique*) documented primitive cultures displaced by the progress of colonization and modernization. Implicit in this notion of salvaging and preserving the primitive is the idea that ethnographers are separated from their subjects by time—the ethnographer is a modern interloper, bringing the harvest of colonialist research back to the museums and archives of the west. The contradictions of salvage anthropology are particularly pronounced for im/migrant or diasporan cultures. Traditional ethnography misses the

constant reinvention that accompanies histories marked by forced relocation and migration.

35. In *Orientalism,* Edward Said broke important theoretical ground, arguing that the Western academic traditions that study nonwestern cultures often perpetuate colonial domination rather than advancing more rose-colored goals of humanist knowledge and mutual understanding. Influenced by such postcolonial criticism, anthropologists have turned to consider the role of the social sciences in promoting domination, questioning the practices of cultural salvage as well as the relationship between ethnographer and informants. At the same time, feminist and poststructuralist scholars have revolutionized the notion of subjectivity itself, pointing to the multiple discursive constructions of the roti eater as authority, consumer of culture, white person, woman, and to the effects of such divided subjectivity on the relationships among researchers and ethnographic "subjects." This critique of the unitary subject has promoted self-reflectiveness among ethnographers about their position among those they study, and about the disciplinary traditions that, as much as any "encounters in the field," inform ethnographic accounts. These two strains of critique, emanating from social movements of decolonization, civil rights, and feminism, have brought ethnography to what is popularly called a "crisis in representation," where the authority of traditional disciplinary practices has been roundly impugned, and we are forced to ask ourselves what our scholarship promotes on a political level, and what we are really able to see and say about other cultures at all.

This encounter of the "West and the rest," where traditional methodologies meet the multiply conscious subjectivities of internal colonization and exile, has changed ethnographic practice. Recent critical work elucidates the contradiction between the desire of scholars to understand and recount consciousness (Spivak, "Can the Subaltern Speak?") and what Trinh calls "the positivist dream of a perfect double" (*Woman, Native, Other,* 55).

Waking up from this dream, or from what many would argue comprises the long Enlightenment nightmare of positivist social science, we realize with a start that the institutions from which scholars draw our knowledge and authority do not necessarily produce expertise across cultural boundaries. What, then, becomes of our desires to understand consciousness; to narrate the conflicts that have come about in the long Western history of contact, mutual influence, and colonization?

CHAPTER 2. PLAYING FOR KEEPS

Conversations with the following people provided crucial information and insights for this chapter: Ellie Favel and Johnny Smith at Heart of the Earth Survival School, Bill Means of the American Indian Industrial Opportunities Center, Jim Clermont, Randy Brewster and Jackie of the Culture of Black Creation Mas' Camp, and Trevor Johns of Basement Recording Studios.

1. For a discussion of the syncretic nature of Afro-Atlantic music, see Hebdige, *Cut 'n' Mix;* Roberts, *Black Music of Two Worlds;* for the hybrid nature of "American" popular culture in the nineteenth century, see Saxton, *Rise and Fall of the White Republic.*

2. E. Hill, *Trinidad Carnival;* Safa, "Preface."

3. Anzaldúa, *Borderlands;* John Martínez Weston, personal communication, March 1994.

4. Valaskakis, "Dance Me Inside," 40.

5. For an excellent discussion of Indian cultural ties to the land, see V. Deloria, *God Is Red.* For an account of current Anishanabe struggles at Mole Lake see Donato, " 'To Allow This Mine.' "

6. Orsi, *Madonna of 115th Street,* esp. 150–162.

7. Howard, "Pan-Indian Culture"; Gamble, "Changing Patterns."

8. Howard and other anthropologists in the 1950s and 1960s stressed the emergence of pan-Indian culture as signaling the demise of specific tribal characteristics and the eventual assimilation of the Indians into mainstream society as an ethnic group. The ideas of Ralph Linton ("Distinctive Aspects of Acculturation") and Anthony Wallace (*Human Behavior*) about revivalism as a contradictory component of acculturation were central to the assimilationist model. This model, however, took a certain cultural teleology as a given, assuming that the direction of history was toward "progress" in the Western sense of the word. Revivalism is not necessarily about assimilation; we must historicize the occurrence of cultural revivals and look for their specific social and political negotiations.

9. Rachlin, "Tight Shoe Night."

10. See Ball, *Indeh!;* Buff, "Gone to Prophetstown."

11. Kees, "Stockbridge Indians"; O'Connell, *On Our Own Ground,* "Introduction"; Perdue and Green, *Cherokee Removal,* "Introduction."

12. Lomawaima, *They Called It Prairie Light,* xiii, 32–33; Child, *Boarding School Seasons,* 4.

13. Mooney, "Ghost Dance Religion"; Hagan, *American Indians;* Hertzberg, *Search for an American Indian Identity.*

14. See Iverson, *"We Are Still Here,"* esp. chap. 1; also Moses, *Wild West Shows.*

15. Rynkiewich, "Chippewa Powwows." See also Heth, *Native American Dance,* "Introduction."

16. See Iverson, *"We Are Still Here,"* 30–49.

17. Hickerson, *Ethnohistory of the Chippewa.*

18. Dyck, "Powwow."

19. Here I think Michel Foucault's sense of the relationship between ecclesiatical and governmental forms of discipline is useful (*Discipline and Punish*). The government sponsored missions to the Indians as part of its Indian policy (especially in the immediate post–Civil War period, with U. S. Grant's creation of the Peace Commission in 1867); in turn, federal efforts to acculturate Indian children dovetailed with missionary efforts.

20. Pratt also founded the Indian section of Hampton Institute in Virginia, which had been founded to educate former slaves. Both sections of the institute, as well as other institutions of this kind, followed then-contemporary race theory in attempting to educate Blacks and Indians to assume a subordinate socioeconomic position in the dominant society.

21. Roger Buffalohead, lecture, American Indian Studies, University of Minnesota, January 11, 1991.

22. Child, *Boarding School Seasons,* 5.

23. Bill Means, interview, Minneapolis, February 1993.

24. Hertzberg, *Search for an American Indian Identity,* 19–20.

25. Lomawaima, *They Called It Prairie Light,* 129.

26. See Gunther, "Westward Movement."

27. Initially discovered by Columbus and claimed for Spain in 1498, Trinidad remained a Spanish possession until the British conquest of the island in 1797. The French influx was due to a peace treaty signed between France and Spain, which encouraged the immigration of Roman Catholics to the island by offering land grants to all settlers, both white and colored. The defeat of Napoleon's forces in Haiti in 1802 and France's concurrent abandonment of its plans for economic dominance in the Americas when it sold the Louisiana Territory in 1803 ironically paved the way for federal Indian removal by giving the United States unprecedented access to lands west of the Mississippi. See Brereton, "Social Organisation and Class" and *History of Modern Trinidad;* Plummer, *Haiti and the United States.*

28. E. Hill, *Trinidad Carnival,* 4–9; Pearse, "Carnival in Nineteenth-Century Trinidad"; Brereton, "Social Organization and Class."

29. Brereton, "Social Organization and Class," 34, 52.

30. Bakhtin, *Rabelais and His World,* 196–277; E. Hill, *Trinidad Carnival,* 11; Nunley, "Masquerade Mix-up."

31. E. Hill, *Trinidad Carnival,* 31–32.

32. Ibid., 20–25.

33. Brereton, *History of Modern Trinidad,* 49.

34. Nunley, "Masquerade Mix-up," 92–94; Lott, *Love and Theft.*

35. Brereton, *History of Modern Trinidad,* 132.

36. Brereton, "Social Organization and Class," 52.

37. E. Hill, *Trinidad Carnival,* 100.

38. Brereton, "Social Organization and Class," 52; see also K. Singh, *Bloodstained Tombs.*

39. It is worth noting, however, that the similarities between these conflicts did not lead to more solidarity among working-class Afro- and Indo-Trinidadians. See K. Singh, *Race and Class.*

40. See Powrie, "Changing Attitude."

41. Even before emancipation, Trinidad had a large population of urban slaves; in 1813, 25% of slaves lived in cities. After the end of the apprenticeship in 1838, favorable wages allowed freedpeople much more mobility than in the United States. Particularly as Indian indentured workers were imported, starting in the 1840s, the Black population tended to be more urbanized in Trinidad than in the United States and in other British colonies, such as Barbados. See Brereton, *History of Modern Trinidad,* esp. chaps. 5–6.

42. Quoted in Pearse, "Carnival in Nineteenth-Century Trinidad," 185.

43. Brereton, *History of Modern Trinidad,* 132.

44. E. Hill, *Trinidad Carnival,* 33–38.

45. D. Hill, *Calypso Callaloo,* 22–43.

46. Stuempfle, *Steelband Movement,* 54; D. Hill, *Calypso Callaloo,* 200–202.

47. D. Hill, *Calypso Callaloo,* 203.

48. Segal, "Living Ancestors."

49. Warner, "Ethnicity and the Contemporary Calypso."

50. Chaney, *Migration from the Caribbean Region;* D. Marshall, "Migration and Development."

51. Manning, "Overseas Caribbean Carnivals," 29; A. Cohen, *Masquerade Politics,* 40.

52. One story of the origin of the jingle dress was told to me by Ellie Favel, a Canadian Ojibwa woman who works as a guidance counselor at Heart of the Earth Survival School in Minneapolis:

> The jingle dress story, the one that the elders gave me the right to tell, is from the Lake of the Woods area. And there's three that I heard ... one from that lake, Red Lake, that area. And there's even one I heard from Sisseton, South Dakota. And they're all a little bit different, but they're all, you know, special, because they're visions and dreams, and the vision was a gift from the Creator.
>
> But the one that I'll share with you is the one I brought from my area. And it comes from a dream that this elder had. This elder had a granddaughter who was raised, and he loved her so much ... but she was really sickly. And he was a real simple man, a kind man, a really down-to-earth person, who prayed a lot. He prayed a lot for his granddaughter. For her to get well. And tirelessly, he did that for many years, and kept praying for her. And then finally, he was honored, and he had this dream, this vision. And, where this beautiful elder man came, you know, with gray hair, and the kindest eyes. And this real sacred person came to him and talked to him. And told him: this dress, that he was to make. And this dress that he was to make to be made real special. The color and the design. And he had to make this with love and prayers. And so he did that, he made it a special way, he made it with love and prayers. And then, when he was complete with the dress, he was to cook all this food that he had in his home and share it with the village, call all the people together, in honor of this dress, after it was completed, so he did that. And he was also to instruct his granddaughter in when she could wear this dress, and when not to wear it. And how she was to conduct herself with this dress, and how she was supposed to take care of it, like it was a spirit....
>
> ... the dress was a spirit. So, she would know how to properly take care of it. So he did that too. When he was complete, with all the instructions, and then the young girl danced with it, and she became well. So that's where that gift came from, to the women. The jingle dress. It's a medicinal dress. And it's to cure what ails the person, you know, who's sickly.

53. Horse Capture, *Powwow,* 27.

54. This interpretation was suggested to me by Ellie Favel, who emphasizes the healing properties of the jingle dress in her work with young Indian women at the Heart of the Earth Survival School in Minneapolis; and also by Debbie Ironshield, a student at Heart of the Earth, who talked about the spiritual dimensions of dancing the Jingle Dress Dance.

55. Ellie Favel, interview, Heart of the Earth School, Minneapolis, April 1994.

56. See Heth, *Native American Dance,* 17.

57. D. Hill, *Calypso Callaloo,* 179–181.

58. A contemporary movie manual advised would-be producers:

> The Red Indians who have been fortunate enough to secure permanent engagements with the several Western film companies are paid a salary that keeps them well provided

with tobacco and their worshipped "firewater." It might be thought that this would civ-ilize them completely, but it has had quite a reverse effect, for the work affords them an opportunity to live their savage days over again, and they are not slow to take advan-tage of it. They put their heart and soul in the work, especially in battles with the whites, and it is necessary to have armed guards watch over their movements for the least sign of treachery. (Dench, *Making Movies,* 92–93).

59. There is some controversy over the origins and authorship of this popular calypso. For a discussion of this controversy as well as background on Decca and other American companies in Trinidad, see D. Hill, *Calypso Callaloo,* 114–144.

60. E. Williams, *Capitalism and Slavery,* 27.

61. See Enloe, *Bananas, Beaches, and Bases;* Nash and Fernández-Kelly, *Women, Men, and the International Division of Labor.*

62. For an excellent account of the show and its relation to contemporary frontier conflicts, see Slotkin, "Buffalo Bill's 'Wild West.'"

63. Gunther, "Westward Movement"; Powers, *War Dance,* 18. As L. G. Moses points out, the timing of the Wild West shows allowed Indian participants to turn the nomadic lifestyle of the traveling circus to their own ends—whether to escape the poverty of reservation life in the late nineteenth century, to meet other Indian people, or to maintain a lifestyle officially outlawed at the time by the Indian Bureau (*Wild West Shows,* 45–46).

64. A fascinating parallel to the Wild West Show is the Canadian Calgary Stampede, which performs a similarly mythologized "Wild West" to this day. See Burgess, "Canadian 'Range Wars.'"

65. Powers, *War Dance,* 161.

66. Lipsitz, *Time Passages,* 233–255.

67. Crowley, "Traditional Masks of Carnival."

68. Nunley, "Masquerade Mix-up," 96.

69. Brereton, *History of Modern Trinidad,* 21, 48.

70. Crowley, "Traditional Masks of Carnival," 264.

71. Stuempfle, *Steelband Movement,* 55.

72. Guillermoprieto, *Samba!*

73. A. Cohen, *Masquerade Politics,* 40.

74. Kasinitz, *Caribbean New York,* 148–159.

75. E. Hill, *Trinidad Carnival,* 97.

76. Though this is the historical narrative of how such costumes as those of Cleopatra and Roman gladiators became popular, it is important to note that it is popularly disputed. "Trinidad put the Ten Commandments on the road be-fore Hollywood ever thought of it," insisted one costume designer (interview, August 1992).

77. Trevor Johns, interview, Basement Recording Studios, Brooklyn, July 1991.

78. Kasinitz, *Caribbean New York;* Manning, "Overseas Caribbean Carnivals."

79. Interview, Jackie, August 1992.

80. Valaskakis, "Chippewa and the Other."

81. In 1884 the U.S. government banned participation in many Indian cere-monies, including the Sun Dance. Under John Collier's administration of the Bu-reau of Indian Affairs, this proscription was lifted in 1933. See Huenemann, "Northern Plains Dance," 125.

82. Sometimes, as Lomawaima points out, boarding schools were sites for cultural innovation and preservation. The Chilocco Indian School in Oklahoma, for example, tolerated stomp dance ceremonies held by students. She writes: "Participation in stomp dances or other covert religious activities was an important way students could retain ties to their home cultures. School authorities frowned on stomp dances, but, for whatever reasons, did not stop them" (*They Called It Prairie Light,* 140).

83. *Peace Pipe* 2 (February 1955), Box 10, American Indians, SWHA.

84. *American Indian Center News* 1, no. 4 (March 1962), Box 4, ibid.

85. Powers, *War Dance.*

86. Jim Clermont, interview, Minneapolis, 1994.

87. Vine Deloria, *Behind the Trail of Broken Treaties,* points out that it was a common tactic of the mainstream media during the 1970s to portray AIM as "outside agitators," urban, educated Indians who returned to reservations such as Pine Ridge to "make trouble." In fact, AIM organizers were often from reservations, and worked closely with ongoing political organizations there. For a detailed case study of reservation resistance, see Peroff, *Menominee Drums.*

88. Bill Means, interview, Minneapolis, 1993.

89. See Roediger, *Towards the Abolition of Whiteness;* Omi and Winant, *Racial Formation.*

90. Basch, Schiller, and Szanton Blanc, *Nations Unbound,* 45.

CHAPTER 3. IM/MIGRATION POLICY,
THE NATIONAL ROMANCE, AND
THE POETICS OF WORLD DOMINATION

I had editorial help with this chapter from Donna Gabaccia, Dorothee Schneider, Ilana Ericson, and the audience at the "Loyal Wives or Cleaning Ladies?: Women and Immigration" at the Social Science History Association meeting in Washington, D.C., October 1997; C. Richard King and an anonymous reader of *Post-Colonial America* for University of Illinois Press; and the Professionally Young Faculty Writing Group at Bowling Green State University: Laura Podalsky, Joe Austin, Rebecca Green, Vince O'Keefe, Vickie Patraka, Mark Hernandez, Jeannie Ludlow, and Val Rohy.

1. See H. Bhabha, *Nation and Narration.*

2. See Harvey, *Consciousness and the Urban Experience.* The percentage of goods produced by the 100 largest corporations zoomed in the first two years of the war, from 30% in 1941 to 70% in 1943 (Nash, *American West Transformed,* 8); this war machine, along with the propaganda apparatus generated to support the war effort, would readily translate after the war into the production and marketing of consumer goods.

3. See N. P. Singh, "Culture/Wars," 510.

4. See Corber, *In the Name of National Security,* esp. 1–39.

5. Sommer, "Irresistible Romance," 75.

6. See, for example, Goldberg, *Racist Culture;* Thompson, *Theories of Ethnicity;* Wald, *Constituting Americans.*

7. For a discussion of the Enlightenment roots of citizenship and the ongoing conflict between the citizen-ideal and social life in civil society, see Alejandro, *Hermeneutics,* esp. 9–41.

8. Thompson, *Theories of Ethnicity,* 64.

9. Lomawaima, *They Called It Prairie Light,* 164.

10. For more information on Bandung and its significance, see Mason, *Development and Disorder,* esp. 31–32.

11. Of course, the history of covert operations in these nations in the post–World War II period is long and brutal. See W. A. Williams, *Empire as a Way of Life;* LaFeber, *Inevitable Revolutions: The United States in Central America;* Chomsky, *American Power.*

12. Quoted in Iverson, "Building towards Self-Determination," 165.

13. Ibid., 166.

14. Philp, *Termination Revisited,* 171, 156.

15. *The Crisis* 59, no. 7 (August–September 1952): 442.

16. *New York Times,* January 6, 1961, 10.

17. See Von Eschen, *Race against Empire.*

18. Among the Jewish components of this alliance were the American Jewish Committee, the Anti-Defamation League, the Jewish War Veterans of the U.S.A., the National Commission on Religion Advisory Council, the National Council of Jewish Women, the Synagogue Council of America, the Union of American Hebrew Congregations, and the United Service for New Americans. In addition, leaders of local Jewish communities often took part in political work as it concerned local elections.

The American Committee for Special Migration was a coalition of thirty-five groups, including the Church World Service and the National Lutheran Council. Other groups included the Catholic Resettlement Commission, the International Longshoremen's and Warehousemen's Union, the American Committee to Aid Homeless Armenians, and the American Committee on Italian Immigrants.

19. For the Bracero Program, see Acuña, *Occupied America,* 260–270; Calavita, *Inside the State.*

20. Rogin writes: "The liberal principle behind such tactics was that coercion emanated only from the government and not from the economy or society" (*Ronald Reagan,* 164).

21. *Congressional Record,* April 25, 1946, 4993.

22. Public Law 40, passed in April 1947, provided for emergency labor through December of the same year. With pressure from western agricultural interests, as well as State Department intervention, an accord was arranged with the Mexican government to continue the importation of labor into the United States; the Bracero Program would continue until 1964.

23. Bell, *End of Ideology.*

24. Quoted in *New York Times,* January 1, 1951, 20.

25. Rogin writes, "The cold war marks the third major moment in the history of countersubversion. In the first moment whites were pitted against people of color. In the second Americans were pitted against aliens. In the third, which revolves around mass society and the state, a national-security bureaucracy confronts the invisible agents of a foreign power" (*Ronald Reagan,* 68).

26. Philp, *Termination Revisited*, 20.

27. Rogin, *Ronald Reagan*.

28. On allotment, see Iverson, " 'We Are Still Here,' " 30–36; Deloria and Lytle, *Nations Within*, 28–36; Josephy, *Now That the Buffalo's Gone*, 131–132.

29. Philp, *Termination Revisited*, esp. 70, 105.

30. The Senate Civil Service Committee, including William Langer (R-N.D.), Zales Ecton (R-Mont.), and Dennis Chavez (D-N.M.), wanted to overturn the IRA and replace it with states' rights and the unrestrained economic development of the West. On the state level, the Governors' Interstate Indian Council supported the same goals (ibid., 70, 95).

31. Ibid., 105.

32. *New York Times*, July 24, 1952, 17. Jean O'Brien-Kehoe noticed the parallel between termination and allotment-era rhetoric; I am indebted to her insight on this matter.

Rich Kees suggests that the concern over "citizenship" during the 1950s focused on the issue of state citizenship rather than that of the nation (personal communication, April 1993). It is true that Indians were not considered to be citizens of the states in which they resided, because of the federal trust relationship. In New Mexico and Arizona, this anomaly was used to make it difficult for Indians to vote. As the debate about termination was disseminated through Congress and the press, however, references to state or national citizenship were dropped. Most Americans, including policy makers, considered the idea of "Indian emancipation" to represent access to citizenship in the nation.

33. *New York Times*, April 6, 1953, 24.

34. Quoted in Fixico, *Termination and Relocation*, 17.

35. Philp, *Termination Revisited*, 105.

36. *Depaoli v. United States* (1944), cited in Philp, *Termination Revisited*, 104.

37. Quoted in Nash, *American West Transformed*, 187.

38. See Proctor, "Censorship," for an account of the connection between uranium mining and indigenous land and labor struggles; also Churchill and LaDuke, "Native North America." For an accounting of postwar land policy, see Churchill, "Earth Is Our Mother"; for water rights, see Guerrero, "American Indian Water Rights."

39. Stoler, *Race and the Education of Desire*, 90.

40. N. P. Singh, "Culture/Wars," 509.

41. See Sollors, *Beyond Ethnicity*, 4–6.

42. Erratic but steady changes in the immediate postwar period toward Asian immigration, particularly war brides, exemplify the kind of debate I am talking about here. In 1942, Japanese and Koreans were allowed to immigrate and naturalize, and given an annual quota of 100 each. In 1943, Congress rescinded *Chinese* exclusion and prohibitions on naturalization, allowing for the immigration of 105 Chinese per year. A 1946 bill allowed for a small quota for Asian Indians and Filipinos. The War Brides Act of 1945 was amended in 1947 to include veterans of Asian ancestry. In 1946, Asian spouses of U.S. citizens were allowed to enter as nonquota immigrants. See Espiritu, *Asian American Women and Men*.

43. Lowe, *Immigrant Acts*, 27.

44. See Lipsitz, *Possessive Investment in Whiteness.*

45. Reimers, *Still the Golden Door,* 17–22.

46. As Candice Bredbenner points out in *A Nationality of Her Own,* the history of the wife as a special candidate for naturalization is long and complex. See also Stoler, "Sexual Affronts," for a discussion of marriage as it functions in a multiracial colonial context to create a boundary for national inclusion and exclusion. The excellent work of the Women, Immigration, and Nationality Group (WINGS) has pointed to the connections between race, gender, and immigration policy; see Bhabha, Klug, and Shutter, *Worlds Apart.*

47. *Congressional Record,* April 25, 1949, 4993. Husbands were not allowed unrestricted immigration until 1952, parents until 1965 (Jasso and Rosenzweig, *New Chosen People,* 412).

48. A common theme in Indian, immigration, and Americanization programs generally. See Sanchez, *Becoming Mexican American;* Lomawaima, "Domesticity."

49. See Lowe, *Immigrant Acts,* esp. 154–173; Espiritu, *Asian American Women and Men,* 7–12.

50. *NCAI Bulletin,* no. 4, 1946. The parallels with the inability of many African-American veterans to take advantage of the mortgage provisions of the G.I. Bill, because of banks' redlining policies and restrictive real estate covenants, is illuminating here.

51. *Congressional Record,* July 21, 1947, 9562.

52. Ibid.

53. Ibid.

54. Ibid., January 16, 1954, 625.

55. *NCAI Bulletin,* July 1947.

56. The operation metaphor, with its particularly Foucauldian and vampiric overtones, is borrowed from Zipes, *Operated Jew.*

57. *NCAI Bulletin,* July 1948.

58. *NCAI Bulletin,* June 1949.

59. *New York Times,* March 4, 1952, 19.

60. The provisions of the McCarran-Walter Act that remain on the books at the present time have been used against such American citizens as the poet Margaret Randall, as well as against gay and lesbian activists. In addition, such controversial nonnational artists as the South African performers Malanthini and the Mahotella Queens, the Haitian band Boukman Eksperyans, and the Scottish pop band Big Country have encountered difficulty entering the country under these regulations.

61. The rhetorical significance of the language of immigration and refugee policy is discussed in Kaplan, *Questions of Travel,* esp. 100–110.

62. Goldberg, *Racist Culture,* 99.

63. "Senator James O. Eastland contended today that the relaxation of refugee immigration requirements would flood the United States with 'criminals and communist agents' " (*New York Times,* September 17, 1955, 10).

64. *New York Times,* April 26, 1956, 13.

65. See May, *Homeward Bound.*

66. *Amerindian* 4, no. 3 (January–February 1956). A *New York Times* editorial, indicative of the lack of support for termination policies among eastern Democrats, criticized McKay's interpretation of the constitution on January 12, 1956: "The circumstance in which our tribal Indian populations find themselves are obviously different from those of any other American citizen, and we therefore think that the Interior Department is straining a point in stating that the principle of Indian consent 'has most serious constitutional implications'" (26).

67. *Congressional Record*, October 7, 1949, 14118.

68. Philp, *Termination Revisited*, 96, 3.

69. Lomowaima, "Domesticity," 203.

70. Quoted in Fixico, *Termination and Relocation*, 49.

71. "Proceedings of the Minnesota Indian Conference," Bemidji, April 11, 1950, p. 14, in Box 10, American Indians, SWHA.

72. *New York Times*, September 16, 1956, 14.

73. Fixico, *Termination and Relocation*, 185. The Klamaths had been awarded a $5.3 million settlement by the Court of Claims in 1938; the award was part of their fitness for termination. See Philp, *Termination Revisited*, 18.

74. *New York Times*, February 7, 1963, 2.

75. Quoted in Ames and Fisher, "Menominee Termination Crisis," 105. Ames and Fisher were both University of Wisconsin faculty members (in sociology and anthropology, respectively), and both worked on the University Committee and Wisconsin Legislative Council for the Menominee Indian Study Committee and the Governance Committee on Human Rights. This coalition attempted to study the conditions for termination and then to implement it. The article is included in the folders of *The Menominee News*, a reservation-based BIA paper, in the Wisconsin State Historical Society, Madison.

76. Ibid., 103.

77. *Menominee News*, August 23, 1956. See also the issues of September and October 1957.

78. Ibid., October 29, 1958.

79. Much of the research on relocation policy and its effects was done in concert with Joe Austin. I have drawn heavily on our joint seminar paper, "The Relocation Programs: Context, Evaluation, and Response," written for Roger Buffalohead's seminar Contemporary Indian Social Movements, Winter 1991.

80. Ablon, "American Indian Relocation," 364–365.

81. Sorkin, "Some Aspects," 30.

82. Price, "Migration and Adaptation," 173. Other studies of relocation in the early period include Ablon, "Relocated American Indians" and "American Indian Relocation"; Clinton et al., "Urban Relocation Reconsidered"; Graves, "Personal Adjustment"; Sorkin, "Some Aspects" and *Urban American Indian*.

83. Gundlach and Roberts, "Native American Indian Migration," 117. For an excellent elaboration of the republican/individualist bias of U.S. social welfare policy, see Bates, "Settling the Industrial Frontier."

84. Philp points out that Dillon Myer overturned Collier's criteria, determining "competency" for termination by the amount of mixed blood, literacy,

and acceptance of white institutions and the degree of local non-Indian support for the program (*Termination Revisited*, 71).

85. Indian agencies placed the population much higher, estimating between 7,000 and 8,000 in the Minneapolis–St. Paul metropolitan area.

86. "Minnesota Indians," Report of Minnesota Legislative Research Committee, Publication 27, March 1950, 44, in SWHA.

87. Following the work of feminist and Foucauldian scholars, many historians of colonization have noted the importance of intimate life to the colonial project. See esp. Gutiérrez, *When Jesus Came;* Mitchell, *Colonizing Egypt;* Stoler, "Sexual Affronts."

88. *Menominee News,* February 27 and March 23, 1956.

89. Fixico, *Termination and Relocation,* 91.

90. Sangari and Vaid, *Recasting Women,* 6.

91. *New York Times,* October 12, 1958, 44.

92. Ibid., August 8, 1956, 12.

93. Immigration History Research Center, Minneapolis, OSIA News Office, Box 2, folder 9. This research is the work of Lee Bernstein, who generously brought it to my attention.

94. Because the timing of the immigration reform coalition coincides with civil rights alliances between African-American and white ethnic groups, Jewish Americans in particular, this is a point that calls for further research. To what extent were Jewish efforts against national origins quotas in line with the broader antiracist agendas of the NAACP? I suspect that this was a cause for division and debate within the Jewish community. A progressive interpretation would see the national origins quotas as posing a racialized threat to both Jewish and African-American communities. This further research project was suggested to me in a conversation with George Lipsitz.

95. *New York Times Magazine,* July 8, 1951, 8. Other senators who supported immigration reform included Philip Hart (D-Mich.); Joseph Clark Jr. (D-Pa.), Richard Neuberger (D-Ore.), Hubert Humphrey (D-Minn.), and Patrick McNamara (D-Mich.). Congressmen Kenneth Keating (R-N.Y.), Herbert Lehman (D-N.Y.), and Emanuel Celler (D-N.Y.), among others, were strong supporters in the House.

96. *New York Times,* March 17, 1959, 37.

97. Ibid., February 10, 1956, 20.

98. Ibid., April 19, 1957, 8.

99. See Davis, *Prisoners of the American Dream.*

100. *New York Times,* January 3, 1956, 7.

101. Jasso and Rosenzweig, *New Chosen People,* 425.

102. *New York Times,* October 7, 1961, 20.

103. For an excellent account of the ways Caribbean immigrants specifically subvert this aspect of immigration policy, see Garrison and Weiss, "Dominican Family Networks."

104. Jasso and Rosenzweig, *New Chosen People,* 185. Current family-sponsored preferences are ranked as follows: spouses and unmarried sons and daughters of U.S. citizens and their children; spouses and children of alien residents and unmarried sons and daughters of alien residents, 21 years of age or

older; married sons and daughters of U.S. citizens; their spouses and children (U.S. Department of Justice, *Immigrant Nation*, app. A). The Immigration Reform Act of 1996 restricted family reunification policies by putting into effect financial requirements. A legal or naturalized immigrant sponsoring a family member was required to earn 125% of the national poverty level to reunite with family members. Federal officials quoted in Pence, "Immigration Law," estimated that such restrictions would have prevented at least 10% of those who sponsored a family member in 1994 from qualifying.

    105. *New York Amsterdam News*, October 3, 1964, 18.
    106. Kennedy, *Nation of Immigrants*.
    107. Fraser, *Unruly Practices*, 22.
    108. Winant, "Postmodern Racial Politics," 121–147.

CHAPTER 4. PERFORMATIVE SPACES, URBAN POLITICS, AND THE CHANGING MEANINGS OF HOME IN BROOKLYN AND MINNEAPOLIS

This chapter draws on the knowledge, generosity, and memories of the following people: *in Minneapolis:* Jim Clermont, Dorene Day, Ron Libertus, Bill Means, Johnny Smith, Norine Smith, and Melinda Hanell; *in Brooklyn:* Jacob Goldstein, Victor Brady, Carlos Lezama, Frank Caramonica, Horace Morancie, Joyce Quinoma, Randy Brewster, and Trevor Johns.

    1. Statistics are from the U.S. Census. It's important that such official figures do not account for illegal immigration. While official census data in 1990 puts the West Indian population of New York City at 370,000, for example, estimates that try to account for illegal immigration and census miscounting put the number much higher, toward 700,000 (*New York Times*, September 6, 1993, 17).
    2. Elaine Neils, who studied the effects of relocation on the Indian community in Chicago, argues that increased migration from reservation to city allowed Indians to return to more migratory patterns of living that the reservation system did not permit ("Reservation to City," 125).
    3. Shoemaker, "Urban Indians," 434.
    4. See Nagel, *American Indian Ethnic Renewal*, 19–33.
    5. It is important to note the overlap between federal internment and relocation policies. As Richard Drinnon points out in *Keeper of Concentration Camps*, Dillon S. Myer was involved as overseer of both projects. In addition, in the Twin Cities, private charities such as the St. Paul Resettlement Committee moved after the war from helping Japanese-Americans to settle in the area to relocating Indians (Shoemaker, "Urban Indians," 453).
    6. Dillon S. Myer, quoted in F. Cohen, "Erosion of Indian Rights," 376.
    7. Gilroy, *"There Ain't No Black in the Union Jack,"* 33–34.
    8. Cornell, *Return of the Native*.
    9. See Kasinitz, *Caribbean New York;* Watkins-Owens, *Blood Relations*.
    10. See Peroff, *Menominee Drums;* also the discussion of the Menominee Warrior Society's activities in the 1970s in Nagel, *American Indian Ethnic Renewal*, 174–175. In addition to the Klamaths and Menominees, four other groups of Indians were targeted for termination: four small Paiute bands, a mixed-blood pop-

ulation of Uintah and Oruay Indians in Utah, the Alabama-Coushattas of Texas, and several small groups of Indians in Oregon (Peroff, *Menominee Drums*, 75).

11. Cornell, *Return of the Native*, 126.

12. Nagel, *American Indian Ethnic Renewal*, 158–178.

13. See Ho, *Salt-water Trinnies*.

14. Neils, *Reservation to City*, 52. In addition, Shoemaker points out that federal relocation was ill timed to coincide with postwar urban overcrowding ("Urban Indians," 453).

15. Kasinitz, *Caribbean New York*, 103–106. Roger Waldinger argues, however, that "ethnic niches" within the deindustrialized economy of New York City still offer economic mobility to many immigrant groups. Most salient to income inequality, Waldinger argues, is racism within the existing economy rather than some economic transformation that disallows upward mobility. See *Still the Promised City?* 1–32.

16. Watkins-Owens, *Blood Relations*, 66.

17. Kasinitz, *Caribbean New York*, 19–37.

18. Watkins-Owens, *Blood Relations*, 83–84.

19. In 1920 only 4% of West Indian men and 18% of the women had taken U.S. citizenship, as compared to 49% of European men and 53% of the women (Basch, Schiller, and Szanton Blanc, *Nations Unbound*, 66).

20. See Basch, "Politics of Caribbeanization."

21. Kasinitz, *Caribbean New York*, 91–92.

22. Basch, Schiller, and Szanton Blanc, *Nations Unbound*.

23. *New York Amsterdam News*, February 28, 1923, 2.

24. Watkins-Owens, *Blood Relations*, 172.

25. Kasinitz, *Caribbean New York*, 25.

26. D. Hill, *Calypso Callaloo*, 114–144.

27. "Resolution Adopted by the 43rd Annual Convention of the NAACP," in *The Crisis*, August–September 1952.

28. *New York Times*, January 6, 1961, 10.

29. See *New York Times*, September 6, 1993, 17.

30. In 1940 the federal census estimated the total Indian population of Minnesota at 12,528. Of these, 875 lived in urban areas, including Duluth, Minneapolis, and St. Paul (Minnesota Division of Social Welfare, Indian Study, 1948, Minnesota Human Service Department Library, Box 10, American Indians, Social Welfare History Archives, University of Minnesota [hereafter SWHA]). Shoemaker asserts that most urban Indians during the 1940s and 1950s lived in the Indian neighborhood of South Minneapolis ("Urban Indians," 444).

31. Alan Sorkin estimates that 23,000 Indians, or 32% of all able-bodied males between the ages of 18 and 50, served in the armed forces during World War II; 90,000 Indian people left reservations in 1943–44 for war work (*Urban American Indian*, 25). In Minnesota, 1,074 Indian men and women served in the military, while 1,800 were employed in defense work ("The Indian in Minnesota: Report to Governor C. Elmer Anderson by the Governor's Interracial Commission," 1952, 55, in Minnesota Human Service Department Library, Box 10, American Indians, SWHA).

32. Iverson, *"We Are Still Here,"* 132–135.

33. Philp, *Termination Revisited*, 99.

34. Iverson, *"We Are Still Here,"* 132.

35. "Chest and Council responsibility concerning the ever-increasing problem of the Indians," Community Chest 8 Council memorandum, September 1, 1955, SWHA. South Minneapolis is still a center of the Minneapolis Indian community, although the Elliot Park neighborhood was partially demolished by the building of Interstate 94.

36. See Neils, "Reservation to City," on Chicago; Weibel-Orlando, *Indian Country, L.A.,* on Los Angeles; and Guillemin, *Urban Renegades,* on Boston.

37. Richard Drinnon, *Keeper of Concentration Camps,* does an excellent job of arguing that the two relocations are deeply connected, by administrative personnel as well as by the operative institutional logic, a kind of bellicose variant of ethnicity theory.

38. Omi and Winant write: "Ethnicity theory is therefore primarily concerned with questions of group identity; with the resolution of tensions between the twin pressures of assimilation (dissolution of group identity) and cultural pluralism (preservation of group identity); and with the prospects for political integration via normal political channels"(*Racial Formation,* 52).

39. "The Problems and Needs of Indians in Urban Centers, with Some Consideration of Reservation Life," an address to the National Conference on Social Welfare, Los Angeles, May 28, 1964, by Kent FitzGerald, Superintendent, Crownpoint Subagency, Crownpoint, N.M., U.S. Bureau of Indian Affairs, in Community Health and Welfare Council, SWHA (hereafter CHWC).

40. DeRosier, "Indian Relocation," 458–459.

41. Dorene Day, interview, Indian Family Services, Minneapolis, January 1994. A 1956 report on Native American applicants for welfare in the Twin Cities found that "some have been given small amounts of $15.00 or $20.00 by some welfare board and advised to move to the city to find employment. In many cases, serious need arises before a pay check is received" (Welfare Task Committee, "The Minnesota Indian in Minneapolis," 1956, 12, in Minnesota Human Service Department Library, Box 10, American Indians, SWHA).

42. Proceedings of the Governor's Interstate Indian Conference, St. Paul, March 14, 1950, 12, ibid.

The "special status" of Indian people led to contradictory policies. In 1956 the BIA offered vocational training programs, for example, but to qualify for them, Indian people had to be enrolled in a tribe or living on a reservation or trust land. Similarly, PL 874 in 1957 said that Indian children would receive school aid if their parents lived or worked on federal property.

43. The program was significantly reformulated twice after its inception: once under the Indian Vocational Training Act of 1956, to provide better job training, and again under a Kennedy task force in 1961, to emphasize employment closer to home. It bears emphasizing here, however, that even a 1955 congressional review suggesting the allocation of more money for industrial and natural resource development closer to the reservation was ignored by the BIA.

44. Horse Capture, *Powwow,* 8.

45. Ibid., 30.

46. Jim Clermont, interview, Minneapolis Indian Center, June 1994.

47. One source estimates that 25–50% of Minnesota Indians left reservations to join the army or work in war industries (Lundquist, *Indians of Minnesota.*)

48. Jim Clermont interview; Johnny Smith, interview, Heart of the Earth School, Minneapolis, November 1994.

49. Quoted in "Bridging the Gap, the Twin Cities Native American Community," Minnesota Advisory Committee to the U.S. Commission on Civil Rights, January 1975, 21, in SWHA.

50. *Peace Pipe,* June 1956, p. 1.

51. Quoted in Basch, Schiller, and Szanton Blanc, *Nations Unbound,* 78.

52. M. F. Jacobson, *Special Sorrows;* Von Eschen, *Race against Empire.*

53. Gilroy, *"There Ain't No Black in the Union Jack,"* 37.

54. D. Hill, *Calypso Callaloo,* 44–64.

55. E. Hill, *Trinidad Carnival,* 100.

56. These balls are still held in the form of parties sponsored by immigrant associations throughout the year, some of them at the time Carnival is celebrated in the Caribbean, some during the New York Labor Day Carnival season.

57. Von Eschen, *Race against Empire,* 13.

58. Victor Brady, telephone interview, New York, August 1993. Brady remembered another incident from his experiences playing pan in Harlem during this period. Victor Brady's Twenty-one Piece Villa Theresa Steel Orchestra performed for Elijah Muhammad, leader of the Nation of Islam. In that context, he claimed, Caribbean steel drums became a symbol of Black pride and innovation. "Elijah Muhammad called me a genuis," he recalled. "He put me on stage and said, 'We don't need the white man. This boy can make music from these cans!' "

59. "165,000 Watched West Indies Labor Day Parade," *Amsterdam News,* September 13, 1958, 18.

60. Kasinitz, *Caribbean New York,* 134.

61. "Anti-Riot Injunction Lifted in New York," *The Militant,* September 28, 1964, in Vertical File, Harlem Riots, Schomburg Center for Research in Black Culture, New York.

62. "Services to newly urbanized Indians," 1961, in SWHA.

63. "Bridging the Gap: The Twin Cities Native American Community," Minnesota Advisory Committee to U.S. Commission on Civil Rights, January 1975, in Box 5, CHWC.

64. Myer spent $2 million under the Johnson-O'Malley Act to subsidize local school districts taking in Indian children (Philp, *Termination Revisited,* 97); in the Twin Cities this idea of mainstreaming often backfired and led to astronomical dropout levels among Indian students.

65. Confusion about who was to provide these services prevails throughout the social welfare literature of the 1950s and 1960s. See "The Minnesota Indian in Minneapolis: A Report of the Indian Committee," Fred Barger, Chairman, November 1956, 6; and "Working draft of plan for improving the situation of Minnesota Indians in urban areas," June 18, 1962, both in CHWC. Similarly, in this period, responsibility for education and health care switched from specifically Indian agencies to general ones with disastrous, and quickly reversed, results. In 1969 a League of Women Voters study found that one-third of social service agencies "were less successful with Indians than with other clients"

("Statement to United Fund Review Committee," September 14, 1969, in Box 4, American Indians, CHWC).

66. A "Welfare Task Committee" in 1956 was made up of representatives of the Hennepin County Welfare Board, the Minneapolis Division of Public Relief, the Salvation Army, American Indians, Inc., and the Traveler's Aid Society.

67. Shoemaker, "Urban Indians," 433–437.

68. American Indians, Inc., was sponsored by the Minnesota Interracial Commission in 1950 (ibid., 453).

69. "Minnesota Indian in Minneapolis," 2.

70. Shoemaker, "Urban Indians and Ethnic Choices," 435.

71. *Upper Midwest American Indian Center News,* December 15, 1961; "To Help Indians: Statements from Sixteen Different Twin City Organizations," Waite Neighborhood House, 1962, in Box 4, American Indians, CHWC.

72. "To Help Indians."

73. Ron Libertus, interview, University of Minnesota, Minneapolis, October 1994.

74. American Indian Center Organization Committee, July 1964, in Box 4, American Indians, folder "American Indian Centers Review, 1969 Study," CHWC.

75. Day may have been referring to a group called the Indian Native Council of Minneapolis Education (INCOME), which lobbied the Minneapolis schools for better treatment of Indian students and more parental control of federal funds. See Max Nichols Star, "Indians Voice School Demands," *Minneapolis Star,* October 30, 1974.

In 1975, Indians at South High School had a 24% dropout rate. Citywide, Indian students had an attendance rate of 83.7%, compared to 90% for the general population. Though Indians accounted for 5% of students in Minneapolis public schools, only 1% of school employees were Indians: 21 teachers and staff, 61 "non-professional staff," no principals, no assistant principals ("Indian Education Statistics," *Minneapolis Star,* February 10, 1975).

76. Norine Smith, interview, Indian Health Board, Minneapolis, January 1994. Smith, then head of the Indian Health Board in Minneapolis, was in direct conflict with the AIM leadership in Minneapolis at the time.

77. See Haar, *Between the Idea and the Reality;* Frieden and Kaplan, *Politics of Neglect;* Fainstein and Fainstein, *View from Below.*

78. See Peroff, *Menominee Drums;* Fixico, *Termination and Relocation.* Philp points out that termination and relocation resulted in an *increase* of federal expenditures through the BIA, rather than the promised "getting the government out of the Indian business" (*Termination Revisited,* 154).

79. Folder, "American Indian Centers Review, 1969 Study," meeting of April 3, 1969, in Box 4, American Indians, CHWC.

80. "Proposal for an American Indian Urban Opportunity Center," 1968, ibid.

81. Emily Peake to Members of the Citizen Community Centers Board, October 24, 1968, memo, ibid.

82. The Minneapolis American Indian Center was the first building designed explicitly for use as an urban Indian cultural center. See Krinsky, *Contemporary Native American Architecture,* 162.

In 1969 Ron Libertus's controversial Model Cities proposal, "Social Development: Provision of Adequate Social Environment," listed the following, divided into categories: "Organizations who service the American Indian public and are Indian in scope and have some board members who are American Indians" (Department of Indian Work, Model Neighborhood, Episcopal Center, Pilot Center); "Organizations who service the Indian public and are Indian in scope with the majority of board members being Indian" (North Side Teen Council, South Side Teen Council, Indian AFDC League, Broken Arrow Service Guild, Sioux Council of the Twin Cities, St. Paul Indian Center, North Side Concerned Citizens, American Indian Movement, Upper Midwest American Indian Center, Indian Education Committee, American Indian Citizen Community Center, Twin Cities Chippewa Tribal Council, STAIRS, Upward Bound, St. Paul Indian Dance Club, Inter Tribal Council, St. Paul Indian Youth Group, Singspiration, Duluth Indian Club) (Box 4, American Indians, CHWC).

83. American Indian Movement to Citizens Community Centers Board of Directors, January 28, 1969, ibid.

84. Quoted in Ebbott, *Indians in Minnesota*, 1.

85. An article in the *Minneapolis Tribune*, May 26, 1969, claimed that the Model Cities program pitted Indian and African-American organizations against each other. Similarly, in the final report of the American Indian Centers Study Committee, the group wondered if: "perhaps another reason for the fact that no solid and productive Indian Center got established is the result of the prevailing opinion that integration of the races was the goal, and that establishing an Indian Center or Centers would lead to separation or self-segregation" (February 6, 1969, 2). Both in folder "American Indian Centers Review, 1969 Study," ibid.

86. *AIM Newsletter*, February 12, 1969, ibid.

87. Pamphlet, May 1975, in Box 4, American Indians, CHWC.

88. Kasinitz, *Caribbean New York*, 38–89; J.R. Mintz, *Hasidic People*, 139–153

89. Hill and Abrahamson, "West Indian Carnival"; Kasinitz and Friedenberg-Herbstein, "Puerto Rican Parade"; Carlos Lezama, telephone interview, Brooklyn, 1992.

90. File "West Indian Carnival," Local History Room, Brooklyn Public Library.

91. Nunley, "Masquerade Mix-up," 166; see also Hill and Abrahamson, "West Indian Carnival," 24; Kasinitz, *Caribbean New York*, 14; Manning, "Overseas Caribbean Carnivals," 30.

92. The Harlem Riots marked the 1960s discovery of northern Black America for the mainstream press. The cover story in *Time*, July 31, 1964, reads:

> No walls surround the ghetto except the invisible ones that can be the hardest of all to surmount. Harlem's Negroes have withdrawn behind the invisible walls, almost out of necessity, into a world of their own, complete with its own pride, its own lingo, and even its own time. In Harlem, CPT means "Colored People's Time," and it runs one full hour behind white people's time.

93. *New York Times*, September 4, 1973, 43.

94. *New York Daily News*, May 2, 1971, B72.

95. *New York Times*, August 18, 1974, B10–11.

96. Ibid., September 3, 1974, 43.

97. *Antillean Echo*, January 1973, 8.

98. *New York Amsterdam News*, September 9, 1978.

99. Manning, "Overseas Caribbean Carnival."

100. Kasinitz, *Caribbean New York*, 33.

101. *New York Amsterdam News*, September 8, 1979, 3, and September 22, 1979, 15; *New York Daily News*, September 6, 1979, 2. The possibility of conflict between Black and Jewish residents of Crown Heights was very real during the late 1970s, though the rumors were probably spurious on this occasion. Responding to harassment of yeshiva students and the murder of Israel Turner in 1975, Hasidim organized "Maccabee patrols" to provide a security they increasingly felt was threatened. In 1978 a sixteen-year-old Black youth, Victor Rhodes, was beaten senseless by a group of young Hasidim. The Black United Front was organized in Crown Heights to counter both the police and the Hasidim. The Reverend Heron Sam, a Guyanese community leader, spoke openly of Blacks' fear of "Zionist expansion" in the neighborhood. See J. R. Mintz, *Hasidic People*, for an excellent account of the politics of race and anti-Semitism in Crown Heights.

102. *New York Daily News*, September 6, 1979, K1.

103. A. Cohen, *Masquerade Politics*, 66–67.

104. *New York Amsterdam News*, August 23, 1980.

105. *Times* (London), September 1, 1976, 1.

106. Joyce Quinoma, Interview, Culture of Black Creation mas' camp, Brooklyn, August 1992.

107. *New York Amsterdam News*, September 22, 1979, 15.

108. *Antillean Echo*.

109. For the differences between Carnival and the St. Patrick's Day parade in New York, see Corrette, "You Can Kiss Me If I'm Irish."

110. Bridges, "Policing the Urban Wasteland," 32.

111. In 1971, Heart of the Earth Survival School and Red School House were founded in the Twin Cities by Indian parents in concert with the American Indian Movement; a state judge had threatened to penalize an Indian couple if they did not enroll their children in school. Title IV of the Indian Education Act amended the 1936 Johnson-O'Malley Act to provide for bilingual and bicultural education. The Survival School's funding comes through these two acts, along with contributions from the tribes, foundations, corporations, and individuals. See Ebbott, *Indians in Minnesota*, 144.

112. This phrase is borrowed from George Lipsitz's important book *Time Passages*.

113. Hokie Clermont and Opie Day, interview, Little Red Schoolhouse, St. Paul, June 1994.

114. Malinda Hannel, interview, Mdewakaton Dakota Powwow Grounds, Shakopee, Minn., August 1994. My count of license plates at these two powwows was revealing. In Hinckley, at a powwow given by an Ojibwa band, the license plates were predominantly Minnesota and Wisconsin, with several from Red Lake, Leech Lake, and Mille Lacs; I spotted a few from Iowa, Oklahoma, and Ontario, and a scattering from New York, Arizona, Oregon, and Louisiana. At the Mdewakanton Dakota powwow, licenses from Minnesota and South

Dakota dominated, with quite a number from Red Lake, Wisconsin, and North Dakota, and a showing from Nebraska, Montana, Missouri, and Canadian provinces.

115. Szewd and Abrams, *After Africa,* 34.

116. See D. Hill, *Calypso Callaloo.*

117. Palmer, "Memories of the Notting Hill Carnival," 21.

118. Foner, "West Indians," 92.

119. Kasinitz, *Caribbean New York,* 155–156.

120. *New York Daily News,* September 13, 1981, B6, and September 9, 1983, KI 3.

121. According to Jerome Mintz, Hasidim filled a demographic vacuum in the early 1960s, as other white ethnics—predominantly other Jews—were fleeing the city and African-Americans and Caribbean people had not yet moved into the area in sizable numbers. As Jewish groups left the city, the Lubavitch Hasidim gained control of the Jewish Community Council of Crown Heights, and for a time were the only effective neighborhood organization able to take advantage of government loan programs initiated to fight urban decay (*Hasidic People,* 141–143).

122. As reported in the *New York Times,* September 28, 1975: "A neighbor said Mrs. Turner was composed, even though she saw her husband fall before her. 'She told me that she and her husband had been inmates in the Auschwitz concentration camp, had seen members of their family tortured and had learned to have strength for things like that' "(quoted ibid., 143).

123. Jacob Goldstein, interview, Manhattan Housing Authority, August 1993.

124. By 1981, whites in Crown Heights, 9.3% of the population, controlled 33% of Community Development funds.

125. Smith, *Fires in the Mirror.*

126. My information on 1994 Carnival comes from "The Politics of Carnival," *Village Voice,* September 6, 1994, 30–32.

127. Ibid., 30.

128. See Institute for Natural Progress, "Unusual and Accustomed Places: Contemporary American Indian Fishing Rights Struggles," in Jaimes, *State of Native America.*

CHAPTER 5. SOUNDS OF BROOKLYN

Many people in Brooklyn generously shared their time, perspectives, and stories with me. I thank these people for reaching across the many kinds of identity that separate us to talk to me. The people whose time and stories made this chapter possible are Judy Henry, Jerry LeGendre, Troy Frances, Clive Bradley, Herman Sooknanan, Tony Josephs, Jesse Miller, and Jamaal King at Metro Steel; Cristol Forde, Gale Francis, Ken "Professor" Philmore, Derrick, Rendrick Roach, Colleen, Mack Scott, and Chocko and Dennis Coffee at BWIA Sonatas; Keitha Thompson, Leslie Ward, and Suzanne of Fort Greene; Earl Alleyne and Heather Findlay at CASYM; Trevor Johns, Tom, and Gus at Basement Recording Studios; Nancy Grey at British West Indian Airlines; Donna Fields at the *New York Daily News;* Les Slater and other members of the Trinidad and Tobago Folk Arts

Society; Dan Simon, Rudy King, Victor Brady, Steve Stuempfle, and Ray Allen, pan historians and promoters; and many other people who talked to me in and around Brooklyn pan yards.

Also helpful were discussions at "West Indian Migration to New York: Historical, Contemporary, and Transnational Perspectives," Research Institute for the Study of Man, New York, April 16–17, 1999, organized by Nancy Foner.

    1. Donna Fields, Public Relations Office of the *Daily News,* telephone interview, September 2, 1993.

    2. In the 1870s, as colonial authorities began clamping down on new Afro-Creole practices of masquerading at Carnival, the Madrasi Hindu fire-pass festival was banned; in the 1880s, such restrictions resulted in both the Canboulay Riots and the Muharram Massacre at the Muslim festival of Hosay (Brereton, "Social Organization," 52); see also K. Singh, *Bloodstained Tombs.*

    3. See Stuempfle, *Steelband Movement,* 45–53. Ancil Neil says that Laventille, among other places, was traditionally known as a "Shango" area because of its association with the most African, lower-class aspects of Trinidadian society (*Voices from the Hills,* 27).

    4. Stuempfle, *Steelband Movement,* 40. Bridget Brereton traces the complexities of Trinidad working-class ethnicity in "Social Organization," 33–55, as well as in *History of Modern Trinidad.* See also K. Singh, *Race and Class.*

    5. Stuempfle, *Steelband Movement,* 47–50.

    6. See Kasinitz, *Caribbean New York;* Nash and Fernández-Kelly, *Women, Men.* Roger Waldinger notes that the gendered division of labor among Caribbean immigrants is particularly salient among the "ethnic niches" of health care work and apparel; in 1990, 44% of West Indian women were employed in such niches, while only 20% of West Indian men found work in the same settings (*Still the Promised City?* 121).

    7. At the same time that West Indian immigrants brought their cultural practices north, increased postwar affluence for the U.S. white middle class funded an expansion of tourism in the economically underdeveloped islands. As the popularity of calypso tunes such as "Yellow Bird" and "Marianne" in the late 1950s and early 1960s attests, tourism led to a temporary surge in U.S. popular interest in Caribbean music.

    Record companies such as Decca and Black Swan recorded music in the Caribbean during the 1930s and 1940s; at the same time, famous calypsonians circulated throughout North America. After the war, African American entertainers such as Harry Belafonte, Ella Fitzgerald, and Louis Jordan and such white Americans as the Andrews Sisters popularized Caribbean music in the States. For a detailed history of the calypso and steel band music craze in the United States, see D. Hill, *Calypso Callaloo.*

    In Trinidad, Laventille bands such as Desperados began to attract corporate sponsorship from both Caribbean and multinational sources during the 1960s. With support from the West Indian Tobacco Company and Coca-Cola, Desperados steel band members attended the First World Festival of Negro Arts in 1966, toured Africa in 1968, and played in the United Kingdom and the United States during 1975 and 1976 (Neil, *Voices from the Hills*).

8. Rudy King, interview, Brooklyn, August 1992.

9. "The 1940s, like the 1870s, was a period of extensive migration, urban overcrowding, and more prevalent prostitution" (Stuempfle, *Steelband Movement*, 70).

10. See Hoetink, "Race and Color" and *Slavery and Race Relations*; Mintz, *Caribbean Transformations*.

11. Williams sponsored the Best Village Competition for steel bands, frequently visited pan yards such as Desperados in Laventille, and in 1965 promoted the passage of the Industrial Stabilization Act, which encouraged both the investment of multinational companies in Trinidad and the support of such multinationals for the steel bands (Stuempfle, *Steelband Movement*, 118–144).

At the same time, Williams's People's National Movement advocated grassroots African forms at the expense of a more multiethnic, inclusive national history. The rival People's Democratic Party (PDP) was led by the East Indian head of the sugar workers' union (Yelvington, *Trinidad Ethnicity*, "Introduction"). Daniel Segal writes: "Thus Williams and the PNM took up the banner of 'creolisation,' but this ideology constructed 'Trinidadian' and 'national' as Afro-Trinidadian-derived culture and labeled practices (such as 'East Indian' culture) which deviated from such a process as 'racist' and 'unpatriotic'" ("Race and Color," 101.)

12. Corporations as diverse as Esso, Mobil, Shell, Pan Am, Coca-Cola, Angostura, Texaco, Guinness, Chase Manhattan, British West Indian Airways (BWIA), Hilton, Carib, and Kirpalani supported the steel band movement in the late 1950s and 1960s.

For an account of the development of the steel band as a grass-roots Laventille form, see Neil, *Voices from the Hills;* also "Steelband," the mimeographed newsletter of the West Indian–American Calypso Association. D. Hill, *Calypso Callaloo*, and Stuempfle, *Steelband Movement*, discuss the association of the steel band movement with the labor uprisings led by Uriah "Buzz" Butler during the later 1930s and early 1940s.

13. Les Slater, interview, Brooklyn, 1992.

14. The dilemma that Partha Chatterjee points out in *Nationalist Thought*—the undermining of emancipatory discourses of postcolonial nation formation by the racialized and capitalistic hierarchies embedded in Enlightenment ideas of liberation—finds a structural echo in metropolitan reliance on nineteenth-century models of ethnicity and assimilation to rationalize urban politics.

15. It has been suggested to me that this situation may be shifting somewhat since 1992; Indo-Trinidadian im/migrants may be returning to Carnival. The subject was discussed at "West Indian Migration to New York: Historical, Contemporary, and Transnational Perspectives," Research Institute for the Study of Man, New York, April 16–17, 1999.

16. This discussion is based on Stuempfle, *Steelband Movement*, 72–75. See also Wilson, "Reputation vs. Respectability"; Abrahams, "Reputation vs. Respectability."

17. For analyses of zoot-suiters, see Kelley, *Race Rebels*, 161–181; Cosgrove, "Zoot Suit and Style Warfare"; Daniels, "Los Angeles Zoot."

18. Stuempfle, *Steeldrum Movement*, 51–52.

19. The existence of these bases was both a spur to the development of political and cultural radicalism in Trinidad and motivation for government repression of both during the war (Brereton, *History of Modern Trinidad,* 189).

20. Stuempfle, *Steelband Movement,* 178.

21. Leslie Ward, interview, Brooklyn, August 1992.

22. See Prell, *Fighting to Become Americans;* Gabaccia, *From the Other Side.*

23. As Paul Gilroy puts it, "gender is the modality in which race is lived" (*Black Atlantic,* 85).

24. As Mikhail Bakhtin has pointed out, such genealogies tend to take the form of an epic story, featuring true heroes and classical struggles between the forces of good and evil (*Dialogic Imagination,* 259–422).

25. At the same time, it is worth noting that the story of pan as the forward progress of Afro-Caribbean culture is also a construction, tending to elide Indo-Trinidadian grass-roots contributions. Daniel Segal notes that the nationalist embrace of Africanized forms ironically tends both to prioritize Afro-Trinidadians and to imply that they are also, somehow, culturally naked without nationalist endorsement ("Living Ancestors").

26. Brennan, "National Longing for Form," 51.

27. For an exigesis of the relationship between such Enlightenment categories and the construction of racist discourse, see Goldberg, *Racist Culture.*

28. See Sowell, *Ethnic America;* Omi and Winant, *Racial Formation.*

29. As Daniel and Jonathan Boyarin perceptively write, "The pathos of notions such as assimilation, cultural demise, and cultural survival grows precisely out of the ways in which they are embedded in political processes of domination and exploitation" ("Diaspora," 705).

30. R. Hill, "Dreadlocks."

31. D. Hill, *Calypso Callaloo,* 203. On one level, then, this is a liberatory process, where nationalist narrative goes about "reclaiming community from within boundaries defined by the very power whose presence denied community" (Brennan, "National Longing for Form," 58).

32. See Segal, "Living Ancestors."

33. I want to hold open here the possibility that what is dismissed by academics as "essentialism" may be a semiotic container for ontological categories that fall outside the rational capacity of Enlightenment thought. See Harraway, "Situated Knowleges."

34. See Radhakrishnan, "Nationalism, Gender."

35. Signifying a loyalty to a nation abroad is quite a different thing than acting patriotically at home, as the Boyarins note: "Practices that in Diaspora have one meaning . . . have entirely different meanings under political hegemony" ("Diaspora," 713).

36. While Brooklyn pan yards can be said to represent a range of im/migrant negotiations, steel band music has also been significantly affected by the transnational circulation of capital, people, and ideas. Musically, the development of the steel band has been influenced by traditions as diverse as European classical music, American jazz, and the cross-pollination of soul and calypso music in soca (*soul calypso*). Continuing a tradition that began as early as the 1930s, Caribbean music today is often recorded, produced, and distributed in small storefront

companies in Brooklyn—B's Music, Charlie's Records, Straker Records. Caribbean musicians often live between two worlds, traveling to perform in both the islands and the mainland. Donald Hill points out that there is a long tradition of Caribbean music being recorded in New York before being shipped back to the islands for distribution. This practice has sometimes functioned to elude government censorship of political or sexually explicit music; at the same time, it contributes to the formation of a transnational culture (*Calypso Callaloo*).

37. Lamuel Stanislaus, telephone interview, August 1993; Earl Alleyne, interview, Brooklyn, August 1993.

38. This decentralization can have both radical and centrist implications. On one level, New York politics became increasingly polarized by race after the divisive struggle over local control at Ocean Hill–Brownsville and the Civilian Review Board referendum of 1966. This ended a phase of civil rights coalition between African-Americans, West Indian–Americans, and progressive white ethnics. See Rogowski, Gold, and Abbott, "Police," and Marilyn Gittell, "Education." Joe Austin brought these discussions to my attention.

39. Stuempfle, *Steelband Movement*, 145–156.

40. Nancy Grey, British West Indian Airways, telephone interview, August 1993; Alleyne interview.

41. Mary Waters asserts that middle-class Caribbean people hold onto their national and ethnic identifications in order to avoid identification with African-Americans, whom they perceive as lower-class and less ambitious ("Ethnic and Racial Identities").

This observation raises several questions. As far as class is concerned, Frances and two of the other young women I interviewed at Sonatas perceive themselves as professionally oriented and college bound. Two of the women were studying to be doctors. But financial limitations make it difficult to stay in college; Caribbean students often wind up studying in the City University system, which slots them into the lower-paying paraprofessions, such as dental hygiene and medical technology. So the racialized landscape of the urban United States plays a role in the class aspirations as well as the realized professional ambitions of second-generation Caribbeans.

As for cultural identification, all the second-generation players I interviewed talked about having two or more groups of friends: a group who played pan, some who listened to rap, others who listened to classical. Frances talked about explaining steel band music to African-American friends in Virginia. Trevor Johns emphasized the ongoing connections between African-American and Caribbean forms: "Bob Marley grew up on James Brown. And if you listen to early Bob Marley, it's straight-up funk, and *that* goes back to the whole gospel tradition."

It is possible that the young pan players I spoke to correspond with a section of Waters's sample whom she characterizing as having "an immigrant attitude toward their identities"; some 28% of the second-generation im/migrants she interviewed "had a strong identity, such as Jamaican or Trinidadian, but did not evidence much distancing from American blacks. Rather, their identities were strongly linked to their experiences on the islands, and they did not worry much about how they were seen by other Americans, white or black" (ibid., 179).

42. See Rosaldo, *Culture and Truth;* Hobsbawm and Ranger, *Invention of Tradition.*

43. Homi Bhabha writes: "The origins of national traditions turn out to be as much acts of affiliation and establishment as they are moments of disavowal, displacement, exclusion and cultural contestation" (*Nation and Narration,* 5).

CHAPTER 6. GENDER AND GENERATION DOWN THE RED ROAD

I am indebted to the insights and kindness of many people who went to pow-wows with me or talked to me about them. They include Dale Kakkak, Dorene Day, Ariana Day, Julie Beaulieu, Gina Artishon, Opie Day, Hokie Clermont, Norine Smith, Karal Ann Coffey, DaLynn Alley, Jim Clermont, Johnny Smith, Ron Libertus, Ellie Favel, Debbie Ironshield, and Fern Mousseaux.

Portions of this chapter appeared as "Gender and Generation Down the Red Road," in *Generations of Youth: Youth Cultures in Twentieth-Century America,* ed. Joe Austin and Michael Nevin Willard (New York: New York University Press, 1998). They appear here by the generous permission of New York University Press.

The term "colonial optics" is taken from the writings of Ranajit Guha, whose excellent analysis of the semiotics of colonialism sets the tone for much of my thinking here. See "Prose of Counter-Insurgency."

1. See Powers, *War Dance,* 59; also Kavanagh, "Southern Plains Dance"; Huenemann, "Northern Plains Dance."

2. Karel Ann Coffey and DaLynn Alley, interview, Powwow Arena, Mille Lacs Band Ojibwa Casino, Hinckley, Minn., July 1994.

3. Johnny Smith, interview, Heart of the Earth Survival School, Minneapolis, November 1994.

4. Green, "Tribe Called Wannabee," 33. As Green further points out, it is common for both whites and African-Americans to claim Indian blood, particularly to claim Indian princess grandmothers. Whites who make this claim, Green argues, do not expect a diminishing of their white skin privilege, but rather an amplification of their sense of individual uniqueness, of historical richness and depth (ibid., 45–47). The moment of photo opportunity, the sighting of the exotic Indian maiden, must not be contiguous with contemporary urban Indians, or the mythology of wildness, of freedom, is undermined. See also P. Deloria, *Playing Indian.*

This ideology of free access to Indian ancestry with social impunity through the bloodline of the mythical princess may well naturalize the moment of photo opportunity. Even for those who do not go so far as to claim actual Indian blood kin, Indians, particularly Indian women, are icons of American beauty, easy to claim as a national treasure. It is important that this free adoption of Indian identity comes through the feminine, through the mythical princess grandmother. The racial boundaries and class distinctions authored by the project of colonization are indistinguishable without the crucial category of gender (Cooper and Stoler, "Introduction," 613). As Ann Stoler writes: "Sexuality illustrates the iconography of rule, not its pragmatics: sexual asymmetries are tropes to depict other centers of power" ("Making Empire Respectable," 635). Colonialist optics, then, are crucially gendered.

See my essay "Tecumseh, Tenskwatawa, and the National Popular"; Churchill, *Fantasies of the Master Race*; Root, *Cannibal Culture*.

5. Horse Capture, *Powwow*, 42.

6. Eric Hobsbawm and Terence Ranger define "invented traditions" as "responses to novel situations which take the form of reference to old situations, or which establish their own past by quasi-obligatory repetition. It is the contrast between the constant change and innovation of the modern world and the attempt to structure at least some part of social life within it as unchanging and invariant" (*Invention of Tradition*, 1).

7. "Powwow" is derived from a Narragansett word meaning a curing ceremony. It passed into contemporary native English to mean "a secular event featuring group singing and social dancing by men, women, and children" (Kavanagh, "Southern Plains Dance," 105).

8. *Healthy Nations*, Heart of the Earth Survival School Powwow, May 1994 (pamphlet).

9. Powers traces the diffusion of the Lakota Grass Dance to the late nineteenth century (*War Dance*, 71).

10. *Pow Wow Time*, 1992.

11. Lipsitz, *Dangerous Crossroads*, 19.

12. See Burgess, "Canadian 'Range Wars.' "

13. H. Bhabha, *Location of Culture*, 91.

14. For a sense of how extensive this circuit has become, see *Powwow 1995 Calendar* or any Indian newspaper.

15. Malinda Hanell, interview, Mdewakaton Dakota Powwow Grounds, Shakopee, Minn., August 1994.

16. See Martin and Seagrave, *Anti-Rock*, esp. chaps. 1 and 3.

17. Horse Capture, *Powwow*, 10.

18. Ibid., 36.

19. The Indian Health Board sponsored a contest powwow in 1992. Cash prizes were as follows: drum contest: first, $1,000; second, $800; third, $600; fourth, $400; fifth, $300. Adult (18–44) dance events (ten events: Men's Senior Traditional, Men's Traditional, Ladies' Senior Traditional, Ladies' Traditional, Jingle Dress, Ladies' Buckskin, Ladies' Cloth, Men's Grass Dance, Men's Fancy Dance, Men's Straight/Southern): first, $700; second, $600; third, $500; fourth, $400; fifth, $300; sixth, $200. Junior categories (11–17): first, $300 (Indian Health Board Powwow Notebook, courtesy of Norine Smith, Director, Indian Health Board).

20. Bob Larson, interview, Fort Snelling State Park, St. Paul, September 1994.

21. Patrick Guineau, interview, Dakota Powwow Grounds, August 1994.

22. Julie Beaulieu, interview, People of Philips Office, Minneapolis, October 1994.

23. See Burgess, "Canadian 'Range Wars.' "

24. Norine Smith, interview, Indian Health Board, Minneapolis, November 1994.

25. Dorene Day, interview, Indian Family Services, Minneapolis, January 1994.

26. Opie Day and Hokie Clermont of The Boyz drum group, interview, Red School House, St. Paul, June 1994.

27. McRobbie, "Shut Up and Dance," 407.

28. Debbie Ironshield, interview, Heart of the Earth School, Minneapolis, April 1994.

29. According to the 1980 census, 24.4% of Indian men and 15.7% of Indian women in Minnesota were unemployed; the disparity is higher in Minneapolis, where 28% of men and only 16.2% of women were unemployed. In the same year 38% of Indian families in Minnesota were headed by women, 57% in Minneapolis (Ebbott, *Indians in Minnesota*, 159).

30. Stoler, "Making Empire Respectable," 651.

31. Fern Mousseaux, Oglala Nation Powwow Committee, telephone interview, August 1994.

32. Gina Artishon, interview, Carol's Diner, Minneapolis, July 1994. For an analysis of connections between blood quantum rules and racism, see M. Annette Jaimes, "Federal Indian Identification Policy: A Usurpation of Indigenous Sovereignty in North America," in her *State of Native America.*

33. McRobbie, "Shut Up and Dance," 409.

34. Rose, *Black Noise,* 163.

AFTERWORD: POLITICAL ECONOMIES OF HOME

1. Kaplan, *Questions of Travel,* 182.

2. See Priscilla Wald's discussion of Gertrude Stein's use of the same metaphor, in *Constituting Americans,* 252–253.

3. Ibid., 279.

4. Lomawaima, "Domesticity," 203.

5. See Fernández-Kelly and Schauffler, "Divided Fates."

6. See Espiritu, *Asian-American Women and Men,* 43–49; Prell, *Fighting to Become Americans,* 17–20.

7. Gilroy, *Black Atlantic,* 85. Prell writes, "Tensions between minority men and women, at least symbolically, represent how each gender understands his or her place in the larger society" (*Fighting to Become Americans,* 19).

8. Connolly, "Tocqueville, Territory, and Violence," 110.

9. Timothy Dunn discusses the convergence of INS, military, and local police forces as a consequence of the War on Drugs, suggesting that the real achievement of this war was not the eradication of the drug trade but the implementation of racialized force throughout the Southwest and California (*Militarization of the U.S.-Mexico Border*).

10. Silko, "Border Patrol State." See also Chang, "Meditation on Borders" and "Toward an Asian-American Legal Scholarship." The momentum of recent legal decisions supports this blurring of rights in favor of the security of the "border patrol state" and the ongoing pursuit of the War on Drugs. See also *Farm Labor Organizing Committee v Ohio State Highway Patrol et al.,* .3, 96CB7580, N.D. Ohio (1998).

11. This number is likely to represent an increase because of the militarization of the border resulting from Operation Gatekeeper. See Anne-Marie O'Connor, "Study Finds Changes in Causes of Border Deaths," *Los Angeles Times,* August 12, 1997. Between 1985 and 1994, between 1,900 and 3,000 persons died at the

U.S.–Texas border alone; Stanley Bailey and his colleagues calculate that this number, representing people of unknown or Latino origin (not Texas citizens), is predominantly made up of undocumented migrants ("Migrant Death at the Texas-Mexico Border").

12. Kaplan, *Questions of Travel,* 110.

13. It's important that these terms are already being revised in academic and policy debates about borders. Would-be protectors of the perennially endangered nation increasingly conflate threats brought by refugees, "illegal aliens," immigrants, and terrorists. This rhetorical success translates into the policy innovations made in the Welfare, Terrorism, and Immigration acts of 1996, but it is continuing as awareness of terrorism within the United States increases. See *Washington Post,* August 9, 1997, A13. Pat Buchanan and Representative (now Senator) Charles Schumer (D-N.Y.) used the discovery of a cache of bombs just above the Atlantic Avenue subway station in Brooklyn to call for a restriction of immigration (Reuters report, August 10, 1997). Both articles were posted on Center for Immigration Studies list, August 11, 1997.

14. See, for example, Brimelow, *Alien Nation.*

15. Georges, *Making of a Transnational Community;* Kearney, "Borders and Boundaries"; Basch, Schiller, and Szanton Blanc, *Nations Unbound.*

16. Schiller, Basch, and Blanc-Szanton, *Towards a Transnational Perspective,* 7.

17. Kaplan, *Questions of Travel,* 110.

18. Bryce-Laporte, "Black Immigrants."

19. Basch, Schiller, and Szanton Blanc, *Nations Unbound,* 8.

20. Kearney, "Borders and Boundaries," 55.

21. For a critical appraisal of the influence of Williams's insights on labor, race, and culture, see Bergquist, *Labor and the Course of American Democracy,* 1–8.

22. Jacobson, *Special Sorrows,* compares the influence of the diasporic consciousness of Polish, Irish, and Eastern European Jewish immigrants on their views of citizenship, race, and foreign policy; see also Winokur's discussion of Charlie Chaplin and the Marx Brothers in *American Laughter* and Jay Hoberman's imaginative history of the Yiddish film industry in *Bridge of Light.* See also Wyman, *Round Trip to America.*

23. Plummer, *Rising Wind.*

24. Gilroy's *Black Atlantic* and *"There Ain't No Black in the Union Jack"* are crucial here. Gilroy writes of the ways in which transnational connections among Afro-diasporic peoples have facilitated the emergence of other networks: "The transnational structures which brought the Black Atlantic world into being have themselves developed and now articulate its myriad cultural forms into a system of global communications" ("Sounds Authentic," 94).

25. Hing, *Making and Remaking Asian America;* Yung, *Unbound Feet.*

26. For crucial discussions of how transnationalism as an intellectual and social paradigm has been shaped from the grass roots, see Kelley, " 'But a Local Phase,' " and Gabaccia, "Is Everywhere Nowhere?"

27. See Bredbenner, *Nationality of Her Own;* Lowe, *Immigrant Acts;* Schneider, "Women Immigrants at the Border."

28. Zavella, "Tables Are Turned," 137.

29. See Roediger, *Wages of Whiteness.*

30. Silko, "Border Patrol State."

31. See my "Building Up Borders."

32. The term "the nations within" comes from Deloria and Lytle, *Nations Within*, but it has a long history in legal rhetoric about Indian nations, dating back to Justice John Marshall's famous term in *Cherokee Nation v. Georgia:* "domestic dependent nations."

33. Silko writes: "The so-called civil wars in El Salvador and Guatemala are actually wars against the indigenous tribal people conducted by the white and mestizo ruling classes. These are genocidal wars conducted to secure Indian land once and for all" ("Border Patrol State," 112–113). She also develops these themes at greater length and depth in *Almanac of the Dead.*

34. Indians became citizens by the Snyder Act of 1924.

35. Lemke-Santangelo, *Abiding Courage.*

36. Gabaccia and Grossman, *Teaching the History of Immigration.*

37. See Barrett and Roediger, "Inbetween Peoples"; Orsi, "Religious Boundaries."

38. Peiss, *Cheap Amusements.*

39. Irma Watkins-Owens points out in *Blood Relations* that many Afro-Caribbean im/migrant women worked in the garment trades, making this point about race, ethnicity, and im/migration in treatments of the period all the more cogent.

40. Bryce-Laporte, "Black Immigrants."

41. Barrett and Roediger, "Religious Boundaries," 4.

42. Peter Kivisto, "Transplanted Then and Now," discusses the transition from the assimilation orientation of early immigration and ethnic historiography to social history's concern with the complexities of transnational identity. Kivisto limits his discussion, however, to changing approaches to the study of European immigrants.

43. For example, she discusses how Progressive reformers neglected living conditions for predominantly male African-American laborers, choosing instead to focus on the "sacrifice of golden boys and girls" of Italian parentage (Hahamovitch, *Fruits of Their Labor,* 38–54).

44. FLOC, for example, works with Mexican farmworkers' unions to attempt to forestall the flight of jobs across the border. Resolution 3 of the Seventh Constitutional Convention of FLOC (Toledo, Ohio, August 1997) calls for ongoing collaboration with Mexican unions to ensure the rights of workers on both sides of the border.

45. Hahamovitch, *Fruits of Their Labor,* 201.

46. Hammar, "State, Nation, and Dual Citizenship," 24–25.

47. D. Jacobson, *Rights across Borders,* 1–18.

References

SECONDARY SOURCES

Ablon, Joan. "American Indian Relocation: Problems of Dependency and Management in the City." *Phylon* 26 (1965).

———. "Relocated American Indians in the San Francisco Bay Area: Social Interaction and Indian Identity." *Human Organization* 23 (Winter 1964).

Abrahams, Roger. "Reputation vs. Respectability: A Review of Peter J. Wilson's Concept." *Revista/Review Interamericana* 9 (1979): 448–453.

Acuña, Rodolfo. *Occupied America: A History of Chicanos.* 3rd ed. New York: Harper & Row, 1988.

Alejandro, Roberto. *Hermeneutics, Citizenship, and the Public Sphere.* Albany: State University of New York Press, 1993.

Ames, David, and Burton R. Fisher. "The Menominee Termination Crisis: Barriers in the Way of a Rapid Cultural Transition." *Human Organization* 18, no. 3 (Fall 1959): 101–111.

Anderson, Benedict. *Imagined Communities: Reflections on the Origin and Spread of Nationalism.* London: Verso/New Left Books, 1983.

Anzaldúa, Gloria. *Borderlands: The New Mestiza/La Frontera.* San Francisco: Spinsters/Aunt Lute, 1987.

Bakhtin, Mikhail. *The Dialogic Imagination: Four Essays.* Austin: University of Texas Press, 1981.

———. *Rabelais and His World.* Trans. Helene Iswolsky. Knoxville: University of Tennessee Press, 1993.

Balibar, Etienne. "Fictive Identity and the Ideal Nation." In *Ethnicity,* ed. John Hutchinson and Anthony D. Smith. New York: Oxford University Press, 1996.

Ball, Eve, with Nora Henn and Lynda A. Sanchez. *Indeh: An Apache Odyssey.* Norman: University of Oklahoma Press, 1988.

Barrett, James R., and David Roediger. "Inbetween Peoples: Race, Nationality, and the 'New Immigrant' Working Class." *Journal of American Ethnic History* 16, no. 3 (Spring 1997): 3–44.

Basch, Linda G. "The Politics of Caribbeanization: Vincentians and Grenadians in New York." In *Caribbean Life in New York City,* ed. Elsa Sutton and Constance Chaney. New York: Center for Migration Studies of New York, 1987.

Basch, Linda G., Nina Glick Schiller, and Cristina Szanton Blanc. *Nations Unbound: Transnational Projects, Postcolonial Predicaments, and Deterritorialized Nation-States.* Langhorne, Pa.: Gordon & Breach, 1994.

Bates, Carla. "Settling the Industrial Frontier, 1890–1940: Being An Historical Study of Anglo-American Social Reformers and Their Struggles to Reconcile Republican Virtue and Industrial Capitalism with Particular Attention to Questions of Property, Citizenship, and the Welfare State." Ph.D. dissertation, Program in American Studies, University of Minnesota, 1998.

Bederman, Gail. *Manliness and Civilization.* Chicago: University of Chicago Press, 1995.

Bell, Daniel. *The End of Ideology: On the Exhaustion of Political Ideas in the Fifties.* Glencoe, Ill.: Free Press, 1960.

Bergquist, Charles. *Labor and the Course of American Democracy: U.S. History in Latin American Perspective.* New York: Verso, 1996.

Bhabha, Homi K. *The Location of Culture.* New York: Routledge, 1994.

———, ed. *Nation and Narration.* New York: Routledge, 1990.

Bhabha, Jacqueline, Francesca Klug, and Sue Shutter, eds. *Worlds Apart: Women under Immigration and Nationality Law.* London: Pluto, 1985.

Bowman, Arlene. "Program Notes." In Two Rivers Film Festival program, Walker Art Center, Minneapolis, 1994.

Boyarin, Daniel, and Jonathan Boyarin. "Diaspora: Generation and the Ground of Jewish Identity." *Critical Inquiry* 19, no 4 (Summer 1993).

Bredbenner, Candice. *A Nationality of Her Own: Women, Marriage, and the Law of Citizenship.* Berkeley: University of California Press, 1998.

Brennan, Timothy. "The National Longing for Form." In *Nation and Narration,* ed. Homi K. Bhabha. New York: Routledge, 1990.

Brereton, Bridget. *A History of Modern Trinidad: 1783–1962.* Port of Spain: Heinemann Educational Books, 1981.

———. "Social Organization and Class: Racial and Cultural Conflict in Nineteenth-Century Trinidad." In *Trinidad Ethnicity,* ed. Kevin Yelvington, 33–55. Knoxville: University of Tennessee Press, 1993.

Bridges, Lee. "Policing the Urban Wasteland." *Race and Class* 25, no. 2 (1983).

Brimelow, Peter. *Alien Nation: Common Sense about America's Immigration Disaster.* New York: Random House, 1995.

Brown, Karen McCarthy. *Mama Lola: A Vodou Priestess in Brooklyn.* Berkeley: University of California Press, 1991.

Bryce-Laporte, Roy Simon. "Black Immigrants: The Experience of Invisibility and Inequality." *Journal of Black Studies,* September 1972.

Buff, Rachel. "Building Up Borders: Regional Fascism in Post-NAFTA America." *Free Society: A Journal of Anarchist Thought and Action* 2, no. 4 (1993): 12–13.

———. "Gone to Prophetstown: Rumor and History in the Story of Pan-Indian Resistance." In *Gone to Croatan: Origins of North American Dropout Culture*, ed. Ron Sakolsky and James Koehnline. Brooklyn: Autonomedia, 1993.

———. "Teaching Crown Heights: The Complex Language of Identity." *Shofar: An Interdisciplinary Journal of Jewish Studies* 15, no. 3 (Spring 1997).

———. "Tecumseh, Tenskwatawa, and the National Popular: Myth, Historiography, and Popular Memory." *Historical Reflections/Reflexions Historiques* 21, no. 2 (Spring 1995).

Burgess, Marilyn. "Canadian 'Range Wars': Struggles over Indian Cowboys." *Canadian Journal of Communications* 18 (1993).

Calavita, Kitty. *Inside the State: The Bracero Program, Immigration, and the INS*. New York: Routledge, 1992.

Chaney, Elsa. *Migration from the Caribbean Region: Determinants and Effects of Current Movements*. Center for Immigration Policy and Refugee Assistance, Georgetown University, March 1985. Pamphlet.

Chang, Robert S. "A Meditation on Borders." In *Immigrants Out! The New Nativism and the Anti-Immigrant Impulse in the United States*, ed. Juan F. Perea. New York: New York University Press, 1996.

———. "Toward an Asian-American Legal Scholarship: Critical Race Theory, Poststructuralism, and Narrative Space." In *Critical Race Theory: The Cutting Edge*, ed. Richard Delgado. Philadelphia: Temple University Press, 1995.

Chatterjee, Partha. *Nationalist Thought and the Colonial World: A Derivative Discourse*. London: Zed, 1986.

Child, Brenda. *Boarding School Seasons: American Indian Families*. Lincoln: University of Nebraska Press, 1998.

Chomsky, Noam. *American Power and the New Mandarins*. New York: Vintage Books, 1969.

———. *The Chomsky Reader*. Ed. James Peck. New York: Pantheon, 1987.

———. *On Power and Ideology: The Managua Lectures*. Boston: South End Press, 1987.

Churchill, Ward. "The Earth Is Our Mother: Struggles for American Indian Land and Liberation in the Contemporary United States." In *The State of Native North America: Genocide, Colonization, and Resistance*, ed. M. Annette Jaimes. Boston: South End Press, 1992.

———. *Fantasies of the Master Race: Literature, Cinema, and the Colonization of American Indians*. Ed. M. Annette Jaimes. Monroe, Me.: Common Courage Press, 1991.

Churchill, Ward, and Winona LaDuke. "Native North America: The Political Economy of Radioactive Colonialism." In *The State of Native North America: Genocide, Colonization, and Resistance*, ed. M. Annette Jaimes. Boston: South End Press, 1992.

Clifford, James. "Diasporas." *Cultural Anthropology* 9, no. 3 (1994): 302–308.

Clinton, Lawrence, et al. "Urban Relocation Reconsidered: Antecedents of Employment among Indian Males." *Rural Sociology* 40 (Summer 1975).

Cohen, Abner. *Masquerade Politics: Explorations in the Structure of Urban Cultural Movements.* Berkeley: University of California Press, 1993.

Cohen, Felix. "The Erosion of Indian Rights, 1950–1953." *Yale Law Journal* 62 (1953): 348–391.

Connolly, William. "Tocqueville, Territory, and Violence." In *Challenging Boundaries: Global Flows, Territorial Identities,* ed. Michael J. Shapiro and Hayward R. Alker. Borderlines 2. Minneapolis: University of Minnesota Press, 1996.

Cooper, Frederick, and Ann Stoler. "Introduction: Tensions of Empire: Colonial Control and Visions of Rule." *American Ethnologist* 6, no. 4 (1986): 613.

Corber, Robert J. *In the Name of National Security: Hitchcock, Homophobia, and the Political Construction of Gender in Postwar America.* Durham, N.C.: Duke University Press, 1993.

Cornell, Stephen. *The Return of the Native: American Indian Political Resurgence.* New York: Oxford University Press, 1988.

Corrette, Leigh. "You Can Kiss Me if I'm Irish, but You Can't Kiss Me if I'm Queer: Constructions of Gay and Lesbian Identity in St. Patrick's Day Parades." Paper presented to American Studies Association, Washington, D.C., November 1997.

Cosgrove, Stuart. "The Zoot Suit and Style Warfare." *History Workshop Journal* 18 (Autumn 1984).

Crowley, Daniel J. "The Traditional Masks of Carnival." *Caribbean Quarterly* 3 (1956): 194–223.

Daniels, Douglas Henry. "Los Angeles Zoot: Race 'Riot,' the Pachuco, and Black Music Culture." *Journal of Negro History* 82, no. 2 (Spring 1997).

Davis, Mike. *Prisoners of the American Dream.* London: Verso, 1986.

Deloria, Philip. *Playing Indian.* New Haven: Yale University Press, 1998.

Deloria, Vine, Jr. *Behind the Trail of Broken Treaties: An Indian Declaration of Independence.* New York: Delacorte, 1974.

———. *God Is Red.* New York: Dell, 1973.

Deloria, Vine, Jr., and Clifford M. Lytle. *The Nations Within: The Past and Future of Indian Sovereignty.* New York: Pantheon, 1984.

Dench, Ernest A. *Making Movies.* New York: Macmillan, 1915.

DeRosier, Arthur, Jr. "Indian Relocation in the 1950s." In *Forked Tongues and Broken Treaties,* ed. Donald Worster. Caldwell, Idaho: Caxton, 1975.

Donato, Marla. " 'To Allow This Mine Is to Disappear from the Earth': Intercontinental Victims of Exxon–Rio Algom Mining Rally behind Mole Lake Anishanabe." *The Circle* 15, no. 7 (July/August 1994): 6–7.

Drinnon, Richard. *Keeper of Concentration Camps: Dillon S. Myer and American Racism.* Berkeley: University of California Press, 1987.

Dunn, Timothy. *The Militarization of the U.S.-Mexico Border.* Austin: University of Texas Press, 1996.

Dyck, Noel. "Powwow and the Expression of Community in Western Canada." *Ethnos* 1, no. 2 (1979): 78–98.

Ebbott, Elizabeth, for League of Women Voters of Minnesota. *Indians in Minnesota.* 4th ed. Ed. Judith Rosenblatt. Minneapolis: University of Minnesota Press, 1985.

Enloe, Cynthia. *Bananas, Beaches, and Bases: Making Feminist Sense of International Politics.* Berkeley: University of California Press, 1989.

Escobar, Arturo. *Encountering Development: The Making and Unmaking of the Third World.* Princeton: Princeton University Press, 1994.

Espiritu, Yen Le. *Asian American Women and Men: Labor, Laws, and Love.* Thousand Oaks, Calif.: Sage, 1997.

Fabian, Johannes. *Time and the Other: How Anthropology Makes Its Object.* New York: Columbia University Press, 1983.

Fainstein, Susan S., and Norman I. Fainstein. *The View from Below: Urban Politics and Social Policy.* Boston: Little, Brown, 1972.

Fernández-Kelly, María Patricia, and Richard Schauffler. "Divided Fates: Immigrant Children and the New Assimilation." In *The New Second Generation,* ed. Alejandro Portes. New York: Russell Sage Foundation, 1996.

Fixico, Donald. *Termination and Relocation: Federal Indian Policy, 1945–1960.* Albuquerque: University of New Mexico Press, 1986.

Foner, Nancy. "West Indians in New York City and London: A Comparative Analysis." In *Caribbean Life in New York City: Sociocultural Dimensions,* ed. Elsa Chaney and Constance Sutton. New York: Center for Migration Studies of New York, 1987.

Foucault, Michel. *Discipline and Punish: The Birth of the Prison.* Trans. Alan Sheridan. New York: Vintage, 1979.

Fraser, Nancy. *Unruly Practices: Power, Discourse, and Gender in Contemporary Social Theory.* Minneapolis: University of Minnesota Press, 1989.

Frieden, Bernard J., and Marshall Kaplan. *The Politics of Neglect: Urban Aid from Model Cities to Revenue Sharing.* Cambridge: MIT Press, 1975.

Gabaccia, Donna. *From the Other Side: Women, Gender, and Immigrant Life in the United States, 1820–1990.* Bloomington: Indiana University Press, 1994.

———. "Is Everywhere Nowhere? Nomads, Nations, and the Immigrant Paradigm in United States History." *Journal of American History,* December 1999, 1115–1134.

Gabaccia, Donna, and James Grossman, eds. *Teaching the History of Immigration and Ethnicity: A Syllabus Exchange.* Chicago: Newberry Library and Immigration History Society, 1993.

Gamble, John I. "Changing Patterns in Kiowa Indian Dances." In *Acculturation in the Americas,* ed. Sol Tax. New York: Cooper Square, 1967.

Garrison, Vivian, and Carol Weiss. "Dominican Family Networks and United States Immigration Policy: A Case Study." In *Caribbean Life in New York City: Sociocultural Dimensions,* ed. Constance R. Sutton and Elsa M. Chaney. New York: Center for Migration Studies of New York, 1987.

Georges, Eugenia. *The Making of a Transnational Community: Migration, Development, and Cultural Change in the Dominican Republic.* New York: Columbia University Press, 1990.

Gilroy, Paul. *The Black Atlantic: Modernity and Double Consciousness.* Cambridge: Harvard University Press, 1993.

———. "Sounds Authentic: Black Music, Ethnicity, and the Challenge of a Changing Same." In *Imagining Home: Class, Culture, and Nationalism in the African Diaspora,* ed. Sidney Lemelle and Robin D. G. Kelley. New York: Verso: 1994.

———. *"There Ain't No Black in the Union Jack": The Cultural Politics of Race and Nation.* Chicago: University of Chicago Press, 1991.

Gittell, Marilyn. "Education: The Decentralization–Community Control Controversy." In *Race and Politics in New York City: Five Studies in Policy Making,* ed. Jewel Bellush and Stephen M. David. New York: Praeger, 1971.

Glissant, Edouard. *Caribbean Discourse: Selected Essays by Edouard Glissant.* Trans. J. Michael Dash. Charlottesville: University Press of Virginia, 1989.

Goldberg, David Theo. *Racist Culture: Philosophy and the Politics of Meaning.* Cambridge, Mass.: Blackwell, 1993.

Graves, Theodore. "The Personal Adjustment of Navajo Indian Migrants to Denver, Colorado." *American Anthropologist* 72 (February 1972).

Green, Rayna. "The Pocahontas Perplex: The Image of the Indian Woman in American Vernacular Culture." *Massachusetts Review* 14, no. 4 (1976).

———. "The Tribe Called Wannabee: Playing Indian in America and Europe." *Folklore* 99, no. 1 (1988): 32.

Guerrero, Mariana. "American Indian Water Rights: The Blood of Life in Native North America." In *The State of Native North America: Genocide, Colonization, and Resistance,* ed. M. Annette Jaimes. Boston: South End Press, 1992.

Guha, Ranajit. "The Prose of Counter-Insurgency." In *Selected Subaltern Studies,* ed. Ranajit Guha and Gayatri Chakravorty Spivak. New York: Oxford University Press, 1988.

Guillemin, Jeanne. *Urban Renegades: The Cultural Strategy of American Indians.* New York: Columbia University Press, 1975.

Guillermoprieto, Alma. *Samba!* New York: Knopf, 1990.

Gundlach, James, and Alden Roberts. "Native American Indian Migration and Relocation." *Pacific Sociological Review* 21 (January 1978).

Gunther, Erna. "The Westward Movement of Some Plains Traits." *American Anthropologist* 52, no. 2 (April–June 1950).

Gutiérrez, Ramón A. *When Jesus Came, the Corn Mothers Went Away: Marriage, Sexuality, and Power in New Mexico, 1500–1848.* Stanford: Stanford University Press, 1991.

Haar, Charles M. *Between the Idea and the Reality: A Study in the Origin, Fate, and Legacy of the Model Cities Program.* Boston: Little, Brown, 1975.

Hagan, William. *American Indians.* Chicago: University of Chicago Press, 1979.

Hahamovitch, Cindy. *The Fruits of Their Labor: Atlantic Farmworkers and the Makings of Migrant Poverty, 1870–1945.* Chapel Hill: University of North Carolina Press, 1997.

Hall, Stuart. "Culture, Community, Nation." *Cultural Studies* 7, no. 3 (October 1993).

———. "The New Ethnicities." In *Ethnicity,* ed. John Hutchinson and Anthony D. Smith. New York: Oxford University Press, 1996.

Hall, Stuart, and David Held. "Citizens and Citizenship." In *New Times: The Changing Face of Politics in the 1990s,* ed. Stuart Hall and Martin Jacques. New York: Verso, 1989.

Hammar, Tomas. "State, Nation, and Dual Citizenship." In *Immigration and the Politics of Citizenship in Europe and North America*, ed. William Rogers Brubaker. New York: University Press of America, 1990.

Harjo, Joy. *The Woman Who Fell from the Sky: Poems*. New York: Norton, 1996.

Harraway, Donna. "Situated Knowleges: The Science Question in Feminism and the Privilege of Partial Perspective." *Feminist Studies* 144 (1988).

Harvey, David. *Consciousness and the Urban Experience: Studies in the History and Theory of Capitalist Urbanization*. Baltimore: Johns Hopkins University Press, 1985.

Hebdige, Dick. *Cut 'n' Mix: Culture, Identity, and Caribbean Music*. New York: Methuen, 1987.

Hertzberg, Hazel. *The Search for an American Indian Identity: Modern Pan-Indian Movements*. Syracuse, N.Y.: Syracuse University Press, 1971.

Heth, Charlotte, ed. *Native American Dance: Ceremonies and Social Traditions*. Washington, D.C.: Smithsonian Institution, 1992.

Hickerson, Harold. *Ethnohistory of the Chippewa in Central Minnesota*. New York: Garland, 1979.

Hill, Donald R. *Calypso Callaloo: Early Carnival Music in Trinidad*. Gainesville: University Press of Florida, 1993.

Hill, Donald R., and Robert Abrahamson. "West Indian Carnival in Brooklyn." *Natural History* 88, no. 7 (1979).

Hill, Errol. *The Trinidad Carnival: Mandate for a National Theatre*. Austin: University of Texas Press, 1972.

Hill, Robert. "Dreadlocks, or The Discourse of the Hair of the Head." Paper presented at American Studies Association meeting, Boston, Nov. 7, 1993.

Hing, Bill Ong. *Making and Remaking Asian America through Immigration Policy, 1850–1990*. Stanford: Stanford University Press, 1993.

Ho, Christine. *Salt-water Trinnies: Afro-Trinidadian Immigrant Networks and Non-Assimilation in Los Angeles*. New York: AMS Press, 1991.

Hoberman, Jay. *Bridge of Light: Yiddish Film between Two Worlds*. New York: Museum of Modern Art/Schocken, 1991.

Hobsbawm, Eric, and Terence Ranger, eds. *The Invention of Tradition*. New York: Cambridge University Press, 1983.

Hoetink, H. "Race and Color in the Caribbean." In *Focus: Caribbean*, ed. Sidney W. Mintz and Sally Price. Washington, D.C.: Latin American Program, Woodrow Wilson International Center for Scholars, 1985.

———. *Slavery and Race Relations in the Americas: An Inquiry into Their Nature and Nexus*. New York: Harper & Row, 1973.

Hongo, Garrett. "America Singing: An Address to the Newly Arrived Peoples." *Parnassus: Poetry in Review* 17, no. 1 (1992): 9–20.

Horse Capture, George P. *Powwow*. Cody, Wyo.: Buffalo Bill Historical Center, 1988.

Howard, James H. "The Pan-Indian Culture of Oklahoma." *Scientific Monthly* 18, no. 5 (1955).

Huenemann, Lynn F. "Northern Plains Dance." In *Native American Dance: Ceremonies and Social Traditions*, ed. Charlotte Heth. Washington, D.C.: Smithsonian Institution, 1992.

Iverson, Peter. "Building towards Self-Determination: Plains and Southwestern Indians in the 1940s and 1950s." *Western Historical Quarterly* 16 no. 2 (April 1985): 163–173.

———. *"We Are Still Here": American Indians in the Twentieth Century*. Wheeling, Ill.: Harlan Davidson, 1998.

Jacobson, David. *Rights across Borders : Immigration and the Decline of Citizenship*. Baltimore: Johns Hopkins University Press, 1996.

Jacobson, Matthew Frye. *Special Sorrows: The Diasporic Imagination of Irish, Polish, and Jewish Immigrants in the United States*. Cambridge: Harvard University Press, 1993.

———. *Whiteness of a Different Color: European Immigrants and the Alchemy of Race*. Cambridge: Harvard University Press, 1998.

Jaimes, M. Annette, ed. *The State of Native North America: Genocide, Colonization, and Resistance*. Boston: South End Press, 1992.

James, C. L. R. "The Mighty Sparrow." In *The Future and the Present: Selected Writings of C. L. R. James*. Westport, Conn.: Lawrence Hill, 1980.

Jasso, Guillermina, and Mark R. Rosezweig. *The New Chosen People: Immigrants in the the United States*. New York: Russell Sage, 1990.

Josephy, Alvin. *Now That the Buffalo's Gone: A Study of Today's American Indians*. Norman: University of Oklahoma Press, 1982.

Kaplan, Caren. *Questions of Travel: Postmodern Discourses of Displacement*. Durham, N.C.: Duke University Press, 1996.

Kasinitz, Philip. *Caribbean New York: Black Immigrants and the Politics of Race*. Ithaca: Cornell University Press, 1992.

Kasinitz, Philip, and Judith Friedenberg-Herbstein. "The Puerto Rican Parade and West Indian Carnival: Public Celebrations in New York City." In *Caribbean Life in New York City*, ed. Constance Sutton and Elsa Chaney. New York: Center for Migration Studies of New York, 1987.

Kavanagh, Thomas W. "Southern Plains Dance: Tradition and Dynamics." In *Native American Dance: Ceremonies and Social Traditions,* ed. Charlotte Heth. Washington, D.C.: Smithsonian Institution, 1992.

Kearney, Michael. "Borders and Boundaries of the State and Self at the End of Empire." *Journal of Historical Sociology* 4, no. 1 (1991): 552–574.

Kees, Richard. "The Stockbridge Indians." Forthcoming.

Kelley, Robin D. G. " 'But a Local Phase of a World Problem': Black History's Global Vision." *Journal of American History,* December 1999, 1045–1077.

———. *Race Rebels*. New York: New York University Press, 1994.

Kennedy, John F. *A Nation of Immigrants*. New York: Harper & Row, 1964.

Kivisto, Peter. "The Transplanted Then and Now: The Reorientation of Immigration Studies from the Chicago School to the New Social History." *Ethnic and Racial Studies* 13, no. 4 (October 1990): 455–481.

Krinsky, Carol Herselle. *Contemporary Native American Architecture: Cultural Regeneration and Creativity*. New York: Oxford University Press, 1996.

LaFeber, Walter. *Inevitable Revolutions: The United States in Central America*. New York: Norton, 1993.

Lemelle, Sidney J., and Robin D. G. Kelley, eds. *Imagining Home: Class, Culture, and Nationalism in the African Diaspora*. New York: Verso, 1994.

Lemke-Santangelo, Gretchen. *Abiding Courage: African-American Migrant Women and the East Bay Community.* Chapel Hill: University of North Carolina Press, 1996.

Linton, Ralph. "The Distinctive Aspects of Acculturation." In *Acculturation in Seven Indian Tribes,* ed. Linton. New York: Appleton-Century, 1940.

Lipsitz, George. *Dangerous Crossroads: Popular Music, Postmodernism, and the Poetics of Place.* New York: Verso, 1994.

———. *The Possessive Investment in Whiteness: How White People Profit from Identity Politics.* Philadelphia: Temple University Press, 1998.

———. *Time Passages: Collective Memory and American Popular Culture.* Minneapolis: University of Minnesota Press, 1990.

Lomawaima, K. Tsianina. "Domesticity in the Federal Indian Schools: The Power of Authority over Mind and Body." In *Deviant Bodies,* ed. Jennifer Terry and Jacqueline Urla. Bloomington: Indiana University Press, 1995.

———. *They Called It Prairie Light: The Story of Chilocco Indian School.* Lincoln: University of Nebraska Press, 1994.

Lott, Eric. *Love and Theft: Blackface Minstrelsy and the American Working Class.* New York: Oxford University Press, 1993.

Lowe, Lisa. *Immigrant Acts: Asian American Cultural Politics.* Durham, N.C.: Duke University Press, 1996.

Lundquist, G. E. E. *Indians of Minnesota: A Survey of Social and Religious Conditions among Tribes in Transition.* New York: Division of Home Missions, National Council of Churches of Christ in the U.S.A., 1952.

Manning, Frank E. "Overseas Caribbean Carnivals: The Art and Politics of a Transnational Celebration." In *Caribbean Popular Culture,* ed. John A. Lent. Bowling Green, Ohio: Bowling Green State University Press, 1990.

Marcus, George, and Michael Fischer. *Anthropology as Cultural Critique.* Chicago: University of Chicago Press, 1989.

Marshall, Dawn. "Migration and Development in the Eastern Caribbean." In *Migration and Development in the Caribbean: The Unexplored Connection,* ed. Robert Pastor. Boulder: Westview, 1985.

Marshall, Paule. *Brown Girl, Brownstones.* Old Westbury, N.Y.: Feminist Press, 1981.

Martin, Linda, and Kerry Seagrave. *Anti-Rock: The Opposition to Rock 'n' Roll.* New York: Da Capo, 1993.

Mason, Mike. *Development and Disorder: A History of the Third World since 1945.* Middletown, Conn.: University Press of New England, 1997.

May, Elaine Tyler. *Homeward Bound: American Families in the Cold War Era.* New York: Basic Books, 1988.

May, Lary. *Screening Out the Past: The Birth of Mass Culture and the Motion Picture Industry.* New York: Oxford University Press, 1980.

McRobbie, Angela. "Shut Up and Dance: Youth Culture and Changing Modes of Femininity." *Cultural Studies* 7, no. 3 (October 1993).

Mintz, Jerome R. *Hasidic People: A Place in the New World.* Cambridge: Harvard University Press, 1992.

Mintz, Sidney. *Caribbean Transformations.* Baltimore: Johns Hopkins University Press, 1984.

Mitchell, Timothy. *Colonising Egypt.* Cambridge: Cambridge University Press, 1988.

Mooney, James. "The Ghost Dance Religion and the Sioux Outbreak of 1890." Bureau of American Ethnology, *Annual Report,* no. 14 (1896).

Mora, Mariana. "Changing Chiapas." *Third Force: Issues and Actions in Communities of Color* 5, no. 1 (March/April 1997): 17.

Moses, L. G. *Wild West Shows and the Images of American Indians, 1883–1933.* Albuquerque: University of New Mexico Press, 1996.

Nagel, Joane. *American Indian Ethnic Renewal: Red Power and the Resurgence of Identity and Culture.* New York: Oxford University Press, 1996.

Nash, Gerald. *The American West Transformed: The Impact of the Second World War.* Bloomington: Indiana University Press, 1985.

Nash, June, and María Patricia Fernández-Kelly, eds. *Women, Men, and the International Division of Labor.* Albany: State University of New York Press, 1983.

Neil, Ancil Anthony. *Voices from the Hills: Despers and Laventille: The Steelband and Its Effects on Poverty, Stigma, and Violence in a Community.* New York: A. A. Neil, 1987.

Neils, Elaine. "Reservation to City: Indian Migration and Federal Relocation." Research Paper no. 131. Department of Geography, University of Chicago, 1971.

Nelson, Gersham A. "Rastafarians and Ethiopianism." In *Imagining Home: Class, Culture, and Nationalism in the African Diaspora,* ed. Sidney J. Lemelle and Robin D. G. Kelley. New York: Verso, 1994.

Ng, Fae Myenne. *Bone.* New York: Hyperion, 1993.

Nora, Pierre. "Between Memory and History: Les Lieux de Mémoire." Trans. Marc Roudebush. *Representations* 26 (Spring 1989): 7–25.

Nunley, John W. "Masquerade Mix-up in Trinidad Carnival: Live Once, Die Forever." In *Caribbean Festival Arts: Each and Every Bit of Difference,* ed. John W. Nunley and Judith Bettelheim. Seattle: University of Washington Press, 1988.

O'Connell, Barry, ed. *On Our Own Ground: The Complete Writings of William Apess, a Pequot Indian.* Amherst: University of Massachusetts Press, 1992.

Omi, Michael, and Howard Winant. *Racial Formation in the United States: From the 1960s to the 1990s.* New York: Routledge, 1994.

Orsi, Robert Anthony. *The Madonna of 115th Street: Faith and Community in Italian Harlem, 1880–1950.* New Haven: Yale University Press, 1985.

————. "The Religious Boundaries of an Inbetween People: Street Feste and the Problem of the Dark-Skinned Other in Italian Harlem, 1920–1990." *American Quarterly* 44, no. 3 (September 1992): 313–347.

Palmer, Leslie. "Memories of the Notting Hill Carnival." In *Masquerading: The Art of the Notting Hill Carnival.* London: London Arts Council, 1986.

Pearse, Andrew. "Carnival in Nineteenth-Century Trinidad." *Caribbean Quarterly* 4, no. 3–4 (March–June 1956): 175–193.

Peiss, Kathy. *Cheap Amusements: Working Women and Leisure in New York City, 1880 to 1920.* Philadelphia: Temple University Press, 1986.

Pence, Angelica. "Immigration Law Raises Confusion." *Arizona Daily Star,* Mar. 31, 1947.

Perdue, Theda, and Michael Green, eds. *The Cherokee Removal: A Brief History with Documents.* New York: Bedford Books of St. Martin's Press, 1995.

Peroff, Nicholas C. *Menominee Drums: Tribal Termination and Restoration, 1954–1974.* Norman: University of Oklahoma Press, 1982.

Pertusati, Linda. *In Defense of Mohawk Land: Ethnopolitical Conflict in Native North America.* Albany: State University of New York Press, 1997.

Philp, Kenneth R. *Termination Revisited: American Indians on the Trail to Self-Determination, 1933–1953.* Lincoln: University of Nebraska Press, 1999.

Plummer, Brenda Gayle. *Haiti and the United States: The Psychological Movement.* Athens: University of Georgia Press, 1992.

———. *Rising Wind: Black Americans and Foreign Policy, 1934–1960.* Chapel Hill: University of North Carolina Press, 1995.

Powers, William. *War Dance: Plains Indian Musical Performance.* Tucson: Arizona University Press, 1990.

Powrie, Barbara. "The Changing Attitude of the Colored Middle Class towards Carnival." *Caribbean Quarterly* 4, no. 3–4 (March–June 1956): 224–245.

Pow Wow 1995 Calendar: Guide to North American Powwows and Gatherings. Summertown, Tenn.: Book Publishing Co., 1995.

Prell, Riv Ellen. *Fighting to Become Americans: Jews, Gender, and the Anxiety of Assimilation.* Boston: Beacon, 1999.

Price, John. "The Migration and Adaptation of American Indians to Los Angeles." *Human Organization* 27 (Summer 1968).

Proctor, Robert J. "Censorship of American Uranium Mine Epidemiology in the 1950s." In *Secret Agents: The Rosenberg Case, McCarthyism, and Fifties America,* ed. Rebecca Walkowitz and Marjorie Garber. New York: Routledge, 1995.

Quadagno, Jill. *The Color of Welfare: How Racism Undermined the War on Poverty.* New York: Oxford University Press, 1994.

Rachlin, Carol K. "Tight Shoe Night." *Midcontinent Journal of American Studies* 6, no. 2 (1965): 84–99.

Radhakrishnan, R. "Nationalism, Gender, and the Narrative of Identity." In *Nationalism and Sexualities,* ed. Andrew Parker, Doris Sommer, and Patricia Yaeger. New York: Routledge, 1992.

Reimers, David. *Still the Golden Door.* New York: Columbia University Press, 1985.

Roach, Joseph. *Cities of the Dead: Circum-Atlantic Performance.* New York: Columbia University Press, 1996.

Roberts, John Storm. *Black Music of Two Worlds.* New York: Praeger, 1972.

Roediger, David R. *Wages of Whiteness.* London; New York: Verso, 1991.

———. *Towards the Abolition of Whiteness.* London: Routledge, 1994.

Rogin, Michael. *Ronald Reagan, the Movie: And Other Episodes in Political Demonology.* Berkeley: University of California Press, 1987.

Rogowski, Edward T., Louis H. Gold, and David W. Abbott. "Police: The Civilian Review Board Controversy." In *Race and Politics in New York City: Five Studies in Policy Making,* ed. Jewel Bellush and Stephen M. David. New York: Praeger, 1971.

Root, Debra. *Cannibal Culture: Art, Appropriation, and the Commodification of Difference.* Boulder: Westview, 1996.

Rosaldo, Renato. *Culture and Truth: The Remaking of Social Analysis.* Boston: Beacon, 1988.

Rose, Tricia. *Black Noise: Rap Music and Black Culture in Contemporary America.* Middletown, Conn.: Wesleyan University Press, 1994.

Rouse, Roger. "Mexican Migration and the Social Space of Postmodernism." *Diaspora* 1, no. 1 (Spring 1991).

Rynkiewich, Michael A. "Chippewa Powwows." In *Anishanabe: Six Studies of Modern Chippewa,* ed. A. Paredes. Gainesville: University Press of Florida, 1980.

Safa, Helen. "Preface" to "Migration and Caribbean Cultural Identity: Selected Papers from a Conference Celebrating the 50th Anniversary of the Center," University of Florida, Gainesville. (Papers housed at Center for Migration Studies, Staten Island, New York.)

Said, Edward. *Orientalism.* New York: Random House, 1978.

Sakolsky, Ron, and James Koehnline, eds. *Gone to Croatan: Origins of North American Dropout Culture.* Brooklyn: Autonomedia, 1993.

Sanchez, George. *Becoming Mexican American: Ethnicity, Culture, and Identity in Chicano Los Angeles, 1900–1945.* New York: Oxford University Press, 1993.

Sangari, Kumkum, and Sadesh Vaid, eds. *Recasting Women: Essays in Indian Colonial History.* New Brunswick: Rutgers University Press, 1990.

Saxton, Alexander. *The Rise and Fall of the White Republic: Class Politics and Mass Culture in Nineteenth-Century America.* New York: Verso,1990.

Schiller, Nina Glick, Linda Basch, and Cristina Blanc-Szanton. *Towards a Transnational Perspective on Migration: Race, Class, Ethnicity, and Nationalism Reconsidered.* New York: New York Academy of Sciences, 1992.

Schneider, Dorothee. "Women Immigrants at the Border: Race, Sex, Class, and the Immigration Service, 1906–1928." Paper presented at Berkshire Conference for Women's Historians, June 1999.

Segal, Daniel. "Living Ancestors: Nationalism and the Past in Postcolonial Trinidad and Tobago." In *Remapping Memory: The Politics of Space-Time,* ed. Jonathan Boyarin, 229–232. Minneapolis: University of Minnesota Press, 1994.

———. "Race and Color in Pre-Independence Trinidad and Tobago." In *Trinidad Ethnicity,* ed. Kevin Yelvington. Knoxville: University of Tennessee Press, 1993.

Shoemaker, Nancy. "Urban Indians and Ethnic Choices: American Indian Organizations in Minneapolis, 1920–1950." *Western Historical Quarterly* 18, no. 4 (November 1988).

Silko, Leslie Marmon. *Almanac of the Dead: A Novel.* New York: Simon & Schuster, 1991.

———. "The Border Patrol State." In *Yellow Woman and a Beauty of the Spirit: Essays on Native American Life Today.* New York: Simon & Schuster, 1996.

Singh, Kelvin. *The Bloodstained Tombs: The Muhurram Massacre in Trinidad, 1884.* London: Macmillan, 1988.

———. *Race and Class: Struggles in a Colonial State: Trinidad, 1917–1945.* Kingston: University of the West Indies Press, 1994.

Singh, Nikhil Pal. "Culture/Wars: Recoding Empire in an Age of Democracy." *American Quarterly* 50, no. 3 (September 1998).

Slotkin, Richard. "Buffalo Bill's 'Wild West' and the Mythologization of the American Empire." In *Cultures of United States Imperialism,* ed. Amy Kaplan and Donald Pease. Durham, N.C.: Duke University Press, 1993.

———. *The Urban American Indian.* Lexington, Mass.: Lexington Books, 1978.

Smith, Anna Deavere. *Fires in the Mirror: Crown Heights, Brooklyn, and Other Identities.* New York: Doubleday, 1993.

Sollors, Werner. *Beyond Ethnicity: Consent and Descent in American Culture.* New York: Oxford University Press, 1986.

Sommer, Doris. "Irresistible Romance: The Foundational Fictions of Latin America." In *Nation and Narration,* ed. Homi K. Bhabha. New York: Routledge, 1990.

Sorkin, Alan. "Some Aspects of American Indian Migration." *Social Forces* 48 (December 1969).

Sowell, Thomas. *Ethnic America: A History.* New York: Basic Books, 1981.

Spivak, Gayatri. "Can the Subaltern Speak?" In *Marxism and the Interpretation of Culture,* ed. Cary Nelson and Lawrence Grossberg. Urbana: University of Illinois Press, 1988.

Stafford, William. *Stories That Could Be True: New and Collected Poems.* New York: Harper & Row, 1977.

Stiffarm, Lenore A., and Phil Lane Jr. "The Demography of Native North America: A Question of American Indian Survival." In *The State of Native North America,* ed. M. Annette Jaimes. Boston: South End Press, 1992.

Stoler, Ann. "Making Empire Respectable: The Politics of Race and Sexual Morality in Twentieth-Century Colonial Cultures." *American Ethnologist* 6, no. 4 (1989).

———. *Race and the Education of Desire: Foucault's History of Sexuality and the Colonial Order of Things.* Durham, N.C.: Duke University Press, 1996.

———. "Sexual Affronts and Racial Frontiers: National Identities, 'Mixed Bloods,' and the Cultural Genealogies of Europeans in Colonial Southeast Asia." *Working Papers of the History and Society Program* 34, no. 3 (Minneapolis: University of Minnesota, July 1992).

Stuempfle, Stephen. *The Steelband Movement: The Forging of a National Art in Trinidad and Tobago.* Philadelphia: University of Pennsylvania Press, 1995.

Szewd, John, and Roger Abrams, eds. *After Africa: Extracts from British Travel Accounts and Journals of the Seventeenth, Eighteenth, and Nineteenth Centuries Concerning the Slaves, Their Manners, and Customs in the British West Indies.* New Haven: Yale University Press, 1983.

Thomas, Robert. "Pan-Indianism." *Mid-Continent American Studies Journal* 6 (Fall 1978).

Thompson, Richard. *Theories of Ethnicity: A Critical Appraisal.* New York: Greenwood Press, 1989.

Thornton, Russell. "Cherokee Population Losses during the Trail of Tears: A New Perspective and a New Estimate." *Ethnohistory* 31, no. 4 (1984).

Trinh, T. Minh-ha. *Woman, Native, Other: Writing Postcoloniality and Feminism.* Bloomington: Indiana University Press, 1989.

Valaskakis, Gail Guthrie. "The Chippewa and the Other: Living the Heritage of Lac du Flambeau." *Cultural Studies* 2, no. 3 (1988): 267–293.

———. "Dance Me Inside: Pow Wow and Being Indian." *FUSE*, Summer 1993, 39–44.

Von Eschen, Penny M. *Race against Empire: Black Americans and Anticolonialism, 1937–1957*. Ithaca: Cornell University Press, 1997.

Wald, Priscilla. *Constituting Americans: Cultural Anxiety and Narrative Form*. Durham, N.C.: Duke University Press, 1995.

Waldinger, Roger. *Still the Promised City? African Americans and New Immigrants in Postindustrial New York*. Cambridge: Harvard University Press, 1996.

Wallace, Anthony F. C. *Human Behavior in Extreme Situations: A Study of the Literature and Suggestions for Further Research*. Washington, D.C.: National Academy of Sciences, National Research Council, 1956.

Warner, Keith Q. "Ethnicity and the Contemporary Calypso." In *Trinidad Ethnicity*, ed. Kevin Yelvington. Knoxville: University of Tennessee Press, 1993.

Waters, Mary C. "Ethnic and Racial Identities of Second-Generation Black Immigrants in New York City." In *The New Second Generation*, ed. Alejandro Portes, 171–196. New York: Russell Sage, 1996.

Watkins-Owens, Irma. *Blood Relations: Caribbean Immigrants and the Harlem Community, 1900–1930*. Bloomington: Indiana University Press, 1996.

Weibel-Orlando, Joan. *Indian Country, L.A.: Maintaining Ethnic Community in Complex Society*. Urbana: University of Illinois Press, 1991.

Weiss, Carol. "Dominican Family Networks and United States Immigration Policy: A Case Study." In *Caribbean Life in New York City*, ed. Constance Sutton and Elsa Chaney. New York: Center for Migration Studies of New York, 1987.

West Indian–American Calypso Association. *Steelband: The Truth*. New York, 1987.

White, Richard. *The Middle Ground: Indians, Empires, and Republics in the Great Lakes Region, 1650–1815*. New York: Cambridge University Press, 1991.

Williams, Eric. *Capitalism and Slavery*. Chapel Hill: University of North Carolina Press, 1944.

Williams, Patricia. *The Alchemy of Race and Rights*. Cambridge: Harvard University Press, 1991.

Williams, William Appleman. *Empire as a Way of Life: An Essay on the Causes and Character of America's Present Predicament, along with a Few Thoughts about an Alternative*. New York: Oxford University Press: 1980.

Wilson, Peter. "Reputation vs. Respectability: A Suggestion for Caribbean Ethnology." *Man* 4, no. 1 (March 1969): 70–84.

Winant, Howard. "Postmodern Racial Politics in the United States: Difference and Inequality." *Socialist Review* 12 (January 1990): 121–147.

Winokur, Mark. *American Laughter: Immigrants, Ethnicity, and 1930s Hollywood Film Comedy*. New York: St. Martin's Press, 1996.

Wyman, Mark. *Round Trip to America: The Immigrants Return to Europe, 1880–1930*. Ithaca: Cornell University Press, 1992.

Yellow Bird, Pemina, and Kathryn Milun. "Interrupted Journeys: The Cultural Politics of Indian Reburial." In *Displacements: Cultural Identities in Question*, ed. Angelika Bammer. Bloomington: Indiana University Press, 1994.

Yelvington, Kevin, ed. *Trinidad Ethnicity*. Knoxville: University of Tennessee Press, 1993.

Yudice, George, and Juan Flores. "Living Borders/Buscando American: Languages of Latino Self-Formation." *Social Text* 8, no. 2 (1990): 57–84.

Yung, Judy. *Unbound Feet: A Social History of Chinese Women in San Francisco*. Berkeley: University of California Press, 1995.

Zavella, Patricia. "The Tables Are Turned: Immigration, Poverty, and Social Conflict in California Communities." In *Immigrants Out! The New Nativism and the Anti-Immigrant Impulse in the United States*, ed. Juan Perea. New York: New York University Press, 1997.

Zipes, Jack. *The Operated Jew: Two Tales of Anti-Semitism*. New York: Routlege, 1991.

PERIODICAL PUBLICATIONS

Akwesasne Notes
Amerindian (1956)
Antillean Echo
Circle
Crisis (1950–1952, 1952–1964)
Menominee News (1953–1959)
Militant (1964)
Minneapolis Star (1974–1975)
Minneapolis Tribune (1969)
NCAI Bulletin (1948–1953)
New York Amsterdam News (1960–1990)
New York Daily News (1971–1985)
New York Newsday (1991)
New York Times (1945–1995)
Pow Wow Time (1992)
Times (London) (1976)
Village Voice (New York) (1991, 1994)

FILMS AND AUDIO RECORDINGS

Bowman, Arlene. *Song Journey*. Film. Produced and directed by Arlene Bowman, 1993.

Litefoot. *Seein' Red*. 1994. Red Vinyl Records, Tulsa.

UNPUBLISHED SOURCES AND GOVERNMENT DOCUMENTS

Bailey, Stanley, Karl Eschbach, Jacqueline Hagan, and Nestor Rodriguez. "Migrant Death at the Texas-Mexico Border." Working Papers of the Center for Immigration Research, University of Houston, April 1996.

Clippings Files, Local History Room, Brooklyn Public Library.

Community Chest 8 Council. Social Welfare History Archive, University of Minnesota.

CHWC: Community Health and Welfare Council. Social Welfare History Archives, University of Minnesota, Minneapolis.

Congressional Record, 1940–1965.

Immigration and Naturalization Service, *Annual Report*, 1963–1991.

Minnesota Human Service Department Library. Social Welfare History Archives, University of Minnesota, Minneapolis.

Neighborhood Files, Municipal Archives, New York City.

SWHA: Social Welfare History Archives, University of Minnesota, Minneapolis.

U.S. Census Reports, 1960–1990.

U.S. Department of Justice, Immigration and Naturalization Service. *An Immigrant Nation: United States Regulation of Immigration, 1798–1991*. Washington, D.C.: U.S. Government Printing Office, 1991.

Vertical Clippings Files, Schomburg Center for Research in Black Culture, New York.

West Indian–American Calypso Association. "Steelband: The Truth." New York, 1987. Mimeo.

INTERVIEWS

Alley, DaLynn. Hinkley, Minn., July 1994.

Alleyne, Earl. Brooklyn, August 1993.

Artishon, Gina. Minneapolis, July 1994.

Beaulieu, Julie. Minneapolis, October 1994.

Bradley, Clive. Brooklyn, August 1992 and1993.

Brady, Victor. Telephone. New York, August 1993.

Brewster, Randy. Brooklyn, Summer 1991 and 1993.

Caramonica, Sergeant Frank. Brooklyn, August 1992.

Clermont, Hokie. St. Paul, Minn., June 1994.

Clermont, Jim. Minneapolis, June 1994.

Coffee, Chocko. Brooklyn, August 1992.

Coffee, Denis. Brooklyn, August 1992.

Coffey, Karal Ann. Hinckley, Minn., July 1994.

Day, Dorene. Minneapolis, January 1994.

Day, Opie. St. Paul, Minn., June 1994.

Favel, Ellie. Minneapolis, April 1994.

Fields, Donna. Telephone. New York, September 1993.

Findlay, Heather. Brooklyn, August 1993.

Forde, Crystol. Brooklyn, August 1992.

Frances, Troy. Brooklyn, August 1992.

Francis, Gayle. Brooklyn, August 1992.

Goldstein, Jacob. New York, August 1993.

Grey, Nancy. Telephone. New York, 1993.

Guineau, Patrick. Sunkopee, Minn., August 1994.

Hanell, Malinda. Shakopee, Minn., August 1994.

Henry, Judy. Brooklyn, July 1991, August 1992, August 1993.

Ironshield, Debbie. Minneapolis, April 1994.

Johns, Trevor. Brooklyn, July 1991.

Josephs, Tony. Brooklyn, August 1992 and August 1993.

King, Jamaal. Brooklyn, August 1993.

King, Rudy. Brooklyn, September 1992 and August 1992.

Larson, Bob. St. Paul, Minn., September 1994.

Lezama, Carlos. Telephone. Brooklyn, 1992.

Libertus, Ron. Minneapolis, October 1994.

Means, Bill. Minneapolis, February 1993.

Mousseaux, Fern. Telephone. Pine Ridge, S.D., August 1994.

Quinoma, Joyce. Brooklyn, August 1992.

Scott, Mack. Brooklyn, August 1992.

Simon, Dan. Brooklyn, August 1991.

Slater, Les. Brooklyn, July and August 1992.

Smith, Johnny. Minneapolis, November 1994.

Smith, Norine. Minneapolis, January 1994.

Sooknanan, Herman. Brooklyn, August 1993.

Stanislaus, Lamuel. Telephone. Brooklyn, August 1993.

Thompson, Keitha. Brooklyn, August 1993.

Ward, Leslie. Brooklyn, August 1993.

Index

Ablon, Joan, 63
Abrahams, Roger, 112
ACLU. *See* American Civil Liberties Union
African-Americans: Caribbean im/migrants and, 82–85, 92, 101–2, 104; conflicts between Jews and, 114–16 (*see also* Crown Heights tensions); immigration reform and, 49, 85; transnationalism and, 174, 175. *See also* Black ethnic identity
Afro-Brazilian culture, 39
Afro-Creole culture: development of, 30–33 (*see also* Caribbean immigrants); steel band movement and, 123–24, 146. *See also* Black ethnic identity
AIDS/HIV, 168–69
AIM. *See* American Indian Movement
Allen, Ray, 127
Alley, DaLynn (Junior Miss Shawnee Nation), 148–49, 170
Alleyne, Earl, 133, 136, 138, 140
American Civil Liberties Union (ACLU), 115
American Committee for Special Migration, 190n18
American Indian Center (Minneapolis), 90–91; Organizing Committee report (1964), 96–97
American Indian Hearse Service, 2–3

American Indian Industrial Opportunities Center (IOC), 27
American Indian Movement (AIM), 11, 42, 97–98, 99, 189n88; Gathering of Nations powwow, 157
Ames, David, 193n75
Anderson, Benedict, 182n7
Anticommunism: im/migration policy and, 46, 51, 59, 65; Indian policy and, 51–55
Antillean Echo (publication), 104
Anti-Semitism, 114
Anzaldúa, Gloria, 24
Arens, Richard, 67
Asians, 55–56, 175, 182n4, 191n42
Assimilation: acculturation and, 26, 86; contradictions in policy of, 50–51, 71–73, 86, 95; as federal policy, 27–28, 46–47; generations and, 172; Hasidim and, 115; immigrant intentions and, 174; individualism and, 64, 78; Native institutions and, 94–100; pan-Indian consciousness and, 26, 185n8; racialization and, 12, 47, 60; transnationalism and, 173–74. *See also* Termination policy
Association on American Indian Affairs (AAIA), 65

Baker, Bertram, 85
Bakhtin, Mikhail, 205n24

Industrial Stabilization Act (1965),
204n11
Internal migration, 25–28, 176–77. *See
also* Relocation policy
Internal Security Act (1950), 59
Intertribal associations, 88–89
"Invented traditions," 34, 41–43,
109–12, 120, 151–53, 169–70, 208n6.
See also Indian princess tradition
IOC. *See* American Indian Industrial Op-
portunities Center
IRA. *See* Indian Reorganization Act

Jackson, Jesse, 113
Jacobson, David, 180
Jasso, Guillemina, 68
Javits, Jacob, 66–67
Jewish community, 1–2, 66, 114–16,
194n94, 202n121. *See also* Crown
Heights tensions
Jingle Dress Dance, 34, 161, 162,
187n52
Johns, Trevor, 107, 131, 206n41
Johnson, Napoleon Bonaparte, 48
Johnson, Robert, 105
Johnson-O'Malley Act (1936), 151,
201n111
Josephs, Tony, 143, 145
J'ouvert (pre-Carnival festival), 30,
112–13, 122
Juju Mas' Camp, 112
Jules, Neville, 130
Junior Miss Shawnee Nation. *See* Alley,
DaLynn

Kaplan, Caren, 171, 173, 174
Kasinitz, Philip, 39, 40, 83, 105, 113
Kearney, Michael, 174
Kees, Rich, 191n32
Kelly, Ray, 115
Kennedy, John F., 67, 68, 69
King, Jamaal, 144
King, Rudy, 123, 130
Kivisto, Peter, 211n42
Klamath nation, 62
Krulwich, Sara, 16, 17

Labor and capital mobility: American
hegemony and, 45–46, 47; demand for
labor and, 3, 49–50; immigration policy and, 49–51, 68–69, 84; migration
of labor vs. capital and, 179; policing
and, 107; popular culture and, 35–36;
steel drum music and, 122; termination policy and, 62. *See also* Bracero
Program; Economic forces, transnational

Lac du Flambeau reservation powwow,
41
Land, and Indian identity, 24, 27, 46, 51,
52, 53, 64. *See also* Relocation policy;
Termination policy
Language, and borders, 173
Legendre, Jerry, 144–45
Lehman, Herbert, 67
Lemke-Santangelo, Gretchen, 177
Lezama, Carlos, 100, 102, 104, 105, 115
Libertus, Ron, 200n82
Lifsh, Yosef, 14–15, 181n1
Linton, Ralph, 185n8
Lipsitz, George, 152
Litefoot (Indian rap artist), 163
Little Miss Shawnee Nation (1994). *See*
Alley, DaLynn
Little Miss Shawnee Oklahoma (1994),
26
Lomawaima, K. Tsianina, 26, 28, 47, 61,
172, 189n83
Lott, Eric, 30
Lowe, Lisa, 3, 55
Luce, Henry, 45

Malliet, Wendell, 83
Manette, Ellie, 127–28, 129, 130, 131,
146
Manning, Frank, 40, 104
Mardi Gras Indians of New Orleans,
36–37
Mark, Robert, 106
Marshall, Dawn, 33
Marshall, Paule, 84
Martínez, John, 24
Mas' bands (costume clubs), 31, 101
Mas' camps (costume shops), 15, 16–17,
112. *See also* Culture of Black Cre-
ation mas' camp
Masquerading traditions ("playing
mas'"), 29, 30, 31, 37, 91–92, 112
Mass culture: Carnival forms and,
35–38, 118–19; colonialism and,
38–43; festival responses to, 23; popu-
lar memory and, 8–10; powwow cul-
ture and, 34, 36, 118–19, 120, 158;
racist influence and, 9–10; rise of in-
dustry of, 35–36. *See also* Media
Master of ceremonies (MCs) at powwows, 38, 168–69
McCarran, Patrick, 50, 52, 53
McCarran-Walter Act (Immigration and
Naturalization Act of 1954), 48–49,
55, 58–60, 65, 192n60
McKay, Douglas, 53, 60
McKay, George, 63
McRobbie, Angela, 162, 169

Text: 10/13 Sabon
Display: Sabon
Composition: Impressions Book and Journal Services, Inc.
Printing and binding: Friesens
Index: Marcia Carlson